Sausage Factory

THE COLLEGE CRIER'S INFAMOUS INTERVIEWS OF THE FREAKS AND THE FAMOUS

Interviews by

T. VIRGIL PARKER
JESSICA HOPSICKER
CARRI ANNE YAGER

Portland • Oregon
INKWATERPRESS.COM

1

Table of Contents

Introduction: Sausage as a Metaphor

The world is full of things we don't want to look at too closely. Even the things we do want to scrutinize, it isn't always for the noblest of reasons. Sometimes we want to give the toupee a little tug, take a peek at Oz standing behind the curtain. Most of us are like that. Winston Churchill warned that people who love sausage should never watch it being made. However, for those intrepid few who positively obsess about sausage; they simply roll up their sleeves and feed the grinder.

Many of the people in this book are among the most fulfilled people on Earth; others are facing demons that would blanch the bones of weaker souls. If you pump all the wonder, pain and glory you can snatch out of life into the grinder, what comes out of the other end may be sublime, or hideous, but will always be profound.

One thing Winston failed to point out about sausage; you never really know what's in there. You might find out that your favorite midnight movie maven got her start acting for the most heralded art film director of all time. You may discover a man who had to make up a song, live, in front of half a million people; or a musician and filmmaker who is worshipped as a god in the South Pacific; an actress who impersonated someone else to audition for her first big acting role; a man who walked barefoot across the Middle East armed with only a guitar; a comedian funding an art museum for Chicanos by stepping in a bowl of cereal. You may encounter a journalist who was a hero for a generation casually grilling lobsters while firing up a fatty.

Physicians may keep us alive. The people we interview remind us to live. As we flail against the tyranny of selfhood we read stories, we watch movies, listen to music, pray, become intoxicated, seek danger. The people who assemble our inspirations are the people who build bridges to the far side of who we are. Are these mere nothings, a diversion? Sometimes. Sometimes we need to be diverted. Sometimes a snatch of a song, a happy ending, a powerful insight, is exactly what we need to take a stab at our own dreams. We take our work too seriously; we don't take our entertainment seriously enough. Enjoy the sausage.

T. Virgil Parker, October 8, 2008

Jethro Tull's Ian Anderson: Knights and Tights

July 2003
By T. Virgil Parker

Since a run through the radio dial never fails to turn up a song that has been played continuously for at least 25 years -think Zeppelin, Floyd- it is very easy to forget that there was a time when Rock and Roll didn't sound very different from R & B, or even Country -think Elvis. The truth is that the 60's and 70's rockers were carving musical landscapes out of very thin air. The intense creativity of that time feeds directly into the groundbreaking efforts of contemporary World, Jam, and Progressive music. As new generations discover the music that their granola-eating ancestors got off on, new musicians launch themselves on the uncharted boundaries of eclectic music.

A brief look at the diverse influences of Jethro Tull sheds light on the unprecedented fascination that 70's Rock still commands. Drawing inspiration from the Blues and -of all things- medieval music, then tossing in a heavy peppering of Hard Rock, a sound like no other emerged. Ian Anderson, a uniquely flute-touting front man, leapt about the stage in

1

lederhosen to create a spectacle that could only capture the imagination.

With over 30 CD's in print, and record sales exceeding 40,000,000 copies, many bands would be willing to sit back and grow fat on the royalty checks. However, not satisfied with being on the Classic Rock short list with standbys like "Aqualung" and "Cross-Eyed Mary," the group never ceased to embark on new projects, their new DVD one of many.

T. Virgil Parker: With 35 years of material to cover in a DVD, most bands would do anything but an all-live project. What led you to such an ambitious undertaking?

Ian Anderson: I was getting a lot of interest from various producers, especially over in America, who wanted Jethro Tull to do a live show and put it out on the DVD Market, but I didn't just want to do a live concert, top to tail, put it in a box and off you go. To capture a live show is almost impossible. We recorded a concert in London which was the bulk of the performance and then we added a few more ingredients from some songs that we did at a reunion of the original 1968 lineup and a couple of things with a string quartet, and some interview material and some other bits and pieces to just make something I hope would be a little more rounded, a little more varied than just a live concert. It wasn't an attempt to capture the all-time greatest Jethro Tull concert ever. As soon as you start recording a live show, it's the unwritten rule that the night you record will not be as good as the night before, or the night after.

TVP: Given the depth and complexity of the material that you perform, how do you keep the band so precise? Is there a lot of intense rehearsing going on?

I.A.: We haven't played together for four weeks, and it's more than two weeks since I've been on stage before an audience. All though it doesn't seem too long, and the bulk of it you remember -it comes flooding back to you rather quickly- there are lot of elements. You really do need to just pick up some of the detail again, and certain areas of improvisation- you need to be able to get your head into the right place to start and finish them, because with the dovetailing of improvisational elements with the more orga-nized, arranged parts, you really have to get the beginnings and ends sorted out in your head. A lot of that I really do need to run through. I usually spend five to seven days prior to a tour doing a couple of hours each day of just playing that music. And that I find very necessary. After two or three weeks of not doing a show there's some serious work to be done, a bit like an athlete training.

TVP: Bassist Jonathan Noyce stated that playing the music is like an extreme sport, that it requires a great deal of con-centration and determination. A lot of what Tull fans have come to expect is that kind of proficiency.

IA: That is true, but it's not about being a machine. It's not like being in a symphony orchestra and having to play everything note perfect every night. It's more of a careful blend between the heart and the mind. It isn't just playing the right notes, it's how you play them, and it is also about the considerable scope that all the musicians have for improvisation. You can just get up and wing it, but that's not quite good enough.

Improvisation doesn't come from nowhere. It still comes from some, albeit very fast, very furious compositional skills. You have a nanosecond to decide about the next note. You have to come up with improvisations that make sense in the context of the music that you're playing. That does require work, but at the end of the day it's not about becoming a perfect machine, and it never will be. There's always looseness about it and a bit of give and take from all the musicians to each other.

TVP: A lot of the bands that are playing progressive music have a "More complex than thou" attitude, indulging in complexity for its own sake.

IA: It is often the case that people just do disappear up their own backsides in terms of creating complex and intricate pieces of work that ultimately aren't going anywhere. I think that's almost so obvious that you would hope that most people would have a built-in self regulator that would stop them doing it, but I'm sure there have been times when we've been as guilty of it as others. Out of sheer enthusiasm you get a little bit carried away with something and you don't realize that what to you may sound fairly straight-forward to the more average ear may sound as oblique or dense as anything from the more avant guarde classical composers. Most of us have a general agreement that we want to hear a good tune. We want to hear something that's got some kind of relevance, some kind of familiarity, but its finding the right balance between providing elements that are within peoples comfort zone but at the same time giving it a little twist that makes it a little more challenging and a little bit more vital, a little bit more original, a little bit more special. That's what the good moments are about, a song that's done right, when you think you've managed to combine those elements.

TVP: You're moving into new territory with your solo work "Divinities" and "The Secret Language of Birds," drawing in more Eastern and more Celtic influence. But if you look at something like "Hunt by Numbers" on the J-Tull.com album that style merges into a purely rock format. How do you keep all these influences in balance and maintain the authentic Tull sound?

4

IA: If you think of it as being like a chef in the kitchen, you can go to the spice shelf and the deep freeze and pull out all kinds of ingredients and stick them together and it may just be an unpalatable mess. You have to find things that compliment each other, you have to find the right flavors, the right colors, the right textures and you have to put those things together and blend them and coax them into something that is a satisfying and pleasing mixture. That's what making eclectic music is all about. You have to do it with some subtlety and some editorial skill so you don't end up with ugly joins between one influence, one prime part of the equation and another. It's nice to be able to feel that you can exercise some taste in the way you do it and hopefully get it right more often than you get it wrong. Having said that, I'm sure I got it wrong lots of times, it's just there are certain songs where I'm pretty convinced I got it right. Those are the ones I enjoy today particularly to play in live concert.

TVP: Have your creative processes changed a lot as the technology has evolved?

IA: To look back on contemporary technology from the early eighties to today, things have gotten a lot easier, a lot faster, a lot better sounding, but essentially we're dealing with the same kind of technology. I still have equipment in my studios that is from the early eighties, still in general use. It still works! Not that I would use it to master an album on, but I have a digital tape recorder which is often used as a backup or something to copy onto, and it is probably 1987 vintage.

We're still dealing with the same kind of computers we've known for quite a few years now, they're just faster, bigger hard disks, do things in a bit more detailed way, but essentially Apple Macs are Apple Macs and PCs are still PCs. Things are not moving with the pace of change that many of us thought they would. How long is it since a man walked on the moon? Jumbo jets have been flying for thirty years. Things haven't changed as much as many of us thought they would. And music certainly is no exception. There's a different gloss on it, a different suit of cloths, different haircut, but it's pretty much the same old stuff. It's very easy to believe when you listen to the lyrics of pop and rock music that there's not a lot different going on out there apart from-you might argue- the sentiments and language of Rap music which has brought something into the equation that wasn't there before. Whether you like it or not is a different matter.

TVP: I have in my possession a Jethro Tull songbook from 1971. The introduction points out that you knocked the Rolling Stones out of the #2 position after The Beatles as the most popular band in the U.K.

IA: That's just some newspaper or magazine doing its usual self-important reader's poll or something. You have to take those things with a pinch of salt.

TVP: Did memories of that period come to mind when you recorded with the original 1968 lineup for the DVD?

IA: Not really. We just got together to play 3 songs; we hadn't played together for 34 years. It was a quick run through and then roll the cameras. I wanted to grab this performance while it was still relatively fragile and there was a little tension in it because it would be all too easy to just over-rehearse something for the cameras. It's really important to have a little bit of tension there. I certainly wasn't thinking in any nostalgic way about any of the original band members or the things going on at the time, I was more interested in trying to remember the right notes to play, as indeed I'm sure my three friends were.

TVP: Now that Mick Jagger has been knighted, do you think you're next in line?

IA: I think there's absolutely no chance whatsoever. First of all, it mostly happens to people who are already well-known figures. There are indeed awards given to public servants who are absolutely not known by most folks; like nurses in hospitals, health care workers, people just doing good work. There are a certain number of those people who do get, not knighted, but given some award by the Queen for services.

But in the case of someone like Mick Jagger, he's obviously one of those very few persistent leading figures in the world of rock and pop music and the fact that Elton John and Paul McCartney had been awarded such things it seemed not unreasonable that Mick Jagger should be treated similarly. But remembering all these guys have had their scuffles with authority, drug busts, lots of sexual shenanigans on the part of Elton John and Mick Jagger anyway, there's a degree of raciness almost. You've got to be VH1 Behind the Music material to qualify for a knighthood these days, as well as to qualify for being on VH1. And I think on any of those counts I wouldn't get close to it because I haven't done any good works, nor have I been conspicuous on a public platform the way that Mick Jagger has. I think it's an absolute dead certainty I will manage to live out my life without being recognized in that sort of way at all. And indeed I would feel completely embarrassed and would have a great sense of being the wrong guy if anybody did say, "Look, um your name's being considered and how would you accept the award and how would you feel about it?" which is of course what happens. They don't want to give awards to people who won't show up, not after John Lennon gave his back. I think I'd be very uncomfortable about such a thing. There are certain qualifications and I don't think I would have them, both good and bad qualifications if you see what I mean, so I'm not really expecting anything like that at all.

Mick Jagger on the other hand, was. He was by all accounts pretty pissed off that some other folks, Sir Cliff Richards, Sir Bob Geldof, Sir Elton John, Sir Paul McCartney, did. I think Mick Jagger was getting pretty pissed off, "Hey, what happened to me?" Well, a lot of people would be saying "What Happened to Charlie, where's Sir Charlie and Sir Keith. Why Mick Jagger and not the other guys? He's after all just one of the band, judging by the lack of the success of his recent solo album, I would have thought he'd be extremely grateful to be part of the band.

TVP: Is there anything unusual we can expect at your upcoming tour?

IA: With Jethro Tull, by and large what is different is on a fairly subtle level. I don't think we're there to suddenly say "Surprise surprise, we're going to show you our new Hip Hop Symphonic Album." People might be a little disappointed.

All Aboard the Hell-Bound Train: An Interview With Hunter S. Thompson

October 2004

By Jessica Hopsicker

Many of you would equate Hunter Thompson with chemical-induced misadventures, as outlined in his most famous work, *Fear and Loathing in Las Vegas*, or the film of the same name starring Johnny Depp. But his most enduring claim to fame is as a sportswriter, novelist, and above all, a political journalist. His recent book, *Hey Rube: Blood Sport, the Bush Doctrine, and the Downward Spiral of Dumbness- Modern History from the Sports Desk* is the unedited compellation of his ESPN sports column. It chronicles the Bush presidency since the election and as it runs its course "on the downhill, hell bound train."

In his Fear and Loathing books, his words evoke a generation; he appears as a kind of Hemingway of the 70's: "You could strike sparks anywhere; there was a fantastic universal sense that what we were doing was right. That we were winning..." Times have changed, and we are now in a century saturated with oil, lies, terrorism, the Bush/ Chaney war machine, and the epidemic of voter apathy.

Now, instead of hope, his words carry a grim yet prophetic tone.

Jessica Hopsicker: Hello.

Hunter S. Thompson: All right, I'll move over here now, two outs at the bottom of the ninth here, the Yankees are behind, no runners on base, Boston's about to win. Ah, where am I, what phone am I talking on?
   Jessica?

JH: Hello. Good evening.

HST: I'm sorry to keep you waiting; life gets confusing around here.

JH: That's all right; I was just about to finish up a beer and leave.

HST: Where are you?

JH: I'm at the office right now.

HST: Where is the office?

JH: In Barneveld, in Upstate New York.

Anita Thompson: Where do you go to school?

JH: I went to Pratt Institute, in Brooklyn.

HST: The art school. Isn't it?

JH: Oh yeah. Studied graphic design for a bit, then decided it wasn't for me and decided to get my foot in the door for journalism, and somehow I found myself thrust headlong into it.

HST: How long have you been at it?

JH: I did take a couple journalism classes in Brooklyn, very interesting. Got into the politics of Brooklyn. But I never thought I'd be doing this.

HST: Well, what the Hell? Why not? I got one of the few things I could do well and get paid for. Also, I got to go to work at two in the afternoon. That was what got me into journalism. You work for a morning paper and you work at night. So once I got a job there and could go to work at two in the afternoon, I never again had a nine-to-five job. That's why I'm a journalist.

JH: That's part of the reason I was thinking about going into the business, too.

HST: Are you a night person?

JH: I can be, every once in a while.

AH: You are tonight.

HST: Well, it helps. Well, let's see. Fire a question at me, and let's see if I can handle it.

JH: After recent round of censorship, a staffer at a certain sports media outlet, was quoted as saying, "Hunter had gone too far."

HST: You talk to people on the phone, you've got to learn to slow down and bite your words off. I know I talk fast, but I'm a good voice critic of other people.

JH: I'm also a bit nervous, too.

HST: Oh, don't worry about it.

AT: You're doing fine.

HST: Do you have any drugs? Do have you any drugs with you?

JH: Not with me, just a bunch of beer and cigarettes.

HST: Well, that won't really work. I'll smoke some pot for you here. It is a nice kind of deep orange and almost turquoise California weed. That should calm you down; you'll get a contact buzz.

JH: Yeah, that'll work.

HST: Feeling any better? I'm getting a little stoned now, so you should start to feel it soon. How old are you?

JH: I'm twenty-one.

HST: Twenty-one, and you've already been through design? That's pretty good. I have a design background.

JH: Really?

HST: Yeah, photography. Taschen Books is publishing a book of my photographs. You know that high-end publishing company in Beverly Hills? They produce very beautiful books. I mean the best in the business, no doubt. They produced that Muhammad Ali book that weighs eighty-five pounds. It's called *GOAT: Greatest Of All Time*. I think it costs eight thousand dollars or something like that. I have an old interview; a piece I did on Muhammad Ali. It's in there; it's one of the essays in the book. It's beautiful. If you ever get a chance to see *GOAT*, it's *Greatest of All Time*. It's really a museum piece. It's wonderful. Like the heaviest, the highest reach in book publishing in American history. It's the largest book ever published. Takes two people to carry it.

Alright, where's that pipe now? Ah, here we go. Little mechanical problem like they have at the air flights. Er, airports. I'm getting nervous myself. All right, I feel better now. I hope you do.

JH: Contact buzz.

HST: Right. But what you mentioned about censorship there, what was that?

JH: After a recent round of censorship, a staffer at a certain major media outlet was quoted saying, "Hunter can go too far at times."

HST: Too far? Well, that's what it's about. If you never go too far, you never have any real sense of adventure. What's too far? That's a matter of taste. Yeah, I believe that's true. Too far is a matter of personal choice. I'm a very down-to-Earth person. I'm a neighborhood "Pillar of Strength." I've lived in the same house here for thirty years. So I'm not really as weird as you may have heard. Are you hearing weird things about me? Why are you doing this, how did you get this assignment?

JH: Well, my sister is a bowling alley waitress; she talked to a local newspaper and said that I wanted to get into journalism. I mentioned that I enjoy reading your work and the next thing I know; here I am, on the phone with you.

HST: Damn, that's fast work.

JH: Yeah. Thrust headlong into journalism.

HST: Yep, that's right. Yeah, you were. Well, I'd like to send you some reading material; I'd like to advance your career if I could. It makes me feel good to communicate with my tribe. I'm a journalist. And I write novels, and I write; what don't I do? I'm a photographer. But right now I'm a political journalist. Have you seen my column in the online ESPN this week?

JH: Yeah.

AT: The book?

HST: What book?

AT: The book.

HST: Oh, *Hey Rube,* that's what we're talking about.

JH: I have yet to read that.

HST: It's a must. First, it's a lot of fun. You don't have to be a sports fan to read this; it is a really brutal political book.

AT: *It's Hey Rube: Blood Sport, the Bush Doctrine, and the Downward Spiral of Dumbness, Modern History from the Sports Desk.* It's the unedited version of his ESPN online column.

HST: Yeah, I do, I write a sports column every week. Is that right? Jessica, you've got to get a little drunk. So what are you most curious about?

JH: I'm just about curious about everything right now. Trying to expand my horizons.

HST: What's your job assignment?

JH: Just to interview you right now.

HST: And get an interview that you can fit on black and white paper and print. Is that right?

JH: Yup, and on the website.

HST: In any case, we will see it in print, somewhere, somehow.

JH: Yup.

HST: Are you a runaway child, Jessica?

JH: Nope, small town girl, born and raised.

HST: What town was that again?

JH: I grew up in Hinckley, a very small town in the foothills of the Adirondack Mountains.

HST: You're a hillbilly! I am too.

JH: It's a good life.

HST: Hmm, what can I teach Jessica here? My beautiful wife is going to explain the set-up for you. It will give you a lead for your piece.

AT: What are we talking about?

HST: *Hey Rube*, I guess. I've written two books pounding George Bush mercilessly.

AT: They call it The Journal of the Bush Presidency. He's been writing this book since the very beginning of the election in 2000, and he chronicles all the chaos that was going on during the election and throughout the whole Bush presidency. And it's a journal that he wrote at the time, as it was happening. Very similar to the *Campaign Trails*, it's not in retrospect.

HST: A good diary of the Bush Presidency, a downhill, hellbound train.

AT: And he also teaches you to gamble, and how not to gamble.

HST: And to shoot. I think we should set up to teach you shooting.

AT: Yeah. Hunter's property here is also the Woody Creek Rod and Gun Club.

HST: Which has many distinguished members.

AT: We called it the Woody Creek Rod and Gun Club after having a barbecue with the neighbors. One of the neighbors was running for county commissioner. So Hunter is actually as involved in local politics as he is in national politics.

HST: It's very important. That's what the Republicans did, in fact. They organized from the ground up, starting when Robertson ran for President. He got beaten. An evangelical preacher in Virginia, Pat Robertson, who runs the Christian Coalition; his party wasn't organized efficiently enough for him to win. I think he won Michigan- some terrifying blunder on everybody's part. He became a serious threat, like Ross Perot in '92. He'd gone from a local boy to a national boy, but he didn't have an organization in place, so he couldn't move from Michigan, for instance, to New York, for the primary, or he'd have to get a whole new organization and teach them all over again. So he figured out that if you organize from the ground up, through his churches, that would give him a base in any city or state and he wouldn't have to teach them the ropes all over again. That's when the Republicans began their Christian Jihad; the crusade. And it's still going on. Bush is a jackass, really. Incompetent, he's an imbecile. I looked up "imbecile" in Black's Law Dictionary, an imbecile, under law, well I can't remember it but it fits George Bush perfectly. It's an intelligence that never develops past sixteen or something like that. It's not a mental disease; therefore you can't hide behind it with an insanity defense. You can't plead insanity and not be executed for murder. But "imbecile" is just a slow-witted half-right yo-yo who is not really sick and can't be cured. You can't cure dumbness. But you can use it. And he got a job as, like, a male model. He was a perfect face for what the religious right and the power mongers wanted. It is like going out and selling Ivory Snow, or like being a Chanel girl; except this is for the presidency. That's ridiculous, you have to like the President or be charmed by him or want to go out and have a drink, get naked with him. If you had to make a choice between getting naked with George Bush or John Kerry, who would you choose?

JH: I'm not quite sure yet.

HST: Oh, don't give me that crap, Miss Undecided. What if you had to do it right now? See this is training, Jessica. You have to make a decision right now.

JH: Kerry?

HST: Kerry. I'm not gonna push you on this, but I'm curious as to why you'd rather get naked-

AT: Than vote.

HST: Yeah, that really has nothing to do with it. But it does, in this country. I don't know what that means for the fact the women's vote is swinging to Bush. I don't know, I'm just jabbering. Ask me a question, Jessica.

HST: Why am I hearing all this noise?

AT: Taking a message, Rolling Stone called.

HST: I'm writing a piece for Rolling Stone and I'm trying to talk to the Editor about the piece.

JH: Does journalistic objectivity still exist?

HST: Only in closed circuit TV camera systems that observe everything that goes on in front of them all the time. You have to be a machine to be objective. Being objective really mandates that you miss a few things. You couldn't see, Richard Nixon for instance, being objective about him. Objectivity is good when you're learning journalism because you have to learn the five W's. You know about the five W's?

JH: The "who, what, where, when, why?"

HST: Exactly. Who, what, where, when, the other one's a tricky one. Why, or-

JH: Sometimes "How."

HST: Yeah, number five is tricky. "Why" is the difference between objective and subjective journalism. "Why" is an interpretive concept. "Where" is not. You know, it happened at an address. I was an objective journalist for most of the time when I was learning it. I wrote for fifteen years before I published a book, which is a kind of measure of success in writing journalism. I think I've published fourteen. But you have to learn. In order to play football, there are certain rules. Mainly it's about getting hired, getting a job. But journalism to me was always a fall back position. And I needed money so I had to agree to work on jobs. My job was to do what the editor wanted. That's how I learned. The editor would pay money. You'd get a check for doing what the editor wanted. But you usually wouldn't get checks for doing just what you wanted. It's a school of hard knocks. Does this make any sense to you, Jessica?

JH: Oh yeah.

HST: So, what have you learned, so far? Wait, who are you going to vote for?

JH: I'm thinking along the lines of Kerry. He seems like the lesser of two evils.

HST: Yeah. In this case, he's a lot lesser. I'm gonna vote for Kerry. I worry, I constantly bitch at him for not being more aggressive and simply more fun. There's no doubt in my mind that Kerry would be a good president and extremely different from Bush, but the main thing is that Bush is not just a likeable cowboy, some "aw, shucks" person, a man of goodwill; a compassionate conservative. No. He's a front man for a gigantic combine of religious zealots and oil billionaires. Voting against Bush is to stop an approaching iceberg or glacier. Bush is taking over; the Bush people. You can't say it's just Bush. You have to have a sense personality to actually win anything. But he is a good, friendly front man, and meanwhile the machine keeps going. People keep getting poorer; losing more jobs, more health insurance, more pension funds. Bush has destroyed the economy in this country. But he has not destroyed the economy of Haliburton, the oil company that Dick Cheney was president of before he became Vice-President of the US. He was CEO. Anyway, you've got a choice of personalities here. I seem to be wandering further and further.

JH: It's alright.

HST: But no, I'm way beyond objective journalism, although I had to learn to be an objective journalist before I could be subjective. And the trick about being subjective is that you have to be employed to do it. Otherwise you're just some kind of silly poet out in the woods. I'm a professional journalist, and a writer. Yeah, it's a job for me. That's the way it should be for you.

JH: What draws you to a subject to write about?

HST: Wow, good question. It's very broad, but it happens to be good. Well, this presidential election is one. Have you read Vanity Fair recently?

JH: No, I haven't yet.

HST: That's an assignment. The assignment is, you should read the June issue.

AT: It has Brad Pitt on the cover.

HST: Yeah, the June issue of this year, from like a couple of months ago, of Vanity Fair, because, well, Brad Pitt's on the cover. Yeah, I'd love you to read about Brad Pitt. No, I have a big story in there, and I was drawn to it. It's about, well it's too complicated to explain to you, but it's about a young girl who's in prison in Colorado for a crime she did not and could not have committed. We're about to get her out of prison. I have a very political approach.

AT: lisl.com

HST: Yeah, write that down Jessica, L-I-S-L.com. The case is right now before the Colorado Supreme Court, and we're awaiting a decision. It's a major case.

HST: ...did she leave?

AT: Are you there?

HST: Jessica, are you writing? Jessica?

JH: Sorry about that.

HST: What happened?

JH: I was looking for a pen, and the next thing you know, I had accidentally pressed the talk button.

HST: Oh boy. Jessica, you really are starting from the beginning here. Do you write pages?

JH: Um, just journalism assignments in school, and stuff like that.

HST: Yeah, but do you write stories?

JH: I do.

HST: Good. Well, why don't you read one of them? No, never mind. This is like teaching a course.

Now, I approach stories that interest me for reasons beyond simple journalism, like, "oh this, would be a good story because it involves the murder of a pregnant mother under treacherous circumstances" like you see them on the news, the Scott Peterson case. No, those things don't interest me. But things that have meaning interest me. Like you had, "cracking the criminal justice system in Denver." I didn't really go into this case with the idea of doing that. I took the case before I planned to write the story about it, so it worked out. I would have had to write the story once I got into it anyway. It happens that when I wrote that in Vanity Fair, it crystallized the whole story and all the details. We did a lot of research on it. That's a key aspect of journalism. We've taken that girl from total doom underneath the Colorado State women's prison, to right on the verge of having her released.

This Bush/Cheney machine in the White House is the most dangerous situation I've ever seen the country in. The country is in worse shape today than I've ever seen it in, and it happened so fast. If Richard Nixon were running against George Bush today, I think I'd vote for Nixon.

JH: Really?

HST: Yeah. I never thought I'd say that.

JH: What do you feel would happen if Bush were reelected?

HST: Well, just more of the same of what's happening now; namely, a looting of the federal treasury. This country has gone from being a prosperous nation at peace, and now four years later we're a broke nation at war. That's a huge turn-around; the effect of a failing economy, although the war-making machine is doing better than ever. Corporate profits for defense companies; companies that make airplanes and security devices and machine guns. Their profits are up two hundred percent over the year before. This is like the tryout period for Bush. Now that he is looking is ahead, I don't think he's going to win. But if he does get reelected, all the directions they've gone in, all the environmental directions, they just indicate a lot of directions. One of them is putting oil rigs, you know, oil pumps, over in Colorado now, in the National Parks, giving away the national parks to mining companies.

JH: I've read the same thing about them mining in Alaska, too.

HST: Drilling for oil in the north shore, that's one of them. And they're doing that; I think it was stopped for a while. Putting oil derricks and pipelines everywhere. It's sucking the energy out of the Earth. And it will run out in about thirty-seven years, according to the scientists who measure stuff like that. The price of a gallon of gas, has gone…

AT: Jessica do you know how much gas was in 2000?

HST: What do you pay now for gasoline?

JH: Well, up in the Adirondacks it's about $2.09.

HST: And what was it when you got your drivers license, do you remember?

JH: Probably like around $1.50 something. Way back when I was around sixteen.

HST: Well now it's over three dollars out here. It's going to five dollars. That's what it costs in France or even England to buy gasoline. But that's sort of like the last gasoline that will be available, ever, because we're running out of oil.

Shit, we're running out of national forests and open land. We're running out of jobs.

AT: It doesn't just affect the price of gasoline in your car, it affects products. Products have to be transported, mainly by semis, and house heating, rent prices go up. Travel, because jet fuel is based on the price of crude oil.

HST: All the premiere airlines are filing for bankruptcy because of the price of fuel. I think the country is headed into the dark ages, and George Bush will be seen in history as the Adolf Hitler of his time. History will show that they committed war crimes worse than Hitler. They'll be put on trial eventually, and they'll be judged. Those religious freaks, let's see how they feel, being judged. Are you religious?

JH: I don't really know yet. I've been spoon-fed a lot of religions, so I'm trying to weed some of it out.

HST: Have you tried Muslim? No, no. One thing that I was about to write here in my own article is, what kind of maniac would declare war on the rest of the world, turning the country into, yeah, like Nazi Germany. People aren't choosing to make the US a bunch of fascist Nazis, but the proof of it keeps coming. We invade countries, and then we wonder why they bitch and try to get back at us through terrorism. The Bush people have created this terrorism, this fear. I have a whole book; remember it? *Kingdom of Fear?*

JH: I want to read that.

HST: You should. Kingdom of Fear and Hey Rube are going to be part of your permanent education. These are two books that are extremely political. Not just that, but if you're going to get into journalism, these are going to be some of your basic texts. What haven't I answered here? What haven't I said? I feel like I'm doing the interview.

JH: What would you consider the foulest lie on the campaign trail of 2004?

HST: The foulest lie, I believe, is the one that says that Bush is going to be a successful President and should be reelected again. That's absolutely 180 degrees off from the truth. He has been a disaster as the President for the country. He's been a good boy for Haliburton, the oil industry. That's what he does, that's where he grew up. He grew up in the petroleum club of Houston, which a huge power center of oil people. That's what he does. But it's not good for the country. What did Clinton do? He got a few blowjobs, and these goddamn religious zealots almost impeached him for it. Then they come in and steal five trillion dollars from the national treasury in the name of war on the rest of the world. What the fuck is that? The lie is really that Bush, Cheney, et cetera, don't deserve to be fired and put in jail. They do. How they would run for President again and get reelected is almost beyond me ability to comprehend. The question now is not whether George Bush is a Nazi or whether John Kerry bled real blood in Vietnam or lied. That's all bullshit, all politics. That's just the presidential year. The question now is whether the American people, the voters, want it that way. Whether we as a democracy approve of having a failed preacher of the oil industry in charge of the country for another four years. I'd be a better Drug Czar than George Bush would be running the country. You think George is stupid? The first time I saw George Bush, I met him, he came into my hotel room in Houston and passed out in the bathtub. Try that for a story. He was drunk. He was not invited, he came into the room with some friend of his who was invited and he disappeared for a while. The next time I saw him he was passed out in the bathtub and he had vomited on his seersucker suit. Yeah, that's a good image. But I've done worse things than that.

I've done terrifying things under the influence of a variety of substances. But, to me, that's the most interesting thing he's done as a human being. The weirdest thing that I've found in this election is that the women's vote is shifting to Bush. The women's vote has been strongly for Kerry in all the polls and predictions. About sixty-forty. But now, in the last two weeks, Bush has swept up about ten points in popularity among female registered voters. And that's the weirdest thing I've ever seen. I'd be afraid to get naked with George Bush. I mean he's not a monster; he's just a nerd. Yeah, a nerd. He's like a drunken teenage kid.

JH: It seems like voter apathy is prevalent today among college students.

HST: I've worried about that for so long. That's a silly excuse for not voting. You live in a country and bad things are happening to it, therefore to you. And you have a chance. This will be our last chance, really, for another four years, to kick the bastard out of the White House, to fire him. And to not vote I think is criminal and stupid, criminally stupid. It's the last time this oil machine is going to be stopped in our lifetime.

AT: The last page in Hey Rube is a tear-out of how important it is to vote.

HST: You have to read something Jessica. Do you have access to a copy of Hey Rube?

JH: I will get a copy of it.

HST: Read the last page first. You talk about apathy, well; apathy is what got us George Bush. Politics is such a vicious business when you're running for President. It's the most powerful job on Earth. Maybe not for long, but it is right now. And people will kill without even catching a breath.

That's what you do in politics, you eliminate people. I've been in politics, writing about it, being in it, running for office, for forty years and I don't have any sure cure. It's like having the Hell's Angels move into your house and having to kick them out. It's kind of hard to kick them out. Here's our chance, and to be apathetic about it is just stupid. It's self-destructive because the apathetic, the dumb, the floaters, are going to be eliminated immediately. There will be a massive crackdown on sex in public. Sex anywhere, really. I've always viewed Election Day as fun. I've always associated it with a kind of action. Pretty girls, getting laid, just fun. The thing to do this year is to get a date right now for Election Day. Be sure you have a date to vote with.

AT: Yeah, bring a date, have some fun.

HST: Hook up with somebody and vote.

AT: What do you think, Jessica? Think that's good?

JH: I think it's a good idea.

HST: You have to make politics fun if you're going to run for office. It has to be fun for people or you won't get elected. It can only be a job for so long and then if it's not fun, you're not going to win. People won't come out and actually vote for you, they'll tell people they will. I think we need some fun in this campaign. I think naked voting should be the new, uh, yeah. I don't think there are any laws against voting naked while you're with a date. That sounds pretty good. Or you don't have be naked to vote, but get naked afterwards. Yeah, wear an overcoat or raincoat to vote. I don't know what the hell I'm saying. I'd like to see what you write about this, Jessica. I want to see it. All this talk about politics is getting me excited.

Afterword: The Curse of the Black Widow Journalist

For four years I have tried to write this down, all wrapped up in the perfect paragraph. It is a convoluted tale of hero worship, death, obsession, and depression. My dreams of grandeur and sense of self-entitlement systematically skived away like a strip of leather by adulthood. I was twenty-one, an art school dropout and soon to be unemployed. Ripe and readily impressionable, I found myself on the phone talking politics with the most savage and beloved voice in American journalism, on the eve of a crucial presidential election. My first interview, ever, was with Hunter S. Thompson. For over an hour I spoke to my hero and I did so little to deserve it. I walked into the College Crier office and simply asked for a job. T. Virgil wanted to know whom I liked to read and when I answered, he offered up an interview with the man. With no mind for repercussions, some of which I am still reeling from, it was an obligation that could not be ignored.

For the following months, I fought and floundered, feeling as though I reached the pinnacle of my career and that was it. It didn't seem possible that I had to do it all again month after month, issue after issue. Then, on a frosty January afternoon, a friend suggested I call upon Mitch Hedberg. A week later, it came into fruition and I began to view this new position as wielding a powerful weapon. For these people, these snippets of conversation I could collect and use them to someday become just as powerful as they were. Authors, actors, comics and musicians, they could all be at my mercy. Sadly, it seemed that fortune would not be so kind. My venture took a tragic turn when I awoke to the news of The Good Doctor's death. I never did report back. Given such a great chance to speak to him when I did, was it my duty

27

to carry the great gonzo flag? Mere months later, such a task proved to be impossible. It was the first of April when I heard Mitch Hedberg died. "Mitch is dead, they're calling me cursed!" I bolted into the office and hollered at T. Virgil upon hearing the grave news. He did little to dissuade me, in fact, with some math of his own; he figured Henry Rollins had three months before the curse claimed him as well. I wondered what I got myself into, had I called upon the wrong God. Was I really cursed? Were these people doomed to die by my hand? I did not want to believe it, but from the beginning, this undertaking was fraught with uncanny luck and great misfortune. Not to mention, shortly after Hunter's interview, the good friend that suggested Mitch Hedberg, T Virgil, and I each had to pull a copy of the interview tape from the wreckage of our cars. It may have been the lure of the state forest not even a mile from my home, where I spent most of my time traveling the back roads fueled by marijuana madness and copies of my father's record collection; that led me to believe this. Either way, it felt as though fate had singled me out. I could have given up and walked away before someone else died and rode out that that perilous three month period in a safe predictable place of employment. Instead, I stuck with it continuing my collection. Though with one great exception, I stopped using the term "journalistic hit list." Someone suggested that I should start calling myself "The Black Widow Journalist" or "The Terminal Journalist." Sometimes, I speak of my previous plight and the unfortunate listener backs away as if talking to them would outright kill them. "I'm fine, I'm not cursed," I would say reassuringly, only after I was certain of that fact myself. "I interviewed a female monster truck driver, George Clinton, and a comic that drinks mustard. They're still alive." So is Henry Rollins.

With such an ostentatious beginning, I had to figure out

how I got there in the first place. I didn't want to be known solely as the girl who interviewed the Godfather of Gonzo and survived or to be branded as cursed- but as a writer. For month after month, issue after issue, year after year, I plugged away like a foolishly determined fly buzzing and bouncing off the window glass looking for a way to escape. Every issue, I threw myself into the world of the insanely famous and the just insane. Researching to the point of fixation, and if the interview did not go as well as I planned, I found myself taking the introduction to the point of obsession. Then when it was finished I would move on to the next one. My work, the collection, made the banality of small town life on a writer's salary a little bit more bearable. However, as each interview ended, I grew increasingly restless sinking further into despondency. Everything I went through happened behind a computer in the same place I lived for the past twenty years. Stomaching a gnawing wanderlust grew increasingly hard to do. When I jumped on board the College Crier, I didn't know how long my sentence was going to be, or if there was one in place at all. Perhaps, I had something to atone for. Who knows if there is a curse placed upon my head, and malevolent fates are waiting to collect. All I know is that these past four years have changed me irrevocably. As for Hunter Thompson and Mitch Hedberg, I owe them a book, at least. On September 17th four years since that fateful start, I called upon Chuck Palahniuk for an interview. I had to do something to mark the occasion and he was after all, number two on the original hit list.

Fishing With Mitch: Mitch Hedberg

February 2005
By Jessica Hopsicker

Mitch Hedberg, now there's a man who knows his toast. He's renowned for his off-the- wall observational humor and uncanny ability to jump between subject matters. His stoner drawl is syncopated with his amazing penchant for saying man and totally. Poignant insights, such as, "I'm sick of following my dreams. I'm just going to ask them where they're going and hook up with them later," make him the epitome of laid-back. His sly sense of humor blended with an unassuming delivery earned him a reputation as a regular on " Letterman," and "Conan O'Brien." TIME magazine even included him as one of the next generation of comedy stars. Just about everyone who has heard of him owns a copy of his CD's, "Strategic Grill Locations" and "Mitch All Together," People eagerly hunt down copies of his independent feature film "Los Enchiladas!" which he wrote, directed and starred in.

He is currently co-headlining an extension of his national theater tour with Steven Lynch, paving their way through 44 cities. When he isn't releasing CD's, appearing in "Almost Famous," gracing TIME Magazine, or co-headlining national theater tours he's just... Mitch.

When he landed at The Egg in Albany on the 13th, we decided to hook up with him.

JH: First of all, how do you feel about being interviewed?

Mitch Hedberg: You know being interviewed is kinda fun after awhile. I think your first reaction to it is a bit of closed off and maybe, ah, talking about yourself can be hard. I've always been the type of person who tries not to talk too much, and talk people's ears off about my life and stuff. So you know in an interview situation you have to talk about yourself. After a while, it becomes very therapeutic. All and all, I like being interviewed.

JH: What about the questions out there that you're dreading I'll ask, the ones you're probably incredibly sick of answering?

MITCH: Well, sure, I try to have a good attitude about that; because I know what someone has asked me million times are questions people want to know. Otherwise, they wouldn't be asking it a million times. I think you've got to have a good attitude about that, but sure, there are many questions I've heard but you know what's the deal. I always try to come up with an answer that's the true answer, but yet has a different take. So what happens is after a while when someone asks questions you've heard before you just try to make sure that you throw in something new about it. You know. But yeah, people ask me where you started comedy a lot and I'll say, "Hey I started in Fort Lauderdale, Florida." Then they'll go, "how'd you get into it?" And I'll say, "Well, because I had nothing else going on." I mean, put it this way man, I was talking to my wife about this, if I had an interview and the person only asked me crazy questions, no one would get any idea of who I was, you know what I mean. So that's what I think is the purpose of questions like that.

JH: All right, as a comedian, do people sometimes find it hard to take you seriously?

MH: Mmm, That's a great question, I like that. I would say, um, I don't think they do. But I think they do, the reason is that sometimes I'll say something and I'll be totally serious and people won't believe you. And you'll be like, "no I'm serious man." I don't have a jockey persona off stage; I don't try to nail or hit people over the head with jokes off stage. So I'm pretty serious, my demeanor is relatively serious, maybe a little too serious at times. I think for the most part onstage you can say something totally true that kinda happened to you that was crazy or something, and people will not believe you. I realized that about being onstage is no one takes you seriously, everyone thinks that everything you say is untrue like if I say, "my sister has cancer," and I go on to tell a joke about it. I mean not that that's a great joke area. Then I get off stage and I'll say, "yeah my sister has cancer" and they'll say "were you serious?!" and I'll go "Yeah man. I was." You know, for the most part everything's cool.

MH: Hey what's going on behind you?

JH: Oh it's my editor, he's on the phone.

MH: Well tell him to get lost... just kidding.

JH: What kind of creative process is involved when it comes to composing your material?

MH: Well, the creative process is very simple. I've tried to

32

analyze it. I would say it's daydreaming, it's daydreaming with a – say, I go off into my head for a while. I just go through the catalogue of events and moments in my life and try to piece them together. I just write something down. The creative process is sitting on the bed with a Coca-Cola or something beside you, maybe an orange, and having a notebook and you just daydream, talk with someone and latch onto a joke. It's kinda like fishing in your head and writing it down. The process is simple, it's not sitting down to write jokes its sitting down to put your mind in a frame where you can catch jokes easier, you know what I mean?

JH: When onstage, how much of your material is actually written down as opposed to how much of it is improvised?

MH: Well, the majority- the bulk of the act is written down stuff, but the more improvised stuff I can get in there the better, as far as I'm concerned. I mean so I'll go onstage usually when I start talking I don't just yell out a joke right away, I'll start- and if I can keep that going, spontaneous, if I can keep that going for the whole show I would. What happens is, after a while you'd be talking and you're doing some loose stuff and people will stop laughing and, you go "well, I need to do something else" so you start telling your jokes and you kinda get caught up in that. So if I could do and entire spontaneous show I would, I just don't think the laughs will be enough. So I try to do as much as possible. The majority of it is written stuff. I would say its 75: 25.

JH: How do you keep the audience enthralled for so long?

MH: How do I get 'em enthralled? You just hope that they are. I mean an hour is a long time to watch somebody; I'm surprised that people will sit through an entire comedy show. I mean, I will do it, I understand it, but the thing is, I think that's a long time to ask people to watch you and listen to you. Say I'm onstage for an hour and 45 minutes into it somebody yells out something and I'll say, "Quiet down sir, you heard the rules, no heckling." I'm basically telling this guy that after 45 minutes of watching me he still can't say anything, you know what I mean? And that's kinda mean, so I'm grateful people watch people for an hour. As far as how I keep them enthralled, I dunno, I just keep doing what I'm doing. A lot of times I think I'm doing stuff that pushes an audience away and yet they're still there, so it's weird, it's- I'm just happy, man. I mean, I'm just so blessed that they do stay with you.

JH: If you could fake your death and collect the insurance money, where would you go and who would you become?

MH: I would definitely become a guy who hangs out on the beach, man. I want to have my moment in the sun, you know. Everyone fantasizes about the beach lifestyle, once it actually happens, once you get to the beach, you might realize, hey its kind of sandy. It's a little annoying and you get a little dirty but I want to find- If I was able to disappear, basically that's what you're saying, and with out anybody knowing where I was I would just lay low. On a Caribbean island or something, and just chill, because I'm really good at chillin'. I noticed that I can sit for hours. I'm really good at that. I think in life that there's too much pressure to produce and have something to show for yourself. I would definitely put myself in a situation where I didn't have to have a lot of productivity.

JH: What is it that prompted you to take up a nomadic lifestyle in the first place?

MH: Well, I love traveling man, I love moving on. I think moving on gives you a fresh start everyday. And I think waking up someplace new is great. What I found when I left home, left behind my parents and my friends I found that it opened me up to being more of a social person and interact with people you find new experiences. I think that you can have a whole life going on and if you're not happy pack up and go somewhere else man. I mean you can't do this your whole life, obviously. After a while, you might have to settle down and establish some roots. I just found that being able to split at a moment's notice and go somewhere else always kept things fresh. I love the nomadic lifestyle, I love hotels, camping, and I like sleeping on beaches, cars, whatever, you know. I'm into it, man; I'm into it.

JH: I also asked a couple of friends if they'd like to ask you a few questions, and here they are:

Many comedians talk about their childhood being the start of their creativity as a means of getting attention from siblings and parents, was it the same for you?

MH: Absolutely, I remember trying to get my parents attention by putting on plays, and all that. Absolutely, it was definitely a means of trying to get attention from everyone. I used to try to get the whole neighborhood to come down and watch us do skits down in our basement. So, creativity is definitely a means to get attention. That's a good point, whoever wrote that question was on to something there.

JH: And here's another one.

When you're forced to play a venue that doesn't lend themselves to your extra curricular activities, do you find that the shows tend to be more robotic? Just telling jokes that you've told before and not really flowing?

MH: It can be, it can be. You try not to, but yeah, that can happen, and it's one of the worst things of all, when you're doing a show that feels robotic. Yeah, that does happen, you try to make sure that you're gonna be flexible and be able to be at ease at any situation. But yeah it happens and when it does, it sucks, there's nothing worse than feeling like you're just being robotic, you know.

JH: Being in one of the few meaningful rock and roll movies, what was it like to play in Almost Famous and to work with Cameron Crowe?

MH: Well, you know, that was an amazing situation for me, I got to see top of the line actors, and I got to sit on the set for two days. My part was very small in film but I was in an integral scene. I got to watch Cameron Crowe and Billy Kriddup and Peter Frampton, for that matter, I dunno, I got to watch these people act and do their thing. I got to learn and I got to realize that acting is not as intense as I think it was, and it can be fun, and I was blown away man. I was blown away. Cameron Crowe is really a creative, cool, cute, guy and it was a mind-altering experience, I'm so glad that it came my way.

JH: Well, last question; is there anything else that we haven't covered that you'd like to discuss?

MH: Albany is a town that I've been coming to more and more lately. And that last time I was in Albany, was when Kid Rock was in to town, and I was hanging out with his bass player, I'm friends with his bass player. I think The Egg is a great venue. I think Kid Rock likes the Egg but he didn't play The Egg. I think they have the weirdest hotel ever in Albany, I didn't stay the last time I was there, but it's right by the airport...

It's got all these strange things in it. I think that Albany is a great city. And college is something I wish I went to, but I didn't so I'm mad. I'd also want to say that USA Today is America's foremost newspaper.

Henry Rollins: 21st Century Renaissance Man

February, 2004
By T. Virgil Parker

Arguably one of the founders of American Punk, Henry Rollins is a prolific writer, activist, publisher, recording artist, lecturer, and some would say- though he despises the term- performance artist. He will not call himself an actor, but you can see him take on nuanced roles in films like *Johnny Mnemonic*, *House on a Hill*, and *Bad Boys II*, to name only a few.

For a strict disciplinarian, his ascent into stardom was unusually spontaneous. Watching the seminal Punk group Black Flag in the early 80's, he threw himself up on stage and sang with them. They liked what they heard. This was the lineup that propelled them into glory and fame.

In '88 Henry put together the Henry Rollins Band and hit the road. This is the group that hit MTV and had a massive hit with "Liar". That band still does a tour now and again and Henry has expanded into his own record company, publishing house, writing books, and the famous lecture series, where you can feel free to check out the only graduate of early American hardcore who's words are good enough for National Public Radio.

Timothy Parker: There are a lot of stereotypes about artists. You negate all of them.

Henry Rollins: I don't know the list that my proclivities happen to negate. But I go against the image of the constant smoking, drinking drugging artist who can't get out of bed.

TVP: Also, you have ideals that extend beyond paper. You apply them to action.

HR: I try. It's easy to talk about things, harder to get it over the wall.

TVP: Yeah, I mean, rather than just showing people how it is; you proactively encourage people to do something about it.

HR: Mostly what I go for is to create an example. You can look around your town and see something wrong, and say "polluted water sucks." Good for you, you don't like polluted water. Do something. The hard part is finding out what to do and seeing it through. That's what I work at: seeing something I disagree with and trying to come up with a solution. We do that at my company, and benefit tours with the band. There's a lot of money we donate to various organizations.

TVP: Do you feel a responsibility as an artist to right wrongs?

HR: To me that's not my job as an artist. I do it as an American. We provide a lot of money for this one orphanage in L.A. because they're down the street, we know them. There's a bunch of kids without parents-they're screwed, they might need some help. We donate a lot to the Southern Poverty Law Center, who battle white power groups via litigation. To me that's just looking out for my fellow countryman. An artist can get some notice. You have a voice that gets heard, more than, say, a plumber's. You can use that dubious power in a good way.

TVP: You work in every conceivable medium. What is unique about speaking as a medium?

HR: I like it because I don't have to be a slave to the snare drum like in a song. I enjoy the discipline of being in a band, being part of a unit, but it's a really great thing to just be up there on my own. I can go one way or tangentially the other; change it up because I won't be messing anyone up. I can be very current and spontaneous. It's easily the hardest kind of performing I do. It's everything but easy.

TVP: It hast to have the same kind of immediacy playing music live. Do you get things from the audience in the same way?

HR: They're not screaming things out. I'm not trying to antagonize them. The fact that they're there listening is inspiring. It gets you cooking.

TVP: Let's compare writing a book with what comes to you before a live audience.

HR: The book thing requires a lot of preparation and coming up with an idea that will be strong enough to carry for several thousand words. So you're working on a premise or a topic or you have a goal. I do a lot of travel writing. That involves getting out there in real time and going to these places, getting the events and the people and putting it onto a page in a way that's somewhat compelling.

On stage I do a lot of storytelling. It won't make you change the character of the story, because you can't stretch it out of truth. What you find say three nights into the tour is that a point in the periphery of the story was actually the main point of the story. You start to light it that way. In one story there are a lot of ways to approach it, a lot of ways to go through. Some of the stories I tell get kind of complex. I end up building all the aspects.

TVP: Do you find the act of touring becomes part of the process of inspiration?

HR: When I tour I watch a lot of news, and I work in a lot of current events. Just in the nature of moving I find that geographic displacement has always been a great tool for creativity and spontaneity. The scene is constantly moving and there is very little that's familiar. I find that I'm more creative on the road than I am off the road.

TVP: Do you get a sense of a current of feeling in America from hitting so many places in the last few months?

HR: You have to remember, you can travel a whole lot, as I do, but your audience is only a certain slice of the American demographic. I'm not going to be getting a whole lot of K.K.K. members at my show. I can't really draw a bead on what they are thinking about. People who buy a ticket to see me do my thing are usually on my side. I don't run into a lot of people who worship Newt Gingrich. In a way I'm preaching to the converted. I find a lot of people who are pretty angry with how things are in America, which I think is very healthy.

TVP: Did you run into a lot of hostility when you were doing the WM3 tour.

[For information on the Memphis 3, three teenagers convicted of killing three children and thought by many to be innocent visit www.wm3.org]

HR: No, not really. There was one day in Memphis Tennessee, which is right next to West Memphis Arkansas, where the incident happened, where we enjoyed a press blackout. The local ticket vendor had been threatened, so we didn't sell a lot of tickets. Fortunately, the venue sold tickets and word-of mouth provided a decent audience. There was a small demonstration in front of the venue, which received a lot of coverage. I did manage to meet one of the mothers of the slain children. She was glad that we were doing what we were doing, which was great to hear. The whole time there was one of those Channel 7 cameras waiting for the fist fight. It was kind of a Michael Jackson day- with the media. The show was fine, but we all breathed a sigh of relief when the bus rolled out of there. We raised a ton of money on that tour. We rocked out, and not one show was anything less than a 9.5!

TVP: How are the efforts toward the WM3 working out?

HR: We gave them about $120,000, which is now with their lawyers. They're now waiting for the State of Arkansas to shuffle some paper around and give them permission to test three pieces of DNA evidence.

TVP: Where is the consensus coming from that the WM3 were wrongfully convicted? What gives you the sense that this is an important cause?

HR: It is pretty evident that these guys didn't get a fair day in court. There was no compelling physical evidence brought against them. There is a strong likelihood that this new DNA testing will be compelling enough to warrant a new trial, or result in them going home.

The three incarcerated boys cannot wait for this DNA to get tested. They want to go to court. They want to show everyone that they're innocent. If I were guilty I would not be all that hot on DNA evidence being tested because it would implicate me. These guys are ecstatic about the prospect because they really want to get out there and show you a thing or two about innocence and guilt. This leads you to think that maybe they're innocent. There is a lot of compelling evidence that wasn't checked out; it makes you wonder why it wasn't. There are so many people who weren't talked to who should have been, one in particular.

My opinion is that they are innocent. Why not give them a fair day in court, innocent or guilty. Every scumbag pedophile drug dealer deserves at least a fair day in court. They deserve due process- that's how we run this place.

TVP: The Punk lifestyle has always seemed to promote drugs. You've used it as a medium to fight drug abuse.

HR: I certainly speak out against them. All the evidence shows me that drugs are a bad idea.

TVP: Did it feel strange coming up through Black Flag. The music industry even to this day can be perceived as not being hostile to drugs. Did if feel strange to be against that, but so close to it?

HR: In those days, and in every band I've even been in, we worked rally hard on the music. All we ever really did was play and drive and play and drive and try to eat three meals a day. We always got the gigs in, but we didn't always get the three square meals. It wasn't even an idea- throwing drugs into the mix. We were an ambitious band, playing hard every night, there was no room for that when you're trying to be excellent nightly.

TVP: Do you think punk has been homogenized, co-opted by the culture?

HR: Anything that hangs around long enough will be, to where you can find all kinds of death video games. Everything is eventually absorbed into modern culture. I'm a 43-year old. The gripe of an 18-year-old might not be necessarily my gripe. I respect them, but it is not my preferred listening at this point. I can't say that I'm an expert on what can be seen as contemporary Punk Rock.

TVP: What do you thing is pushing the edge now?

HR: It all seems to be pretty palatable these days.

TVP: Can you talk to me about "Shock and Awe, My Ass"?

HR: I took exception with the way this war was sold to us. At one point I was sitting in this bus, where I am sitting now, watching the news. A General was talking about how we would shock and awe the Iraqis and bring them a light show the likes of which they'd never seen before. I thought, what is this, a Direct TV sports package? Are you selling me ultimate fighting on Pay Per View? Or, is this a war where there's going to be American and Allied K.I.A. and along with the bad guys there's going to be dead women and little children, which happens in all wars?" If we're going to war, can't we be a little grave and serious, unless you're insecure and don't believe in what you're selling. It made me terribly angry that this is the way we chose to talk about what is now 500 American dead. It was sold like, "We're going to kick some ass!" I'm not with that. A soldier wrote to me and told me he heard about my thoughts on the matter. He said that that was to pump up the troops. I said that it's the kind of things a soldier should hear, but not civilians. When you're on CNN hearing this, the whole world hears it. I don't want the world to perceive this country that way. We should be careful how we speak of these things out of respect for what will happen and what it will mean to the world.

TVP: It seems like the media and the administration were singing the same song.

HR: I don't agree. Some of the media was gung ho with it. I remember one Marine being interviewed who said, "I feel bad for all those people being hurt by Sadam, but isn't he Iraq's problem?" I thought that was interesting coming from a Marine. There are many people who are not in support of this war. Everyone supports the troops, as we should.

TVP: You are doing a lot of acting in very mainstream action type films. It looks like you're funneling a lot of money into artistic projects that don't get the attention they deserve.

HR: I've been doing that for years. Whenever I do an acting gig, it's always a good story, because I'm not an actor.

TVP: What makes America so prone to seek the lowest common denominator in the art and media that's being consumed?

HR: Of any country I've been to with an active media and an active consumer population we do go more for the easiest and least valuable stuff. The U.S. and England, which is just as inundated with magazines and TV and all that.

We're just born and raised to consume in mass quantities. Lots of food, lots of TV, lots of movies, it can't all be good. If you're going to serve someone a lot of food it has to be cheap, processed junk. The same is true of media.

TVP: What can people expect of your current speaking tour?

HR: I'm going to be talking a lot- for two hours. Stories of where I've just been and stories of things that are going on now, nothing that I did last year.

TVP: What kind of musical projects are you working on now?

HR: I'm doing this until April, so that's all that I'm thinking about.

Unleashing the Beast: An Interview With Henry Rollins

By Jessica Hopsicker
March, 2005

Henry Rollins, what doesn't that man do? Besides fly or turn water into wine or even hot air balloon ride for that matter. No, the man isn't God, but he's still pretty damn cool. The Crier was lucky enough to catch this globe-trotting, publishing, punk rocker, talker, namedropper, TV and radio show host after a recent trip to Siberia.

JH: Between roles in various movies and TV shows, owning your own publishing company, having a weekly radio show and "Henry's Film Corner" on the IFC, embarking on USO tours, and not to mention The Rollins band; is there anything left that you want to embark on?

Henry Rollins: yeah, I'd like to be a better writer, that's what I'd like to do. I'd like to work on that more. It's very time intensive, it takes a lot of discipline, and in the future I would like to see what I've got, you know in that respect. And that I'd like to really spend more time on a single book project, and see what it really takes. But I have no ambition to direct, or do anything like that, hot air balloon. Pretty much everything I do it takes up all my time. I don't know if I'm really good at any of it. I give it all my best shot.

JH: You've basically never stopped moving since your rise to fame as the as the lead singer of Black Flag. What is it that keeps you so obsessed?

HR: I like working, I like what I do. Interesting- and I come from a minimum wage working world, and so, that being said I know what I left behind, and this is infinitely more interesting. Both my parents were very busy hard working people. So I was raised in that environment. So working a lot is just kind of what I know how to do. I can't think of doing it any other way really.

JH: Tell me about the USO Tour.

HR: Well, I've done a lot of them, actually. The USO contacted me in the fall of 2003 and asked if I'd like to go out and meet some soldiers and I said, "yeah." Because even though I disagree with the war in Iraq, and I don't like the president's policies, a lot of his foreign and domestic polices I have problems with. But with that being said, I don't have a problem with the soldiers. They are employees and they go where they're told. So I have no problem going out to meet them. They sent me out on a trip to Afghanistan, Kyrgyzstan, and Qatar. And I came back from that and said, "that was great, can I have another?" And then after that I went to Iraq and Kuwait, and asked if I wanted could go out again. I went to Honduras. Then again I asked and I went back to Afghanistan and Kyrgyzstan. I was in Abu Dhabi that last trip in December. In February of this year I spent a day with wounded soldiers in Bethesda Army Medical Center, I believe that's what it's called, and the Walter Reed hospital. I think the next USO Tour will be South Korea and Japan, and that is in June when I get back from Australia.

JH: I heard you were just on vacation in Siberia.

HR: Well, I wouldn't exactly call that a vacation, I went to see if I could endure a week alone on a train going across Siberia. I did the entirety of the trans Siberian Rail, went from Moscow to Vladivostok. One week on a train and I got a lot of writing done. It'll be a chapter of a travel book I'm working on. So, there's not a lot to do vacation wise in a train car... especially in Siberia. Interesting, it was interesting and it was my 5th trip to Russia.

JH: You're writing a travel book?

HR: Well, yeah, it's a bunch of different chapters going here and going there and a lot of the USO stuff is in it. There's no way you're going to spend a week in Baghdad and not have a bunch of stories. I will be doing a lot of traveling this year. Hopefully, I'll get a moment free, and I'll be in Vietnam and Cambodia later in the year. And where ever else the USO has me. I travel to about 1-3 different countries a year that I've never seen before. I try to at least.

JH: Where did you come up with the idea for "Henry's Film Corner?"

HR: I didn't, the producers did actually. The guys at this company called Swift River, they approached me with the whole thing kinda storyboarded out. They said "we'd like you for the show, what do you think." And I said, "this seems really interesting." So they pitched it around. We ran a 12-minute version of the show to show people. The Independent Film channel said, 'Okay we like it. Here is a budget make a half hour version, like a broadcast version and we'll see how we like it." And they did like it and said

"Great, well congratulations, have a show, and that's what happened. So it wasn't my idea.
   Going

JH: And how did Heidi come into play?

HR: Oh, Heidi works here at my office; Heidi has been here for about eight years. They said to me one day that we need somebody on the show for you to bounce off of. Someone you can have a rapport with. I said, "well I got somebody for you, come over and meet Heidi, she's got more personality than any of us know what to do with. And they came over and they met Heidi and went "whoa." I said, "Yeah that's what we always say." She is a very amazing person, I think. And so, she's the one that gets all the fan mail. On my radio show a bunch of times, when she was there, she got all the mail. Now she's got a place on the TV Show as well, and that's cool.

JH: Are there any films out there that you want to trash but are afraid to?

HR: I'm not afraid to trash anything. It's America, trash on. If were to trash something, I wouldn't necessarily trash it. I would rather just critique it, have fun and be informed. Like, if I were going to rip a film, I would sit and watch it carefully. And if I don't like it I would be very sure I don't, and I'll tell why. I wouldn't just bucket the thing and go "this sucks," which is kind of boring and stupid. I'll pin point why, same thing if I like a film I'll break it down. If you've seen the show and the films I go after- I'm right. I mean it's not like somebody can say, "I Robot was really good, you just didn't watch it right." And no, I watched it and it sucked. It wasn't will Smith's fault or any of the other actor's faults. It was a dumb idea. Not even the concept isn't bad, its men running on from cartoons all day. It's just not on. So if you go from that premise, then you can unleash the beast. So, no I'm not afraid to say what I want, that's what I do.

JH: All right then, what about Constantine? It seems bad reviews for that are hard to come by.

HR: It's not really like you're going to get me to go. Heidi was dragged to it over the weekend and she told me about it not an hour ago. She said she was laughing so hard someone kicked her chair. (laughs)

JH: Really

HR: Yeah, she said it was awful. And there's no way, unless I had to see the film for the show. There is no way I'm going to pay $9.50 to stand in line and go see Constantine. Not unless someone came back and said, "Oh my god, you gotta see this film." There's no way. It's nothing against Keanu, I have met him on several occasions and couldn't meet a nicer guy- I just don't really get off on his movies.

JH: And what's The Rollins band up to these days?

HR: I'm going to be doing some song writing with Chris Haskett of the band this month and next month in New York, and well, we'll see if anything happens. When you get older the songs don't come as easily as they used to. So we'll have to see what's left at the bottom of the can.

Hey Mister Mustard
Man: Mark Kikel

September 2005
by Jessica Hopsicker

Do you know the Mustard Man? Perhaps not, that is unless you've been to Portland/Vancouver area, or caught him on the Tonight Show, downing a bottle of mustard. He's the fling-fling wearing, mustard chugging, stoner comic from way out yonder on the West Coast. It was a bizarre twist of luck to hook up with this original individual. We were then engaged in a rather long-winded conversation; covering everything from the swinging lifestyle of a 43 year old man, how corporate America is not always the answer, a possible tour with Tommy Chong, and his homage to the dearly departed Mitch Hedberg.

Jessica Hopsicker: I guess we should start with why the Mustard Man?

Mustard Man: Just about everyone in Portland knows who the Mustard Man is. I was just Mark Kikel, married, had a daughter and I was working as an environmental consultant. The highest level I reached was Senior Project

51

Manager, which meant leading large-scale asbestos and lead removal projects.

JH: Sounds like fun.

MM: Yeah... but I kept doing comedy, I'd hit the open mike, you know, so I'd stay fresh. Then in 94' Mark and Brian, KLOS Mark and Brian, I don't know if you've heard of them, they have a radio show they simulcast all over the country and actually have a star on the Hollywood walk of fame. Anyway, they were having a contest, a "What would you do to hang out with Mark and Brian Contest." I volunteered to drink a 32oz bottle of mustard while playing the theme from the Lone Ranger on my belly button. They loved it and the next thing you know they're up in Portland broadcasting from their station there, and 10 million people were listening to me drink a bottle of mustard in the studio live at 7:00 in the morning. Brian just spit out "Oh you Mustard Man you!" The name just kinda stuck.

I went to Harvey's Comedy Club that night- I did 32oz at the radio station, and then we crashed this Portland morning show called AM Northwest, they had no idea we were even coming and I drank another 32oz of mustard in front of their studio audience. And about that time, I'm higher than a kite, because the vinegar thins your blood out really bad, and the doctor later said I was suffering from acute anemia-

JH: Wow!

MM: Yeah... It's not something you do; it messes up your digestive tract horribly. What I have learned through the years is that when I do the mustard thing, which is basically for publicity, is don't digest- I now drink a glass of water with baking soda in it and find some private place were I can expel. I don't let that stuff go through like I let that

80oz and it basically changed the way I live. So I did the Mark and Brian thing and became the Mustard Man, Mark the Mustard Man Kikel.

The Mustard Man is beginning to leak out. "I'll be darned; he's on the Tonight Show." If you made a list of all the comics from Portland that have been on the Tonight Show, I'm the only comic on that list. But then there's has to be an asterisk at the end of my name, then you have to look down at the bottom of the page and it would read, "asterisk did not tell joke only drank mustard." Because I'm not going to pretend like I'm some sort of big shot and tell jokes on the Tonight Show. All I did was this stupid mustard thing I do for publicity and exposure.

One of the things I do to make money is make and sell these pokers and clips to all the functioning alternative shops in the Portland and Vancouver area. As a matter of fact, they are in Oregon, Washington, and Montana and I also take them on the road with me and sell them, they're called Joker Pokers, toys from the bins of Good Will. They're pretty cool, and you can check out some other interesting items at www.themustardman420.fanspace.com.

I'm getting ready to launch a tour called the Funny 420 Tour, I'm middling with this guy Arlo Stone. He knew Mitch and was actually there the night I met Mitch, but Arlo's like the local hippie political expert around here, this guy looks at the simple plain and finds the absolute absurd in it. He's so political; he delves into the stuff and makes it easy to understand in a really funny way. Arlo's great. I also picked up this young hot shot from Portland, his name is Richard Bain, and he's going to be our emcee. So what I have done is package up a whole comedy show and am selling it, and booking venues here in the Portland Vancouver area, and probably go as far north as Seattle and see how far down I5

I can take it, hey, and probably hit some of the colleges. Hit up a few of the venues that Mitch did.

JH: So you have pretty much cornered the market on Mitch Hedberg Memorabilia I heard.

MM: My Mitch Hedberg collection is to me, right now, nowhere near a monetary value. It's a shrine, definitely a homage that I'm paying to him and trying to gain some inspiration and yeah, he's just an awesome guy, was an awesome guy, was- … I'm still not used to saying that. Since Mitch's death- wow, we felt it. I know this is going to sound stupid but it really was a disruption in the Force- I mean I couldn't stop crying for a good week. Every time I'd think about it I'd start crying. I only met him that one time, I mean I saw him perform on TV and all that stuff but that one night- I can't say that it didn't influence me a great deal because it did. He was incredible, a good man and a great comic. It was a sad day for comedy… the camaraderie. We lost one of our generals and no one will ever be able to replace, to fill that void. The only thing I can do is to continue what I already do. If I'm onstage and someone thinks I'm piecing my material on something and thinks of Mitch. I would just be honored to be in the same thought as him. I never got to open with him, and I have always wanted to work with him.

JH: Is there anyone you'd like to work with in the future?

MM: I got a lady, Mary Jane from Mary Jane's House of Glass, and she's real good friends with Tommy Chong. He's off probation in September and wants to hit the road and he's looking for an opening act. Mary Jane told me to pack it down with my new head shot, DVD, the whole nine yards. She's already talked to him about me, and the

Tonight Show didn't hurt at all. So it's very feasible that I could be touring with Tommy Chong this winter.

JH: Wow, that's cool.

MM: Or, opening with him on tour when he hits the road. He was doing a show that got shut down, because people were not respecting his probation. He can't be associating with certain elements. He has to play the game all the way through to the end of his probation. He's dying to get out on tour. So, I'm very lucky to have that connection. Something like that could be what it takes for me to finally go nationwide.

JH: Will it be hard to maintain a relationship while you're bringing your show to so many clubs?

MM: My girlfriend's name is Megan and we've been together for 2 ½ years and that's been the longest relationship I've had other than my marriage. And I absolutely love her, she's 15 years younger than me. It's not like I chase around younger girls. The joke I tell is "I love, her she's 15 years younger than me, she's bi- and I don't mean polar." For a 43-year-old guy I do have a lot of fun.

JH: Indeed.

MM: I have been described as one-of-a-kind. It's weird I've had someone call me a pimp one day and later I was called a hippy. I combined the two and I like to be called a hippy. I wear the tie-dye and color coordinated bright yellow sweats, my hemp jewelry. I wear gold but it's not bling bling its pieces of gold that women have thrown back at me in anger. So I like to refer to it as fling fling.

I'm making a living, I'm not rich, but I'm making a living now doing stand up comedy and just developing- I've finally metamorphosed into the Mustard Man, which is pretty much this big friendly stoner type guy. So anyway that's pretty much the new thing I'm getting ready to go to Seattle hit a bunch of clubs, I'm focusing on this funny 420 tour and coming to New York in September. I couldn't be happier where I am sitting right now. Don't get me wrong, I wouldn't mind having a couple movies, or a half hour comedy special under my belt, but you know what that's just stuff I need to go out and get and I'm working on that…. So do you have any questions, I guess I have rambled

JH: No, I think you pretty much just covered everything.

MM: Did I? – Is this what you call an easy interview?

JH: Yeah.

MM: Okay. I had a feeling that I was just going to ramble and answer everything you had to ask.

JH: Pretty much.

MM: Cool, cool. Well, I can't tell you how excited I am and how grateful. This is really cool, kinda weird, I mean a West Coast comic appearing in an East Coast paper. I believe there's a reason for everything and the fact that'll be in New York shortly. Who knows, maybe I'll get a week of gigs at colleges out there.

Richie Havens: Grace of the Sun

November 2004
By T. Virgil Parker

If you've ever seen the Woodstock movie, you'll see him at the beginning of the concert blowing away an audience of half a million people; a feat he was forced to carry off impromptu. Pushed back onstage over and over again to fill the void of missing bands, Richie Havens blew through every song he knew. Imagine looking out at an audience that spans the horizon and then looking into yourself for something, anything. He started playing some chords and then built the song that represents the entire alternative generation of the sixties: "Freedom." This bit of spontaneous inspiration assured him a permanent place in the world of music, and perhaps history.

In an era awash with divisiveness, war and bad vibes (now, as well as then), his mere presence has always been mysteriously healing. Richie Havens is one of those rare people whose energies fill a concert hall before he says a word or bangs a pick against the strings. People describe his concerts as a spiritual experience.

Presently older than many people who keep their teeth in a jar, his profound energy is evident in his most recent CD. Grace of the Sun is possibly the best effort he's ever put forward; a compelling disk that carries a powerful message of togetherness and good will that easily transcends our petty differences.

TVP: One of those random but perhaps synchronistic moments happened while I was driving here. Bob Dylan was on National Public Radio doing his first live interview in 20 years.

Richie Havens: Too Much!

TVP: He pointed out that for a long time some his most profound music was completely dead to him for a number of years. That doesn't seem to have been a problem for you. You've been carrying your vibe at 200 percent for the last 40 years. How?

RH: I'm convinced that it's been a continuum. It's one thread that I've managed to keep weaving into the present. That thread is sharing what was given to me by others. It's the people who inspired me to do what I've been doing, that carries me along.

TVP: You expend more energy in five minutes than most people do all day.

RH: I don't notice it because it doesn't feel like I have that much energy when I walk in the door. It's always the audience.

TVP: You ever get the feeling that you send out energy and get it back?

RH: Absolutely. When I first started in the Village. I learned that personally. I even gave it a metaphor: it's like breathing.

I walk on the stage, they applaud, and they exhale. When I sit on the stool and start playing I'm exhaling the energy and I'm inhaling. This breathing process goes through the set. They give it to me. I always know the first and last song I'm going to sing. Whatever's in between the audience has made me do.

TVP: Let's take half a million people and give you the opportunity- really the need- for complete spontaneity The song *Freedom* appears out of nowhere. Did you feel almost possessed by the spirit around you?

RH: Completely. It started nine months before Woodstock happened. The guys who were trying to do it kept looking for a town to do it in. They always came back saying they had a town to do it in. Two weeks later the press would be writing about that town changing their mind and saying no. This went on for nine months. What the press didn't realize is that they were building an audience, because every time an announcement went out that the location was refused, more people found out about it. By the time they got to the last town, Woodstock, which said no, there was two weeks to go before it actually happened. Due to the press, the farmer Max Yasger heard of their dilemma and came to them.

The forum was actually created for what happened because of the way we were being radicalized by the press each time they announced another shutdown.

Then there wasn't going to be a Woodstock, for about five hours. There was no way to get to the stage. All of the other bands were at the hotels, with no way to get to the field, by car or truck or anything because of all the people

They found a farmer who had that small bubble helicopter and the promoters knocked on my door. I had the least stuff, so they could take me over and put me on stage.

That's how I got over there. Flying over those people, I looked down and thought "If this picture hits the newspaper tomorrow, we've won. We would be now above ground, un-relegated to the underground.

TVP It was almost a birthing process.

RH: Exactly. And it was. God knows they only expected 70,000 people.

TVP: Do you ever wonder about the two sides of the legacy of Woodstock?

RH: Every divine happening lacks managerial oversight. It just happened. People came to be together and to hear music.
   All of the West Coast bands who were there, 90% of them had never played on the East Coast. Something happened there that was very special for the audience as well the musicians.

TVP: I, while not really trying, conducted a social experiment by going to Woodstock 99, which was hedonism at its worst, and then heading over to Bethel Festival, the site of the original Woodstock. The two events could not possibly have been more different.

RH: For 26 years, those concerts had been going on at that field for free. The locals were able to go there and have their own concert. Anywhere from 10,000 to 45,000 people would show up. The vibration of that place, and the happening aspect of that concert was carried on for 26 years before the second official Woodstock happened.

TVP: To many people who are associated with the social movements of the sixties, there's a perception of sort of a psychic battery that's been charging down for the last 35 years.

RH: That's the view of the press. They haven't had over half a million people on the first day of any concert since.

TVP: You've taken that energy and somehow continually renewed it.

RH: I've been carrying what I'm doing from the very beginning. I spent seven years in Greenwich Village on stage every night for seven days a week, playing thirteen sets a night, passing the basket like everyone else that was down there. Few of us were getting paid a salary by anyone. There was a steel drum band who were the big stars at the Village clubs, and they were getting paid $125 a week- the whole band! You could live, at least.

The point I'm trying to make is that from that point on, I've been able to do exactly what I'm doing- sharing songs that changed me personally.

TVP: You have preceded the independent music trend by thirty years.

RH: Yes. In 1970 I had my first label. It was only because there was a promotion guy at MGM who was trying to renegotiate my contract for a $15,000 advance. This was my third album coming up. I had to meet with him to set up a bunch of interviews. This was the first time I'd been in the building, even though they'd been doing my albums for three years. I got up there and met the guy. He said that I was one of the few people actually making money for the record company and that I should ask them for my own label. I had no idea what to do with my own label. He convinced me that it was possible. I figured out that I could get several people that I knew -who wouldn't get picked up anywhere else- onto the label. We ended up with a $700,000 contract, in 1970.

TVP: At this point, the only other musical act to have done that was The Beatles, I believe.

RH: That's right. I started the label recording my albums, and I ended up recording three other groups, and it worked for them as well. I just learned to do what I did for myself. I'd take the bands into the studio, do the music, record it, and take it to the next step.

TVP: So, again, it just happened.

RH: And if it hadn't I wouldn't be here right now. I played all the time whether I had an album to support or not. I outlasted five presidents at MGM and they rebuilt the company around myself and a couple of other artists. I've been very fortunate to have people looking out for my albums when they come along.

TVP: You are an activist who transcends politics, and a musician who transcends show business.

RH: Yes. I realized that I was out of show business when I stopped singing Doo Wap with my friends in Brooklyn. When I heard the music coming out of Greenwich Village I was then in the communications business. That's what I've been in since then, music that has a meaning; that has a message that anyone can tap into.

TVP: I can also point out that many people perceive you as a spiritual leader while transcending religion.

RH: A lot of people say that the experience they have at the shows is very spiritual. I had a grandmother who made me go to church as a kid. It set me on a path of what I call comparative religion studies, which I did for like 17 years on my own, trying to find the roots of where religion came from, what the purposes were, and to find out in the end that they were all the same. I accepted that all religions perceptually were the same. They all point to the same direction; we are all working on becoming human beings.

TVP: I was curious about your recent album *The Grace of the Sun*. Did you intentionally release that under the sign of Leo?

RH: No, but it is a good thing. When it comes back to me in hindsight, there's something terribly magical about it.

TVP: The album is shot through with solar images; even the structure of the music is somehow solar.

RH: It really is, and I didn't realize that. The songs that I wrote came to me practically instantly a few weeks before I finished the album. I don't sit down to write anything. I stopped doing that when I first hit the Village, people ware singing with a global perspective and the global aspect of our oneness. That changed my life. I decided that I was never going to try to write like that, I didn't. A title would hit me in a taxi, and because of the title, I would understand what the song was. I'd go home and write the song down. The songs came out whole; they came out with a total understanding of what had to be said.

TVP: There's a profoundly organic sense to the album as a whole. Even the covers feel like a natural part of the album.

RH: People said they'd heard *All Along the Watchtower* somewhere before, where is it? I'd say that it was a Bob Dylan song. They'd say that when they heard it, it didn't sound like Bob Dylan.

I tell them I sing it to the best of my ability with the

emotion that it gave me when I first heard it by the original artist, rather than the interpretation that Jimi Hendrix did.

TVP: This album is more contemplative than much of your work, but if anything it's more energetic than anything you've done.

RH: This album was done spontaneously because we always believed that recordings should be performances. My best albums have always been when I have been able to produce them myself. Everyone on the record was in the room when the tape was rolling.

TVP: So it was almost live.

RH: That's always the best way. You always get the natural and normal dynamics of a whole band.

TVP: I've heard that you have a project called the Natural Guard. Can you tell me a little about it?

RH: The Natural Guard actually came out of another children's project I had with a friend who was a Navy Seal. He once told me that he didn't trust grown ups at all. He could only trust in children. Having confided that to me I understood what an innocent person he was. His father had put him into that Navy at the age of fourteen to get him off the streets. He was the youngest Seal ever trained- but they didn't know that. Because of that training he was able to see what needed to be done, but also because of that training he was going to stay with a challenge and bring it to a conclusion.

One day I asked him what he really wanted to do with his life. He said that he wanted to have a museum for children, where they could come and touch things from the ocean, and learn how to teach people how not to destroy the waters they live around. We built this museum mostly with stuff from that he had gathered from around the world. It was called the North Wind Undersea Institute. He brought this stuff down, antique bottles, a cannon he had found. We must have had 200 sets of shark teeth from a lot of different species. We were able to put together some very interesting exhibits. He thought that children should know that pollution of the water was killing off all this life. The museum became a place where we got 30,000 kids a year to come through for about six years.

These kids would all come in with their classes and we did an exhibit called "The Right to Live." It was on whales. Little did we know that we had created the first historical analysis of Yankee whaling. We traveled to all the whaling towns around and we found out that none of them had any historical museums or displays about the whales, only the whalers- the culture of the people who were whaling. We tried to find information on the whales. My friend had me paint pictures of all the different whales for the display, but that we would hang an empty frame for the extinct species with a label indicating the date of extinction. The kids would say "Where's that whale?" and their parents would have to tell them.

He made a black coffin in the shape of whale, and he had tombstones around in for all the extinct whales.

In the classes at the museum we asked the children what an environment was. They always said that rain forests were an example of an environment, and they didn't live in one because they live in a city! We had to tell them that anywhere they lived was an environment. They had parks and squirrels and birds right in their own towns. That was a way of giving them a viewpoint of their own community. That's what the Natural Guard came from. We had to extend that out to kids anywhere: seeing your own community as an endangered environment.

TVP: With that comes a responsibility for your own environment.

RH: That's right. And consider yourself as the most endangered animal in it. The Natural Guard was one of the first three environmental justice organizations. We actually got the Points of Light Award from Hillary Clinton. These kids change their own environment. They find out what's wrong with it and come up with an idea to change that.

Our job was to get non-profit chapters running and find children who wanted to join Natural Guard. The second day we opened the door we had fifteen kids walk in the door, and they never left for six years. We ended up with fifteen chapters around the New Haven area.

These kids created such a furor of change that everybody had to sit up and take notice. The support that came from that was essential for donations and for help. We wanted the support to come from the communities and not from the government. The places that count on government grants are lucky to last a year.

An eight-year-old kid might ask if we can grow a garden to feed the homeless. They actually did it. They grew three gardens and grew food in the middle of New Haven Connecticut, which I never thought was possible. They supplied the soup kitchens that summer. They did that for six years. They found out that lead poisoning was a problem there and designed a coloring book to raise awareness. That coloring book ended up going out to all the schools in the state.

Out of sixteen kids in the first group, eleven of them went to college. These are kids living with single parents in communities where kids shoot kids. One of them is in Harvard studying to become an environmental lawyer.

TVP: What is your advice to musicians starting out now?

RH: Only sing songs you love because they actually impart knowledge to you. Sing songs that you love because you'll sing them the best.

Michael Franti: Barefoot Bodhisattva

May 2007
By Jess Hopsicker

Some time ago, I had the pleasure of standing there and watching the man walk past me. It all happened so slowly, on the deck of the lodge at the Mountain Jam, a northeast hippie fest nestled on Hunter Mountain. I remember how the seconds stretched into minutes. I stood there, open-mouthed as if I was about to speak but I was mesmerized. It was from the way he carried himself, to the bottom of his feet. Amidst the misty driving rain upon the mud-slathered mountain, his bare feet were clean. For all I knew they never touched the ground. I craned my neck to watch the doors part before him, and once he left, the spell was broken. Time returned. "Michael Franti," my festival friend muttered beside me, "damn I wanted him to sign something." It made me wonder if he was as entranced as I was.

"Uh-huh" I answered, slowly coming back to my senses, my face flushed, "the man's a god."

I was crushed to have missed his show earlier, and was

later regaled with stories of how he leapt up onstage during Keller Williams's set along with 1000 beat-boxers. Corralled in the ticket room, I witnessed the exodus after the show, as the wide-eyed spectators lined up to leave; they mumbled his name with admiration.

My first encounter with him was purely superficial, but the moment stayed with me. A year later, the chance arose to conduct an actual interview the "god" Franti, and little did I know how right I was about his divinity. Michael Franti is a minstrel, storyteller, songwriter and a human rights activist: a real barefoot bodhisattva. In a time of global turmoil, his message is simple, peace through music and human contact. "We can bomb the world to pieces, but we can't bomb it into peace." Reach out with a kind word instead of a WMD. In 2004, armed with a guitar, he took a camera crew to the war-torn world of the Middle East. Instead of the few biased media feeds we Americans receive, he witnessed and embraced the human wreckage first hand. In the footage shot, a music video / documentary entitled I Know I'm Not Alone, his message is growing in popularity.

Another anniversary of "Mission Accomplished" passed us by. What good is one man's mission of peace going to accomplish when everyone else it seems to be preparing for the end of the world?

Through music, he spreads his message. It's up to us to listen, dance, sing along, and pass it on.

JH: You have a real social responsibility as an artist; do you pay a high price for that?

MF: I think all of us have a social responsibility no matter what walk of life we come from; I'm able to mix music with what I do so I always have fun doing it. I don't think about it as being a high price. I think of it as being a great opportunity in my life.

JH: Is it hard to stay underground with so much respect behind you?

MF: At times, but every time I come home. My kids and my family life humble me, digging in my garden and stuff at home.

JH: In 2004 you toured around the Middle East, with just a guitar; did you go in with any preconceived notions, or with an open mind?

MF: Well, I tried to go in with an open as mind as possible but I'm the kind of person that really questions our government's motives about entering Iraq. I didn't feel that they were justified. When I got there I saw the pain and suffering on both sides. The Iraqi families that lost everything, they lost their homes they lost family members, and they didn't have access to food, healthcare or an education. I met US soldiers that thought they were going over there for one reason, and then they found out that those reasons were lies. I guess the way that it really changed me, is that I've done a lot of work connecting with veterans and military families.

JH: Was the whole process cathartic and were you pleased with the outcome?

MF: Well, making the film was a very cathartic ritual, we had over 200 hours of videotape, and we had to get it down to an 86-minute film. The whole process, as I watched over the footage, took me back to the places where I was, and sometimes while I was there I didn't have a chance to stop and feel and emote everything that was happening at the time, and when you get back home and you relive it. So what I did, I wrote songs, they ended up being in the film, and they helped express my emotions about it.

JH: From you being there first hand what kind of media disinformation have you witnessed?

MF: Well, I guess the main thing is disinformation by omission. We have yet on the American television to see the effects that the bombing has on the lives of individuals, we don't see their homes, the buildings; I guess the other misconception is that they want us to be there. Most Iraqis want us to leave.

JH: Do you think the American people have grown a bit apathetic, or desensitized as result?

MF: We Americans are a bit like people anywhere else, just trying to deal with the six inches in front of our faces, trying to take care of our families, going to school finding a job, and trying to get to that job on time every day. Its difficult for people to connect sometimes, what happens with politics in America is that it so greatly effects us as well as the rest of the world; in this time of climate change, war and economic instability.

JH: How did they treat you as an American, but not one that they'd necessarily expect?

MF: Most people treated me with incredible generosity. I was really amazed at just how many people would open their homes for me. They would invite me in for food; offer me a place to stay for the night. There was incredible generosity that I rarely witness in this country.

JH: Is there another project you are working on?

MF: Right now I'm writing songs for a new album that were going to record in July and August. It won't come out for a while yet. We just launched a YouTube TV channel called FrantiV, sort of like my last name, with a V at the end.

As I travel around on tour I meet all kinds of interesting people that I'd like the world to know about. The first two episodes have Dennis Kucinich and Jack Johnson They're launched now.

JH: How do you build your sound?

MF: Well, usually what I do is find a guitar riff a drum grove or a base line, sometimes it could a phrase, just a little words I could put together, could be a little melody. I start to build up from there once I have a song written, usually in its raw form I could pick it apart and take it from there.

JH: Is there anything grand planned for the Mountain Jam?

MF: We always try to make every show unique, I really like Mountain Jam, and I love that part of the country. I love being up on the mountain. The only thing about the Mountain Jam is that you never know what the weather is going to be like. Sometimes it can add to the spontaneity of the performance. Whatever the weather is we try to bring enough fun and positive vibes out there. That's what I like about that festival is that the people that go. Always go into it with a sense of humor about the weather, whatever comes is going to be fine.

Cheech Marin: The Freedom of Cheech

By T. Virgil Parker

I guess when we think about Cheech and Chong there a few things that spring immediately to mind. For me the scene in Up In Smoke in which a stash of "Labrador" is retrieved by following a dog around is one of these. Other things don't come to the forefront of our consciousness, such as Disney, such as art curation.

As always when considering talent, we have to look out for unexpected diversions, deviations, detours. This is where anything worth our attention originates. The easy assumption that dope jokes is all there is to Cheech Marin would be like saying that Golf is about balls.

If you watched television between 1996 and 2001 you couldn't miss the irony of seeing Cheech Marin alongside the aptly named Don Johnson playing the roles of detectives in Nash Bridges. I offer this up as an example the enigmatic nature of the man.

You have almost certainly spent some time with him without knowing it. His rather extensive animated voice credits include a gig as a hyena alongside Whoopi Goldberg in The Lion King.

His comedic vision is obvious, and more than worth a little pruning from Tickmaster to check out their current tour, or any tour, ever. The painstaking irreverence of this work made Cheech and Chong the most successful comedy troupe in history.

When you talk to Cheech Marin, the most obvious thing is hefty dose of good will he effortlessly generates. This is not the Desmond Tutu variety, but more like you're being let in on a wicked, hysterical prank.

T. V. Parker: First I'd like to congratulate you on being one of the few English majors who is not in the food service industry.

Cheech Marin: Very good! That's true.

TVP: It looks to me like your face means "detective" to a lot of people, and to a lot of other people it means "pot head."

CM: That is a byproduct of my work ethic. I don't set goals, I just eat what's on my plate.

TVP: You look for some compelling feature of the character?

CM: I usually get to make up my own character. If they like me they put me in different situations, as far as acting goes. I was thinking about that the other day. I don't set goals. I have not ever. I just kind of do the next job that's there. Just living in the moment, which is really good. And it has buoyed me for all these years.

TVP: Well, a goal can kill creativity in a way.

CM: Yeah, I think so. I'm Chicano, I have to have three jobs.

TVP: Do you think comedy is easier from the outside of mainstream culture?

CM: No. Comedy is comedy. You either laugh or you don't, that's the criterion. All the other stuff is bullshit.

TVP: So many things are invisible to people who aren't forced to think about who they are, though comedy is as hard as it gets.

CM: Drama is accumulative, but comedy has to be immediate or it doesn't work. The analogy is like the slot machine. Every time you put a nickel in, you have to have two nickels back; otherwise it doesn't work.

TVP: Did you start out doing street comedy?

CM: No. I was always funny though. I was a funny guy. My whole family was funny. Everybody in my family, all my cousins that I grew up with, they were quick-witted and well read, and had a really outsider's viewpoint.

TVP: You grew up in a time when the counterculture was almost the only ethical choice there was.

CM: We were the first ones that were like hippies, and then we're always hippies, you know? We didn't change from being straight and then becoming a hippy.

TVP: Right. Most people these days started out as hippies and then they became CEOs.

CM: Exactly. That damn pendulum, you know? But what are you gonna do?

TVP: Some of your early stand-up work, I'm thinking

circa 1978, is as edgy as anything that's ever been done in comedy.

CM: Well, thank you.

TVP: Do you think that the development of the characters of Cheech and Chong almost made things easier or smoother?

CM: You know, yeah. There's just different periods. When we started in records we were doing multiple characters. Multiple characters, and the ones that were really the strongest that we emerged to let live in the movies were the lowrider and the hippy guy. And as we developed, our movie career was just on those two guys. Or, we did other characters, but those were the mainstays. Developing movie jobs is very different form developing stage jobs or writing jobs or even TV jobs.

TVP: It looks like just about on a daily basis you've got a show. Do you find yourself going into old improv habits?

CM: We're improv guys from day one. That's just our rhythm. It changes. That's what's great about working a lot, it changes every day, almost imperceptibly, until suddenly this other thing comes out. But that's the only way to get it out.

TVP: It's pretty clear that even in the movies there was a lot of jamming going on.

CM: It makes for more natural rhythm, especially in comedy. We brought that rhythm into the film lexicon. We could sustain it for a whole movie, however limited the premise. The premise wasn't the star. It was these two guys juggling. That was the star.

TVP: Are you blown away that these shows are selling out left and right?

CM: Not blown away, because I suspected there was a great audience out there. But the amount of them, and there are multiple, two, three, four shows in some cities. That's surprising.

TVP: It's amazing because your own work is so respectable and so serious. It's got to feel strange to go back to doing something you were doing when you were a kid and just have the paint come right off the walls.

CM: It's amazing. You know, I missed it. It was like an asset that I couldn't access. I owned half of it and I couldn't make any use of it or enjoy it or take it out for a ride when I wanted to, you know? And Tommy; we both did stuff, I did a little bit of standup but not much, he went into the standup world. But it was like we each had half of a treasure map. The only way you could access the treasure was that you had to put the two halves together, and then the doors opened up. It was like Raiders of the Lost Ark, or some shit. [Turning to television]. Oh man, Camilo Villegas just made like a hundred foot put.

TVP: Wow.

CM: Dang. See? Latinos are taking over the world; I'm just the forefront of the wave there.

TVP: That's the one thing I've never been able to find exciting, golf. I don't know why.

CM: You gotta play it.

TVP: They say that seventy percent of the world's business deals are transacted on the golf course.

CM: I don't doubt it. Well, I don't think it's the deals exactly, or the transactions, it's the sizing up of each other. You can tell a lot about somebody by the way they play golf.

TVP: You can tell how good I am at carrying golf clubs around…

Now, working creatively with someone, there's no other relationship like it. It's like being married, but without sex. Has that been strange, to end up working with Tommy again? Has he changed a lot? Have you changed a lot?

CM: Yes and no. I've changed a lot, and there are some aspects that are the same. There are some aspects of our particular dynamic that was the cause of our genius, and the cause of our demise as well. We have two strong personalities. It's nice to come back at this age after everyone has done what they're going to do. That speaks to our maturity. We've come back at a different level, but with a lot of the same good and bad things. We've managed to exorcize the bad things, right now.

TVP: That's wonderful, because people are so excited by this.

CM: It's fun being on stage. It gets physically wearying after a while because we're older, but being on stage in front of crowd, I mean the thing is, we just really do it and I think that's what we were best at, of anything we did, the stage show.

TVP: You're directing right now.

CM: Every once in a while. Not too much, but I do.

TVP: How different is that from putting together a comedy piece? Does it draw on the same skill set?

CM: No, no, they're different. The story has to be told through the camera. Once you realize that, it's a whole different thing. It has to be told through the camera, so you have to know the technical ends of it in order to articulate your vision of what you're trying to accomplish better.

TVP: Do you ever feel compelled to voice political opinions artistically, or do you find that boring?

CM: I'll endorse somebody. Tommy and I both endorsed Obama; we thought that was a good move. If I'm asked, I'll voice my opinion, but you know? Oh, politics. Would you like an Allan wrench or a crescent wrench? I don't know, it's a wrench, you know?

TVP: I think it's going to be a lot harder for comedians now that we have somebody who is so much harder to make fun of.

CM: Yeah. You'd be getting charged with doing black jokes. "No, they're presidential jokes! The president walks into a watermelon patch!"

TVP: You're an art collector, and really, you seem to be an authority on Chicana Art.

CM: Chicano is a variation of the word. There are a zillion definitions of how the word came to be, but originally it was an insult from Mexicans against Mexicans. The concept being that the Mexicans living in this country had left the country and were no longer truly Mexicans, they were something smaller, they were something less. They were Chicanos. Little satellite Mexicans living in the US. Everybody has a different explanation of the definitions of the word, but I like mine.

TVP: Because it's used both as a point of pride and as an insult, too.

CM: Yeah. It depends on where you were in relation to the border how much of a source of pride it was. Chicano, if you were just in Texas along the border, that meant you were low-class. It was calling you low-class, and as you got further away, into LA or California or anywhere north of that, it was the only thing that really described me. When I was a kid, the other kids were like, "hey, Mexican!" I've never even been to Mexico. I don't speak Spanish, nothing! When I heard "Chicano," that's where it started. That's me, that's what I am. I'm a Chicano. And that was the same time as the movement. But I've always called myself Chicano.

TVP: The definition I've always heard is, Mexican ancestry but born in America.

CM: Yeah, that's what it is. You can actually become a Chicano if you're experience in this country outweighs your experience in the other country. Like, Carlos Santana was born in Mexico but he's a Chicano, because he has been here much longer than he's been there. He came here as a young kid.

TVP: Can you claim Diego Rivera?

CM: Diego Rivera is a Mexican.

TVP: But he moved to New York.

CM: Yeah, but only for a short period of time to do work, then he moved back to Mexico.

TVP: True, but I thought I would help you justify picking up some of his work.

CM: "Hey man, you've got enough shelf space! Give the

Chicanos some!" That is what it was all about. It was about getting these Chicano artists, who were really good painters, I mean they were world class men. They were some of the best painters going, and I know art.

TVP: And they were pretty much unknown.

CM: Unknown. I come from show business, it's all about advertising. People gotta know you're there and know your name and what you do. I said, "You couldn't love or hate Chicano art unless you saw it," so my goal was to get it seen. That's what we're in the process of doing. We just did a big giant national seven year tour from coast to coast, all major museums. The Smithsonian, the D. Young, the Weisman. The LACMA. We just closed at LACMA here in LA. So that part of it has been hugely successful. I continue to collect and show these guys that are good.

TVP: And it all came from rolling a giant doobie?

CM: Yeah, baby! You know, that came from before the doobie. I was always into art. From a young kid I couldn't do it, and so I thought, "I really want to learn about it, 'cause I like it. So I learned it on an academic tip. I used to the library and I took out all the art books and just looked at them. Read the little stories and blah blah blah. That's how I got into world art.

TVP: You probably know more about art than an artist, because they're all about processing the experience.

CM: Yeah. They're all about process, too. My last wife was a painter, so I lived with her for like twenty years. You get a real insight of the painter's life.

TVP: Did you ever piss her off so that she would do an interesting painting?

CM: Oh yeah, or a series of them.

TVP: What do you see yourself doing in the next ten years?

CM: I would like to direct a couple more movies. And I'm working a legit play version of Cheech and Chong's story, basically how we got together. It's a very funny story. It will be a musical a la Spamalot, and I'm working on that right now. And like to write. I've got a couple book deals that I have to get to. But this thing interferes, the tour. I'd like to write a novel. I'm working on one right now.

TVP: And you've got three children's book deals?

CM: Yeah, three children's books that are coming out. Two of them have already come out and the third one is yet to, with Harper Collins. It was a character idea. I did two children's albums of music, and the publishers heard them said, "Would you like to do a series of books on them?" I said, "Hey, might as well." So you know, I was an English major, like you said at the very beginning!

TVP: Yeah, headed right back to where you came from.

CM: Yeah, one of my three jobs.

TVP: I have to ask you, how do you do voice-overs for Disney and do Cheech and Chong at the same time?

CM: You schedule them at different parts of the day. It's something I was raised to do, because Cheech and Chong albums were animation without the animation.

TVP: That's true!

CM: In that voice world, that's what we did.

TVP: Aren't you doing an animated Cheech and Chong project now?

CM: Yeah! What they're doing is, they're animating some of our earlier bits in flash animation. They're funny. I saw the first one the other day, they're very funny. Because those voices come through, you know. It's a very interesting process. I haven't visited those albums in a zillion years.

TVP: Here's a concept that was developed our office today: Cheech and Chong need to do a reality TV ghost hunting show.

CM: That'd be great!

TVP: That would really work.

CM: Yeah.

TVP: And the ghosts wouldn't even have to be there.

CM: Yeah, really. You could have guest star ghosts, but they don't have to be there either.

TVP: So, looks like you're good at multitasking.

CM: Yeah, Catholic education. That's what it is.

TVP: It seems that your life is about as fulfilling as it can possibly get.

CM: Well, you know, it has its ups and downs. Right now I'm at a little groove. I got a really beautiful, lovely, intelligent, Russian classical pianist girlfriend. So that's all good. Kids are off. They've got like pensions and all that shit.

TVP: Passive revenue?

CM: Yeah.

TVP: That's all good stuff.

CM: It's all good, yeah!

TVP: It does seem like there's a sub-text that Mexican-Americans seem not to have reached to the forefront of American consciousness the way other minorities have.

CM: You know, it is not only inevitable, it's unavoidable. There are eleven to twelve million illegal immigrants primarily from Mexico here in this country. And that's just the illegal ones. There's an equal amount of legal ones, and then the citizens that have been here for long standing. It's the biggest wave of immigration ever in the history of the country right now. What makes it different from the other waves of immigration is that it's in every state. Every single state has a large and growing Latino population that's vital to that state.

TVP: And it's taking longer to be absorbed, as well.

CM: Yeah, but they're going to be absorbed all the time. Whenever they start having funerals, there's eight new people who are going to come to the funeral. So it's unstoppable, but it's influential. You can influence this, but you can't stop what's going to happen. In the next fifty years it's going to transform into a heavily Latino influenced and populated country.

TVP: I think culture is always the forefront of that. Always.

CM: Exactly. Those are the advanced sensors of any movement: The culture of any country. The only things we leave behind as a culture is our museums and our art. There's no museum to the art of the business deal.

TVP: That's right, I was going to ask you about that! Is that in the works? LA in general doesn't have a lot of art museums.

CM: They do. They have some, and they have some very good ones, but they're struggling like all others. MOCAH, the Museum of Contemporary Art History, was struggling financially, and that will kept safe somehow, but LACMA of L.A. County is a world class museum. There's the Getty, which is good. Huntington. They've got a lot of museums, they're good.

TVP: Yeah, a lot, but it's not like the east coast. You trip over an art museum every time you turn around.

CM: Yeah, but they're getting more and more. That's kind of what I'm doing now. I'm starting to organize Latino collectors so they can be a force in the museum world. We'll buy our way in, just like everybody else did. That's the American way, and it makes sense to me.

TVP: I think you're in a position to take pride in the way you're presenting an under-represented minority.

CM: It is! It is one of the most prideful things I've ever done, because it brought to the forefront these artists, these deserving artists, you know? Like discovering somebody in the movies; Pee Wee Herman, or whoever. It feels good.

TVP: That's great. Is there anything else you want to plug?

CM: Let's see. We have a DVD of the concert tour coming up. We're going to shoot it in March, and it will be out shortly thereafter, I'm sure.

TVP: That's excellent.

CM: We're going until some part of the beginning of April, April or May, and that's it.

TVP: Are you doing Europe, too?

CM: No, I don't think we're going to go do Europe. We just got offered Australia, and we turned it down. I think we're going to take some time off. I think we're going to work on a movie, and if we want to get the kind of movie that we want to do out by the time we want it out, I'd say we have to start working on that now.

TVP: Yeah, I would say that's gotta happen.

CM: So we'd like to do that. And we've got a bunch of other boats in the water that we're trying to push in at the same time. We can't tour forever. We're fucking ancient, you know?

TVP: Not ancient. I mean, you're not B.B. King, but there are better things to do.

CM: Yeah. But touring is fun. That's the thing I missed; having my finger on the pulse of the country from being in every city every day.

TVP: It's like being a rock star without having to tune anything. It's mind boggling, the way it's being received. I want to congratulate you on it all.

CM: Thank you. It's been great. What amazes me is that we haven't been on stage or touring essentially in over thirty years, and we announce a tour and it sells out immediately without the benefit of a hit record or a hit TV show or a hit movie, nothing. Zip.

TVP: With the economy tanking like it is, that's amazing.

CM: People are thanking us for getting together. We hear that every day. They needed a laugh. They needed a pure laugh and we're it right now, so cool. America needs a hug.

TVP: Yeah, I'd say.

CM: And we needed some new buds.

TVP: Yeah, that's right. Nancy Reagan is just beginning to wear off.

CM: I love that Bush had a shoe thrown at him. That is just fitting. I bet his dad used to throw shoes at him too. He fucking ducked like a pro!

TVP: Yeah, his dad's probably a better shot.

CM: That's the best movie ever made, him ducking.

TVP: The thing I loved was the Iraqis protesting with shoes up on long poles. It was most surreal thing I've seen in quite a while.

CM: Yeah, it was funny. What a doofis. What a fucking doofis, this guy. And we elected him twice.

TVP: Twice! You know, all my friends said they were going to leave America, and instead they just told people they were Canadian.

CM: It's like getting botox. It's not a full face lift, just a little botox.

Rachel Miner: Major Talent

November 2007
By T. Virgil Parker

People go into showbiz for a variety of reasons, but often for the booty, or the bling, or the ego massage, maybe all three. The omnipresent blitz of merely OK performances is a testament to the existence of actors who are a little too dazzled by the marquee to take a good long look at the script. There have always been people who seem to have been born to walk the boards. You occasionally find them in community or street theatre. Fortunately for us, Rachel Miner's community, and her street as it were, happened to be Broadway.

As a third generation actor, it isn't surprising that she felt a calling. That the call came in at an age when most of us can't form sentences is more than a little unusual. At the age of two, she decided to act. At eight, she started working. By ten, she started a five-year gig on *The Guiding Light*. Say what you will about soap operas. You don't get to shoot a scene 20 times; special effects don't come to the rescue. You act, and act, and act.

Perhaps the single greatest testament to her devotion to the art of acting is that she made zero effort to cash in on her publicity-saturated marriage to Macaulay Culkin and stoke it into a glitzy part. Instead, she took acting-intensive Indie roles: effort high, publicity and cash nearly non-existent.

Her cameo part as the kid sister of the femme fatal in *The Black Dahlia* is an example of making maximum impact in minimal space. However, it was her work in Showtime's *Californication* that totally grabbed my attention. The insidious way her character, Secretary Danni, emerges from obscurity into Svengaliesque intrigue is marvelous to see.

T. Virgil Parker: There's probably not a time when you don't remember acting.

Rachel Miner: I do remember the time of wanting to act really badly as a little girl. But I have been doing it a long time!

TVP: It's so much a part of you now. How much of your work is intuitive and how much of it is based on study of the character?

RM: That's a really good question. I think a lot of it is intuitive. I think probably about, I don't know, maybe a 70/30 proposition. Seventy percent intuitive and thirty percent work, which doesn't mean it's not a lot of work; it's just that when it comes down to the day of shooting it's so much intuition. I'll notice if I'm talking to someone who's just starting out, they're just getting used to the cameras and lighting and where you have to stand and all that stuff. A lot of that is second nature after a while on set, you know? That factors in, too.

TVP: At this point I'd think that you'd be looking at, say, literally inhabiting a character.

RM: Yes.

TVP: So do you ever feel inhabited by these characters?

RM: No, actually, I don't. I find it pretty easy to portray a part, and I think it will affect you physically sometimes, oddly enough. Especially if you're playing a character who's really unhappy or you're going through a lot of grief and things like that. It's draining physically, but I don't find it affects me too much. There's certain aspects that might creep in that are fun. If I play a particularly outgoing character or happy character I notice that I tend to be a little more excitable in life. Things like that.

TVP: The way you perceive the world have a lot of depth, in terms of having so many different realms of experience to draw upon when you're perceiving the world.

RM: Right.

TVP: Presumably the richness with which you interpret a character is going to increase all the time.

RM: Absolutely. Every day, everything you do, you run into different people with different life experiences and it's one of the fun things, I think for anyone. If you're awake and alive and looking around the world, you get to see a little bit through different people's eyes and your view is constantly broadened. Your perspective of the world is broadened. You have more and more to draw on as an artist, certainly, and as a human being in your opinions of the world. So yeah, I find that I learn something new every day.

TVP: There is a moment in one of the Californication episodes in which your character is just beginning to put the screws into her boss, Charlie. You can detect this sense of overcoming fear. It's only an instant, and I thought, "Wow, how hard do you have to study and interpret a character to get that authenticity?"

RM: You know, I don't think it's, for me, especially with that character, a matter of hard study as much as it's just being there in that moment and inhabiting that person. I think those little moments of honesty tend to come in more by just doing it for me. Just being there and going through that scenario as that character. What would go to your mind naturally if you kind of set up a good base of the character in a scenario, and as you're going through it, you experience that moment of nervousness a little bit? Do you know what I mean?

TVP: Yes, absolutely, but I was thinking: that's more aware than I've seen an actor off -the-cuff in a television program.

RM: You've got a really interesting perspective.

TVP: You are probably uniquely suited to describe the difference between a big budget and a no budget movie. What works and what doesn't work?

RM: One of the things I love about a low budget film is that because it's a smaller group of people, and the circumstances are more trying in terms of actually getting the footage, in terms of actually getting the scene shot, you've got a lot more work to do in a day. You're forced to constantly be there. You're constantly working with other people. You're not in your trailer waiting for your scene, you know? That's the biggest difference, which I find to be positive in that, it's important in acting not to be isolated. For me, at least. That's what works: To feel alive, to communicate with other people, and to be present. So I actually like that lower budget film making kind of forces you into that. And I think it helps in that way. I think, on the other end, when technically there's a lot more difficulties it can detract from a performance. The camera reads everything that's going on in your head. You really have to work on not being distracted by those technical difficulties, and exhaustion, and hunger, and you know, what's going on around the set. the little dramas of trying to get things accomplished. When you have a budget, one of the good things is that there tends to be a different level of crew around you. I can't stress how much of a difference it can make for a performance actually showing up on screen when you've got a brilliant cinematographer and you've got a brilliant design and everything because an actor can only do so much if it's not picked up correctly by the lens and you're eyes aren't lit right. It won't read to the audience. So there's definitely a positive side to a bigger budget as well.

TVP: You can probably grab just about any Indie part out there, assuming it's not for a midget or something. You must go to certain lengths to choose scripts.

RM: I think I'm going to hire you as my representation! I don't know. There are a lot of great actors out there, and it's a big field. I certainly get some offers and stuff, but sometimes, yeah, there's a great amount to choose from, and sometimes there's not. I do my best to pick a part that's interesting that I haven't done before, but I don't think I always know what I'm doing. There are many different factors in making those decisions. That's another area I learn more about every day. Figuring out who I want to work with, what project I want to be doing next, and how that project is going to come together.

TVP: So you've got two scripts in front of you. One has a great character; the other is a great story. Which one do you choose?

RM: Well, in order to make that a fair question, I'm going to say all other factors are the same. It would depend on the level of truth in that, but I think it is important to actually have the good story. One of the things I love as an artist is being able to tell the full story and I think if you pick selfishly based on character alone and how much fun it would be to actually play that character, it doesn't necessarily mean anything because as an actor you're not actually out on your own. It's so much about the whole project that you're working on. I think in that scenario I would actually go with the story.

TVP: You can take a small part, like in, say, *The Black Dahlia*, and literally turn it into a showstopper. Everyone comments about the scene where you open the door. Is that stage experience, do you think that allows you to take a moment, because that's something you see a lot in theater, is that a moment become positively imprinted.

RM: I've noticed that from working with actors, especially some English actors who've done a lot of stage, that there's not such a sense of, "it's all about me and my character." It becomes a sense of the group working together and you each enjoy just the little moments, the little gems that you have, and enjoy being part of an ensemble. So you might well be correct, that that comes out of stage experience. I really couldn't say, I think that it's just; I know I enjoyed working with those actors and film makers and that character was fun, and I just enjoyed that moment. I'm not sure exactly where that decision comes out, to just enjoy playing the character regardless of the size of the part.

TVP: There's a lot of complexity inherent to the way

you approach any character. I'm thinking about Bully, for example. Certainly a bad guy, if you will.

RM: Absolutely.

TVP: But one that you empathize with because she's obviously staring into the great void and it's staring back at her. How much can you convey through gestures and word about carrying a landscape of expression? Is that on your mind when you're playing a part like that?

RM: I think the most important aspect of working a character is the empathy that you were discussing. I think that you don't have to like the person or agree with the person as an audience or an actor, but you certainly have to understand them fully. I don't think about what mannerisms I'm going to use or how I'm going to move physically or speak or things like that. I know some actors kind of work that way, from the outside in, and they work really well. But for me, I like to work from the inside out. What's going on in their head? Playing a character like Lisa in Bully, you have to understand how she thinks. It has to make sense when you're embodying that character. That's really what I work on. It's just, what's going internally as a way of viewing life. And then individually within that scene it manifests, and that's where specifics and voice and all that come from. If you assume a certain view of the world and you assume a certain emotional experience, your voice changes and your physicality changes automatically.

TVP: I wouldn't be surprised if your biochemistry changes as well.

RM: I bet. It's amazing how much you affect your body. I remember doing a play where I played a prostitute with a really rough life. Getting physical aches and pains, and

94

I think I got an illness, and stuff like that. You're putting your body through a ringer. You tighten up certain muscles when you're in a certain emotional state and stuff like that. I'm sure it affects every aspect of you.

TVP: You're not exactly a method actor. There's even an amount of artifice in method acting. But you seem to organically come to a similar place.

RM: I'm not hugely studied in the area, but I guess the difference in what I've heard about the method is you're drawing off of your own life experience more than what the character is going through, or in order to embody what the character is going through. I'm sure I do that, I don't think it would be possible to exclude my own experience of emotion and life when I'm making those calculations, but I try to think about it from a different view. Not so much how I felt when such-and-such happened but how this character would feel.

TVP: What's a very exciting project for you?

RM: There's nothing more exciting than working for people who inspire you. To me, the most exciting thing is when you're surrounded by other artists who are inspired as well because you float at that point. It's amazing how much work goes out the window when there's excitement all around, when everyone is enjoying creating this world together. Beyond that, I think the projects I long to do are the projects that are similar to then ones that have truly affected me, things that will hit an audience in the same way that I've been moved by films. Films that change your perspective of the world, that make you look at humanity in a different light. You leave having had your view of the world changed. I think that's exciting, too.

TVP: What films blow you away?

RM: For all different reasons, some of the films I've watched recently like; Hotel Rwanda blew me away. I just watched *Elizabeth: The Golden Age*, and I think that blew me away the performances especially. I watched The New World, that blew me away, and I also love The Lord of the Rings and big epic fairy tales. Those will blow me away. I watch films constantly and I'm constantly moved. And from all different types of films that are well executed.

TVP: What plans do you have coming up in the next few months?

RM: I wish I had greater plans! I don't know, it's something that I look at a lot. It's a funny art/business, and I have many ideas, but not as many plans as I probably should. You know, because there's also the aspect of so much of it being in the hands of luck and other people's creativity too, and what's going to make it's way to your doorstep. My plan is to keep working and keep working on what I do, because I always want to be better. When I watch my performances, I always see things that I could change. When I watch projects I see things that I could have done better. So I just keep trying to do that and hope that it winds me up on more and more interesting things.

TVP: What was *Tooth and Nail* like?

RM: That was an interesting one. It was a project that was pulled together really quickly. That was definitely an Indie. I think we're all like, how's this going to come out? What's it going to be like? I was playing another character that was interesting to embody, had good and bad aspects, so I spent a lot of my time trying to figure out how to make that real.

TVP: Are you looking at directing down the road a bit?

RM: You know, I've thought about it. I respect directors so much because it's quite a challenge to hold together the whole team. And think that because having grown up on sets, I definitely am impelled towards that, but also away from it, because of the responsibility and the details. Being on the set you get to watch everything that works and doesn't work. On the one hand I probably have certain knowledge that would be very useful, and on the other hand I'm also aware of how many ways even a really talented person can go off. I start to think, I'd be in prep for two years trying to make sure I don't let anyone down.

TVP: Imagine investing that much of your life on a project.

RM: Yeah. But it's definitely something I thought about for the future. And I think it would be being inspired enough to write something that was really passionate, or finding a project I was so passionate about having it made the way I saw it that I was really pushed past any worries about that experience and toward a need to get it made.

Mary Gaitskill: Critics Line Up to Get Her Wrong

October 2006
By Carri Anne Yager

We are all more than willing to accept that there is oppression and pain in the world. A much harder realism to accept is one that acknowledges the utter totalitarianism of selfhood. This autocracy is the subtext that forces the hand of many writers. We long for neatly polished identities- straight out of the box. We demand that they be unsullied by chiaroscuro, but what we really need to know is that our departures from the constructed norm, from stasis, are all that we can rightfully call authentic. Few writers have the audacity to stare straight into this void and foliate the edges, leaving the secret center intact. For any but real artists and revolutionaries, the impulse to provide camouflage is too overwhelming. The result: The world in much fiction, and all other media, is softened by failing to acknowledge the fully emergent individual. Faced with the near unanimity of these unfleshed characters, we automatically call our own interior ironies into question.

I suspect this is why many people call Mary Gaitskill's

fiction 'dark'— a word devoid enough of content to imply a desire not to go certain places. What's really being avoided, I suspect, is the acknowledgement of the entire package of selfhood, warts and all. There is an almost predictable point at which even the most eloquent attempts to interpret her work seem to veer into the suburbs of denial. Realism still demands the kind of closure we think is quaint in Victorian novels. Even in her early short fiction, *Bad Behavior*, we see external conflict saturated in characterization that does anything but simplify and resolve. With her most recent novel, *Veronica*, we find the immense payoff that comes with digesting the sometimes excruciating truths she unveils. We see undiluted personhood in her characters. To encounter Mary Gaitskill's fiction with the honesty it demands is like scratching a very bad itch.

Carri Anne Yager: Given what must have been frustrating interpretations of your work in the past, have responses to your later books become more in step with your intentions?

Mary Gaitskill: Any time you write a piece of fiction it will be interpreted in ways that you don't intend. It's difficult, it's painful, but it's part of the turf. I would never change my writing based on my advance projection of other people's interpretations. Just thinking about it makes my head hurt. And no, nothing has become more in-step with my intentions, which is probably good, even if I do find it irritating. I've read reviews in the past, but in the case of this book I haven't read many. I did read the first paragraph of the Janet Maslin piece in the New York Times because where I teach at Syracuse they have a showcase where they put up books by faculty and, because my book is just out, they put up the review. So when I looked at it, I read the first paragraph. I don't like to complain about it because I understand it's a good review. People have told me it is, but she says it's really dark and terrifying and there's no tenderness whatsoever--she also compares it to Burroughs and the director David Cronenberg. That suggests to me that she doesn't know how to read, on top of it being a really strange misreading. Another review which I unfortunately did read was the one in Slate, the online magazine. It was a positive review, but my God, She thinks it's all about people being punished for having sex.

CAY: Oh, Calvinism?

MG: Yeah, it was the one where she called me a Calvinist!

CAY: Yeah, I read that.

MG: I mean it is a good review in the sense that it's very respectful, and she clearly had a very powerful reaction to it. But I just don't understand that interpretation. It seems all projection on her part. The book is not about people being punished for sex, it's not about being punished for anything in the usual sense of the word, it's just about people experiencing what can happen to one in life. I really liked that she referred to the image, the vision Alison sees of cosmically chewing teeth eating everything, but if you were going to put a denomination on those... I don't think the chewing teeth have a denomination, but if you were to give them one, it would be more like Hindu. The teeth are more like a glimpse of Kali, The Destroyer. Kali doesn't destroy to punish, she destroys because that's her job. And she's necessary for the Creator.

CAY: You have mentioned that you were driven to write because of a need to communicate. How old were you when you started writing?

MG: This is kind of a cutesy story but it is true: When I was six and I first learned how to write, I wrote a story. It was what I first thought of what to do with this new skill, and then when I was a kid I wrote stories. I wasn't serious about it, it was just like kids doing drawings. I think I started writing stories in a serious way, with an idea that I wanted people to read them when I was about eighteen. But I really had no skills at all. I had no idea what I was doing. And I was very poorly read. When I was in high school and junior high, and even elementary school, I read a lot and I often read above my age level. But when I was a teenager, things changed, and I didn't read much. I read, but it was stuff that you would buy in the grocery store check out line--a best seller or something. Occasionally I would pick up a classic, but my reading was really spotty and I had no idea what I was doing. Then I went back to school and slowly figured out how to put basic skills together. So I'd say I started learning seriously when I was about twenty-one.

CAY: What happened that made you develop your focus? I was just wondering if you took a certain class in college that opened you up and made that difference, so to speak, or was it something that you discovered on your own?

MG: Well, I think whether you take a class or not, it's always something you discover on your own. The most helpful thing to me in school strangely enough was that before I went to university, I went to a community college--I had not graduated from high school so I could not have gone to a regular university. Also, my father taught at this community college and part of the deal with his contract was that his children could go there for free. My writing at that point-- well, I had to be in the remedial program. Community college teachers are not busy like university professors are and they're not being harried by students trying to get their attention. Most of the students in the community college were there taking vocational stuff. They took the Liberal Arts classes because they had to. Or there were those like me who were planning to take the Liberal Arts classes and transfer to a university. But they just weren't as ambitious or as likely to try to get stuff out of the class as university students are. So I approached this one teacher and told him, "I want to learn how to be a writer" and he was just thrilled. Probably the stuff that I was doing with him would seem really babyish to me now. But it was immensely helpful. It was the first time anyone had told me that I was talented. He seemed like an intelligent person and I don't doubt that he was. He took me seriously in a way that I hadn't been taken seriously before, so that was incredible, especially coming when it did. I was in a really uncertain time and it was a big thing for me to go to the community college. To get that reaction from an authority figure was really galvanizing.

CAY: I'm glad for that.

MG: I would've found another way if it hadn't, but the way things were, that was a very important connection for me. When I went to university, they didn't have as much emphasis on creative writing as they have now. But I took a few classes and I actually didn't like the workshops. They made me really uncomfortable--though I did meet one teacher, who I did like. Have you heard of Gayle Jones?

CAY: No.

MG: She wrote a couple of books in the 70's called *Corregidora* and *Eva's Man*. Her most recent book is called The Healing. She was very amazing and eccentric and one of the first people who made me feel I was in the presence of a genuine writer. And she took me seriously too. She was one of the only African-American professors there. She was not an academic, and I think it was hard for her to be in that environment. But when she told me she liked my story--and she didn't dole out praise easily—I went home and put on music and danced.

CAY: In order to create such realistic fiction, you bring the reader to places that are uncomfortable to face. Is it also hard for you to deeply contemplate these darker aspects of life, or do you feel relieved confronting them?

MG: Most of the time I don't think about it in those terms. But this relates to your first question because what surprised me about the response to Bad Behavior- it still does in the case of that book- is that it didn't seem to me that my subject matter was especially dark. It seemed to me that I was just writing about things that people deal with pretty regularly. I mean, not everybody has a boss that spanks them for typing mistakes, but many people have experienced the cruelty of office politics and the weird feeling of being sexually attracted to something that's humiliating and not knowing what to do about it. I think a lot of people have had that one way or another. It didn't seem to me that I was writing about things that were that strange, so I was surprised. It seemed to me, and it does still seem to me, that the book overall has a gentle tone. It doesn't seem to me to be hard or cold. There have been times that I was writing about something dark, and it was hard for me; certain sections of *Two Girls Fat and Thin*, and this last book, Veronica. I actually had a nightmare about Veronica, which I didn't realize was about the book at first. It was when I was finishing the manuscript. I don't think it was only about Veronica —when you have dreams, your unconscious often blends things together strangely but- do you know the Black Dahlia murder?

CAY: I've heard of it, yeah.

MG: It's a really horrible murder that took place in the 30s. I dreamed I was digging up her body and reburying it. There was a literary critic present and he was saying, "What are you doing? Don't you know this is illegal? Don't you know you could get in trouble for this?" And I said, "I know, but I have to do it. You should just get out of here. It's something I have to do." I woke up very frightened and disturbed. The reason I think it was about Veronica, although there are other things too, is that it was a book I had originally written in the 90's, which I was literally digging up and doing again. But the dream overall was frightening and I think there were things in the book that were frightening- -AIDS, death, abandonment, and self--estrangement. It's not that I sat there and felt frightened when I was writing them but those are very heavy things.

CAY: I have some experience with confronting things from my own past and working them out with words. I find it hard not just to go there but once there, I find it hard to come back to normal life and I wondered if that was a problem for you.

MG: I'm glad to come back to normal life. I like to have normal life around me, but it's hard to mix the two. I have to be very alone to do the wording. It's kind of like I have to go to a place that doesn't mix with normal life. But I'm glad to get back to normal life.

CAY: When you are in the state of mind that is necessary to create that fiction do you alter the normal, scheduled events in your life in order to accommodate the need to keep going?

MG: Yes.

CAY: That must be tough when you're teaching as well.

MG: Yeah, it is.

CAY: Many of your characters undergo experiences wherein they are victimized, or helplessly witnessing someone else being victimized. One quality that adds power to these scenes is that the situations are left unresolved. Why is it important to leave them unresolved?

MG: I think in general it's better to leave a story open than slam it shut. There might be some stories or situations in which it's nice to slam it shut, but in general I like the open quality better. That's whether the story is about a bad experience or not. One of the things I like about Chekhov's stories or the stories of a Japanese writer, Haruki Murakami--their stories are often open to the point that while they have unity and integrity you can't quite say what it is. When writing is good it allows and honors the mysterious to be present. It doesn't come up with too many answers. Because there aren't really answers. I mean there may be answers temporarily in life but there are no answers with a capital A--life is too strange for that and it changes too much for that. I think stories should honor that, and do honor that.

CAY: It's been said that your characters try to break out of lonely worlds by seeking intimacy with strangers. Do you see your characters this way?

MG: That's true of some of the stories I've written. What's wrong with that analyses is that it sounds like that's the character's entire motive, and most of my characters aren't doing that. I don't know if I've even got any character doing that consciously. The character in Two Girls Fat and Thin, Justine, does get involved with a stranger and you could say that it's to have a feeling of intensity that will alleviate loneliness, but she doesn't seek him out. She just bumps into him and responds to him. The girl in "Secretary" is a lonely person, but she doesn't seek out the situation with her boss, it's happened. She responds to it. You could say she's using the experience to break out of loneliness, or try to, but I think her motives are more complicated than that. She's somebody with a need for intensity and doesn't know her own sexuality well enough or understand the situation that well. I guess what I don't like about the comment is that it's reductive, or only part true.

CAY: You create ambivalent characters. Do you feel it's important to subvert the reader's identification process?

MG: I don't think of it that way. I feel that in life I am often surprised by people. I think of them as one way and they turn out to be another. And then sometimes I come back around to my original idea of them.

CAY: There are parts of *Veronica* in which the narrator, Alison, may come off as judgmental. Because of the power of Alison's voice as a narrator, do you think readers might confuse her voice with your own?

MG: Perhaps, but I honestly don't think she's so bad considering where she's come from and what she's experienced. I don't think she's a moral paragon either, but I think the judgments she makes are very typical. I think they're the kinds of things that go through people's heads. She seems morally average to me. And in fact, for somebody her age, the fact that she stays friends with Veronica and supports her as best she can is what redeems her as a person. But I think that most people think the kind of things she thinks. They might not be thoughts that you take seriously, but they run through your mind. Remember, Alison judges herself very harshly for some of her unkind thoughts. And, she thinks some very kind, generous thoughts as well. I don't think she ever thinks that AIDS is there to punish people for having sex, it's more a fear. There's a section where she's thinking, "We tried to be so liberal and they were always about death" and so on and so forth but those are the kind of thoughts that I believe everybody at that time had. AIDS at that time brought up really deeply buried feelings about guilt and terror; about sex and feelings that people thought were over, because for the last twenty years or so before AIDS reared its head, for the first time in history, really, people thought they could have sex without severe social or medical consequences. It seemed to change the way people thought and felt about sex and yet when AIDS happened I think that those deeper, darker, very primitive fears came roaring back in a big way. I would guess a lot of people had those thoughts. Alison's not happy with those thoughts either; she's really surprised and ashamed. To me Alison's worst characteristic is that she's vain and she lets her life become about her beauty, but I also think that for a beautiful girl with little connection to her family, and who is searching for excitement, it's a very understandable flaw. If I were sixteen and was told I could be a model I would probably be very sarcastic about it and talk about how stupid and sexist it was but I would have done it- who could say no to that kind of money, especially a girl from a working class family? When I read, I don't feel I need to identify with narrators or like them. I can very much enjoy books narrated by or about people that I wouldn't necessarily like or want to spend time with. In fact to me it's a plus to be able to be inside the mind of a person and spend time with a person on a page that I wouldn't in life. In life I could never get to that deep place inside them that the writer can. So I'm not necessarily trying to get the reader to identify with the characters. Some people do, but that's not a goal of mine.

CAY: And you're not especially trying to make the reader question the narrator either?

MG: No, I'm trying to present the narrator as accurately as I can. When I was in Alison I was always trying to feel my way around what Alison would think and feel and respond to in a given moment. I was trying to be as accurate about that as possible. I don't think about other people's reactions or getting people to question things or like or dislike at the time that I'm writing. I'm just trying to be as accurate and real as possible about the person I'm describing or bringing to life. I feel that other people's reactions are none of my business at that moment.

CAY: Pain and sex seem closely connected for your characters, and you have said that sexuality and sadness have a natural connection. Do you believe they exist close together deep within the human psyche, driving our actions?

MG: They can be, yes. I think that sex can also be connected with joy and procreation and rage and fear and love and strange things that we can't even identify really. Basically sex is connected with anything deep within people. Just the act of procreation and coming into a physical being has a hint of death to it because that physical being is going to die at some point. So, I think that they're connected and it's a connection that gets overlooked sometimes or that people find frightening.

CAY: Do you believe consensual sexual pain (as in S&M) and pain evoked by art are both cathartic in a similar way?

MG: I don't know. I kind of doubt it. They may be cathartic but I don't think in the same way. I think that anything you do physically with your body by nature is very different from what you do in your mind or with art.

CAY: Do you think it's part of human nature to be aroused by things that we cannot explain to ourselves or justify morally?

MG: Yes.

CAY: Do people need to experience injustice before they believe in it?

MG: Yes and no. I think that people can understand in their minds that injustice exists and be indignant about it but I don't think they really understand it until they experience it themselves.

CAY: So maybe they understand, it but in a faraway, abstract sort of way?

MG: In a relatively superficial way. It's a much deeper understanding when you have experienced it.

CAY: Since we're on the subject, what do you think of the situation with Hurricane Katrina as it pertains to that kind of social problem?

MG: Well, it's horrific. I don't know if I've got adequate words to describe it. I think that people who are not in that situation can never understand what it's like regardless of how you might understand it in your mind. This may seem like a digression, but bear with me: I'm reminded of a reviewer who said that Alison's feeling of hope or generosity in the end was false because the whole book was so dark that her hope at the end couldn't be true. And it's true that Alison's desire to be helpful- the image of herself as a bird giving breadcrumbs to others- comes too late for her to be able to do anything practical with it. There aren't that many people in her life she can help in a practical way. She has no money, unlike Daphne who sends money to her sister. But to me it counts that she's having that thought. And truly, anybody can help people. After Katrina we heard a lot of stories of rape and violence which I'm sure happened, but I think there were other things we didn't hear about. I'm sure that there were people who had nothing and no ability to offer practical help, but who offered warmth and kindness to their neighbors who were also without houses, water and food and were just stranded somewhere. I'm sure that people did things like put their arms around each other and comfort each other. And that kind of help, even though it's of no practical use, can be as powerful as knowing that somebody far away is going to be writing a check to supply relief. I'm sure that the people in that situation were able to offer comfort to each other in a way that couldn't be offered by people outside because people outside didn't understand. To have someone who's going through what you're going through, and knows exactly what it's like, put their arms around you and hold you while you're crying is a much more powerful experience emotionally than for someone to come in- even though you might very much appreciate the person coming in to rescue you- they can't really understand what's happening on a gut level, unless they've gone through it themselves. Though that's not totally fair to the rescuers, they had their own hell to go through.

CAY: Injustice is a recurring theme in your writing. You have demonstrated several situations in which people can't help what is happening to them. For example, it seemed to me that Alison found Veronica's family shocking, and I wonder if readers might also find it hard to imagine a family situation so terrible. I can't help but wonder if people interact with literature differently depending on their backgrounds. Do you think defense mechanisms play a role in a reader's interpretation?

MG: Yeah. There's some quote from... I think there was one volume of stories by Chekhov where he quotes someone and I don't know who it is, but it's about how, "the man who is not suffering will do anything to avoid seeing the man who is. And the man who is suffering, as soon as his sufferings are over, he will also do anything to avoid seeing the man who is suffering." And I think that's really true, even of people who are working with suffering people. There's some suffering that does not have a solution, and that's something that people just don't want to face. It's very human.

CAY: Do you think things have improved over the years for women, or do you think the same old problems lurk beneath a different surface appearance?

MG: I think they've changed since the 20's or 30's in certain ways but I think there will always be a power struggle between men and women. I don't mean that in a dark, hideous way. I just think it's a clash between two fundamentally different forces. Men and women are very, very different physically. I don't mean they're from different planets. They are the same species and it's true that the similarities are more than the differences. We all have arms, legs, feet and heads (laughs) but nonetheless, it's like a cosmic opposition almost, and this always will result in a clash.

CAY: Do you think people use judgments regarding "making right choices" as an excuse to isolate people when they are most in need?

MG: Sometimes, yeah. But it's also true that you can't leave out the question of choices altogether. People do make choices, and the complicated thing is that when people make wrong choices or choices which are going to increase their suffering -which people do constantly- usually there's some really complicated thing going on in them wherein they either don't see another choice. But also I think there's really complicated questions of- did you ever read a book called *Random Family*?

CAY: No.

MG: It's a very interesting book and very disheartening in many ways. It's about a woman who spent a lot of time living with a very poor, extended Hispanic family in the Bronx and she obviously liked them a great deal and they came across as very likable people but you saw them constantly making unbelievably bad choices. This one woman was on a waiting list to get on SSI, which would have enabled her to get really cheap, decent housing and she at the last minute just said "no." She went to live in an even worse place than she had before, which was so bad she wound up moving out of it almost immediately. In the book you felt that part of the reason that the people made those kinds of choices was that they didn't want to abandon the other people who were in poverty. They felt in some way that by getting something better, they were abandoning their family, for example. A friend of mine said the same thing. She mentored a Dominican girl in her neighborhood. At first the girl was improving in school, kind of wanting to do well in school and improve her chances in life and then suddenly she just started fucking up everywhere, left and right. And my friend couldn't really understand it, but what she thought was happening was that the girl didn't want to abandon her family and her friends. And she felt like by doing better, she would. That's just one example. I think there's lots of internal reasons that people willfully make what look like really stupid choices and not just poor people, either. It's hard because on one hand you can't just say they couldn't do any better, I mean they did make the choice. But on the other hand, unless you could be inside their mind, you don't know why they made that choice.

CAY: It's hard to speculate on the outside...

MG: Yeah, it's a very difficult question. There's self-destruction, but. I don't think anybody really understands what self-destruction is. It involves a lot of things, and it's different things for different people. I have felt that way about close friends of mine, I mean white people who came from middle-class backgrounds. I've gotten angry at them because they make certain bad choices over and over again and there I am left watching this downward spiral. It's extremely painful to watch. It seems like it was avoidable, and it's difficult not to get angry with the person, so I guess I understand the impulse to blame.

CAY: It struck me in the novel, and in life, that AIDS has tested human character, pressing people between their judgments and their loved ones. Would you agree?

MG: Yeah.

CAY: I thought you did a great job of developing Alison's character throughout the novel, and demonstrating the way time changes our perspectives. Are you optimistic that society can grow as Alison did?

MG: I don't know. Right now I'm not very optimistic about society, period, or human kind, period. But I think at moments society does grow. There are certain times when society does really reach a good moment, and does genuinely progress, and things get better. It just always seems like it goes to shit again quickly (laughs).

CAY: Do you see that happening with Hurricane Katrina?

MG: I see that happening with the whole government now.

I think that's not an anomaly. Was it Bill O'Reilly that got on the radio afterwards and said, "Well, if you're poor, you'd just better take care of yourself and stop being poor because, otherwise, you're going to die." I do think that's become more and more an attitude, even though very few people would come out and say it. I think it's very prevalent, and the shameful handling of Hurricane Katrina was one of the more grotesque manifestations of it.

CAY: I'm curious to see how it's going to affect thinking. I wonder if it will be a passing phase where people are taking an interest in the poor, or if it will have a lasting effect.

MG: You mean you think there's a positive side to it?

CAY: I think it's interesting that this is making people think about something they have wanted to stay in denial about. I wonder if it will last. I think there's been a lot of media coverage on it, and it's starting to be discussed: the American poor. I've noticed that media will cover issues that exist in other countries but the way it's being presented, it looks as though our culture is better and more advanced. I think we have a lot of the same problems that we look at other countries and judge and criticize. I think that American poverty is more controversial because... referring back to something you had said in your e-mail conversation with Rick Moody; it's disloyal to appear sad or unpatriotic. I have found that if you stick your neck out for the poor, people think you are unpatriotic or you don't support capitalism. Therefore you're not to be trusted.

MG: The outpouring of charity towards the victims of the hurricane I think is good, but the difficult issue to me is, people have always been capable of generosity in the face of really horrendous material suffering like that. The Bush people have always encouraged this idea of private charity, and private giving as opposed to governmental giving. To me, that's the knotty issue: how much is the government responsible for caring for citizens in that physical way? That's why the thing happened. There wasn't any care about the infrastructure of the levees and no systematic attempt to get people out of there. They were told to get out but they had no means to get out. Why didn't they have means to get out? Only the city, state and federal government could have provided that. I think that on an individual level, American people can be very generous, write checks and volunteer. I think the question is, "Is that enough?" or "What responsibility does the government have for this?" The government responsibility is being dismantled, and has been for some time. Now the disaster is being presented as, or evidence that, the federal government obviously doesn't work, so that's one more reason it should be dismantled.

CAY: I have seen more attention given to the subject of the American poor in the media. It seems to me that more people are taking an interest in the subject. I think there are people thinking for the first time about what it might be like not to be able to get into a car and leave your home if something bad were happening.

MG: I think it's true that even as Americans have become more and more poor there's still a feeling that real poverty doesn't exist except for a tiny minority. Most people, I've read, regardless of their income will define themselves as middle class. If people are waking up to the truth, then that's good.

The Real Circus World: An Interview With The Amazing Blazing Tyler Fyre

June 2006

By Jessica Hopsicker

A s a kid you've more than likely coasted down the road on your bike with no hands or standing on the ripped banana bike seat bearing a satisfied smile. "Yup, I can totally join the circus." That is, if it wasn't a school night. Reality has a habit of working like that. Some people later, well into adulthood, have given up on the dream. While in therapy, they would pass it off as a childhood delusion. Their real world exists behind a desk, crunching numbers or selling, living a life that is stable, constant, and financially secure. Others believe that it is no way to live, as if there's something toxic about homeostasis. Home for them is on the road. Some people after years of denial and a formidable education still manage to find the circus.

The title of Tyler Fyre usually comes with the words Amazing and Blazing attached to the beginning. It bears no stretch of the imagination. As a veteran of the Coney Island Circus sideshow he has accrued numerous awe inspiring talents and death defying titles, such as glass and fire eating, sword swallowing, Bed of Nails, Escape Artist, Human Blockhead, Carnival Talker and Master of Ceremonies. He strode the boards and led some of the world's foremost Circus's and Sideshows including Coney Island, his own project the Lucky Devil Circus Sideshow, Bros. Grim, Circus Una and the Bindlestiff Family Cirkus. He performs 800- 1,000 shows each year including award ceremonies, festivals, and tattoo conventions. We were lucky enough to catch up with this Lucky Devil in Las Vegas during Exotic World, where Dancing Girls from all over the globe vie for the Miss Exotic World Crown. He has come a long way from his education as playwright to one of the most renowned talents to grace the sideshow world today. Maybe the purpose of college isn't to get the almighty piece of paper, but as a means to answer the age-old question: Do you live to survive or live to be alive? That's when The Amazing Blazing Man got philosophical among other things.

Jessica Hopsicker: So Mr. Fyre, how is Vegas treating you?

Tyler Fyre: It's fantastic. I love it up here, in just a minute I'm heading up to the rooftop pool to kick back for a little.

JH: Sounds nice, what made you want to do this, and do you get that question a lot?

TF: I do, and it's a fair question, because really what makes anyone want to do anything? It's the grand question, of is there free choice or pre destination? Is there such a thing as fate or destiny or do you really decide every choice in your life? I don't know, I just love the circus since I was a kid and it's a miracle that I get to travel all over the country and all over the world making people happy…and sometimes scare them.

JH: I saw you swallow and pull back up a string of razor-blades, it was really gross and disturbing, but cool.

TF: You know its kind of like a car accident, you want to look around- I get a lot of people that put their hands over their eyes but peek through their fingers like little kids, I love that.

JH: Is there anything that you wouldn't dare do?

TF: That is a great question; I got to say that answer changes every day. Every day I wake up and there is some idea that pops up like "Hey, no one has ever done a stunt like this before, I wonder if that's possible." Or "boy it would be really fun to do this but man, it sounds really stupid." I don't know it changes every day. I like to change up the acts and design new stunts, that's what makes the whole thing fun. And when I come across something that seems like it would be impossible it seems like "whoa I wouldn't dare do that, it's a terrible idea." I find that those are the ideas that stick with me the longest until I can figure out a way to make them happen. That's what makes them fun.

JH: It's like testing the boundaries of human existence in a way.

TF: That's exactly the way I see it, testing the boundaries of human existence. Taking something that is physically impossible pushing it into the realm of the possible. It's like miracles... without being Jesus.

JH: You originally studied to be a playwright; your heart wasn't in it I guess.

TF: Hmm, you have all the dirt in the Tyler Fyre department, it's true, it's true. I went to New York University's Tisch School of the Arts for playwriting and I found out

I hated it. Well, I shouldn't say I hated the world of the-atre people, which would sound bad. But I found out that it wasn't a way I wanted to live my life. I wanted a little more excitement than keeping myself locked in a room all by myself writing, writing, writing, and then having it read by other people. I wanted to be out there in the world with the other people. That's where I wanted to be instead of writing action scenarios for other people and fictional char-acters to live out; I wanted to live them myself. But I must say it's not like I totally wasted my college degree. That's not entirely true. While I was in school, I made my first friends in the real circus world they carried me through and introduced me to the people that have made it all possible. I took a circus class and had a great teacher by the name of Hovey Burgess who taught me how to juggle and how to tightrope, and how to do trapeze and from there he taught me how do be a success at fire eating. From there I met Todd Robbins and Jennifer Miller the bearded lady. It all did sort of spiral out from the fact that I did go to college for four and a half years.

JH: Like you said before, predestination, that's what I think.

TF: There you go. Did you choose this path for yourself was it pre-set for you? It's a big question- it'll take college kids to answer that.

JH: I suppose it would… And oh! Lucky the Painproof Man says hi.

TF: Hey hey! Oh my god! I had the best party with Lucky the Painproof Man. We played Philly at the Burlesque-A-Pades tour with The World Famous Pontani Sisters, Fish-erman Xylophonic Burlesque Orchestra, Corn Mo, and all these great dancing girls and acrobats. The last show of the tour was in Philly and I met Lucky after the show. We talked online a little and he came out. We had a party; we went out to some go-go club and ended up at a naked party after. God, that was a good night.

JH: Yeah, must've been… say will you be going to The Haunt in Ithaca anytime soon?

TF: The Haunt in Ithaca, we played there twice and loved it up there. We had a blast both times in Ithaca. It all nice, there is that river that runs out there and the deck, and the people are really cool. Yeah, we had a great time playing up there. The first time we played a couple of years ago, and it was a Saturday night, no I guess it was a Friday night, before the Saturday of Easter weekend. Easter weekend is the traditional opening weekend of the sideshow in Coney Island. It's the weekend you look forward to all winter when it's cold and you're poor and you like "God, I just want to be back in show business again, I can't wait for Coney Island and carnival season." It's the weekend to look foreword to. It's a big tradition with big crowds. As it happens we have a show that Friday night. With this party called Bound, Wilhelm K throws it. I think it's like six hours from NYC, and we drive up and do the gig. We were like "seriously we have to go back right after this," we were having so much fun. After the show we stayed and partied, met everyone and they're really cool. Then we loaded up the whole show, which is a big van full of stuff, and we drive back overnight. The suns up before we reach New York City, we get into Coney Island and that is opening day of the Sideshow Season.

You have to give up things like regular meals and sleep when you work in the sideshow. Really, I don't miss it at all. You got to get that out of you mind right from the beginning. If you're still thinking I need 3 meals a day or I need breakfast in the morning or I need more than four hours of sleep every couple days, and then you're screwed. If you take moments like that as a luxury, or you're like, wow didn't this work out great, the truck broke down near a diner so we got to eat, or whatever, then it started to rain last night so the show closed early and we got six hours of sleep. Think of them as little miracles that come at you every now and then you can't come to count on those or expect those. No, no, regular meals and regular sleep right out the window.

JH: Yeah I need to learn how to do that, it's unhealthy to carry vendettas first thing in the morning.

TF: It's all in the mind, really, it's all in the mind. You switch your mindset around to thinking you don't need it all the time and its just a little luxury you'll be fine. It's only when somebody wakes you up and you're all mad like "why'd you have to wake me up this is my day off." And you're all bitter and angry that's what really sucks the energy out of you. You're not going to win that fight anyway you're already awake. If you think of it as being more of adventure it is fine.

JH: How do you think the sideshow has changed over the years?

TF: I think the sideshow has changed over the years just as much as women's bathing suits and men's hats have changed over the years. The sideshow is entertainment. What is going to sell tickets and make people excited and bring people into the show now? Back in the early part of the century it was albinos, and everyone's like "wow! I've never seen an albino before!" There were elephants and giraffes before TV, the most bizarre creatures you can possibly conceive when you live in America, and are used to horses and cows. It's the same thing, but now there is television and the internet and you have seen a lot of those things. Like Siamese twins and sheep's heads in jars. You've seen all that now so it's about seeing something else. It's marketed differently; all entertainment has changed over the last hundred years, so sideshow has changed in just the same fashion. Don't fight the change. Of course, it's not like it used to be. I'm not making 50 dollars a week like my heroes from 80 years ago, that would be terrible, and you want it to change. You want it to keep up with the times as some kind of new thing.

JH: And what's your future shaping up to be like?

TF: My future is shaping up one day at a time, just like they tell me at the meetings. Um… it's good. I just got my tour schedule for the summer. When I left Coney Island a couple years ago to be on another show called the Bros. Grim Sideshow. I still live right down the street from the Coney Show where I spent seven years. It's still my home base and close to my heart. I left for another show so I could go back on the road. The Bros. Grim sideshow, we filmed a new television show with it last year. Really, television is the new midway. People don't flock to the carnivals to see the brand new creatures, and products that they can buy that you have never heard of before. All that happens for us now on television, through Nip Tuck, Fear Factor, and late night infomercials. That coverage was what made sideshow great. We still have it, it's just in a different form. So the Bros. Grim made a TV show last year, and it looks like that's getting picked up. So we'll be filming the TV show while taking the big top on Ozzfest this summer.

JH: Nice

TF: I think that's the question that you were just asking,

How has the sideshow changed. It's because we have moved beyond the midway, whereas people want shocking entertainment now. And where is shocking entertainment? It's rock and roll. There wasn't rock and roll when the sideshow started, it didn't exist. Now, you can get huge crowds of people to flock to an outdoor festival. They want to be shocked and amazed and have an amazing memorable day. Well, you can find that at Ozzfest because that's where we're going.

JH: Great we can plug that too. Is there anything else we haven't covered?

TF: Yes, you can love television and you can love everything about the new world but don't forget live entertainment. Live entertainment is where it actually happens where you can sit in the same room and breathe the same air as the people that are entertaining you. It changes everything! Seeing a concert live compared to seeing a video, seeing a play that is not televised. Definitely when you're dealing with death defying stunts and strange people being in the same room with them changes everything. It will change your life.

Clint Borgen:
Pummeling Global Poverty

February 2008
By T. Virgil Parker

Y ou pull up alongside a new Jaguar and say "lucky bastard!" There are plenty of places in the world where
you'd be saying the same thing when you drag yourself up
alongside someone with a bowl of rice. Of course we do not
feel good about this, but thinking about it for very long can
take the polish off those shiny new toys we Americans love.
So many of us change the subject, or believe that it can't
happen to us. We are ambitious, smart. We would find a
way out of starvation.

I suspect that our padded resumes and slick networking
skills would do precisely jack for our waistlines in: Malawi,
Somalia, Comoros, Solomon Islands, Burundi, East Timor,
Tanzania… To participate in an economy, you must first
have any economy at all.

I'm not implying that you need to feel guilt about what
success you do have, far from it. Grab what joy you can.
But, what better way to celebrate your good fortune than
by saving a few lives with pocket change, saving a few

thousand more with a couple of phone calls to your government representatives?

Clint Borgen has done a lot more than that. His volunteer work in Kosovo refugee camps as a college student opened his eyes to the way so much of the planet lives. Not having the resources to launch the project, after graduating he did a gig on a North Sea fishing vessel, tucking the resources away and turning the ship's kitchen into an office for what has since become a worldwide poverty eradication network; a hefty one at that. He has a truly viable plan to eradicate world hunger. Also, Clint may be the only NGO director with groupies following him around. Talking with him is highly energizing, after a few minutes you want to go to www.borgenproject.org and get to work.

T. Virgil Parker: I don't want to take up too much of your time because x number of people will starve if you're not out there doing what you're doing. So, first question: For the cost of a handful of B2 Bombers, you can end world hunger.

Clint Borgen: That number compares with the World Food Program, their annual budget. They are able to assist like a hundred million people for what is spent on two B2 Bombers. So the impact of the largest relief agency on the planet is pretty amazing, but you look at what the US could do with what they spent on two B2 bombers, it's pretty astonishing. If you look on our homepage, the estimated cost in world hunger is at nineteen billion dollars a year, yet the largest military contract in this country gets more than that. The US defense budget is like five hundred and fifty billion. So needless to say, for a fraction of what we spent on military endeavors, we could drastically reduce poverty.

TVP: I only recently discovered The Borgen Project, which means I must have been living under some kind of rock, because it's really making waves.

CB: We're still pretty young so we're not totally out there, but it's definitely getting a little more buzz these days.

TVP: It strikes me that no one has ever attempted a sexy high-end relief project before. How did you develop the persona of the Borgen Project?

CB: A big influence is looking at what it would take to mobilize, and I kind of looked at campaigns, like political campaigns, particularly presidential campaigns. People are more inclined to mobilize around an individual, a personal organization, so that was definitely taken into consideration. Using the internet obviously was a huge component. We're very web-based; everything we've done has been based around tapping into different community groups out there and mobilizing people in those districts, to just create a product that was appealing to more of mainstream America.

TVP: There's nothing in your background that would imply a corporate mindset.

CB: No, uh-uh.

TVP: But what I see is every bit as hardcore as a Fortune 500 company.

CB: Yeah, correct. One of my big things is I feel a lot of people go into these issues very well-intentioned but not necessarily competitive with how a business might approach it. To have an impact you kind of really need to be hard hitting and make things happen. Maybe not so "do-good-erish" might be a nice way of putting it. That's kind of the influence behind adapting to what businesses do and looking after that angle of, "what's it going to take to have an impact?" and not so much "what is the more 'do-gooder' persona?"

TVP: Where did you get the inspiration to make it that edgy? I've seen presidential campaigns. They're in your face in a certain way, but still in a very stodgy kind of way. But what you're doing is right on the edge. It looks to me like Madison Avenue might have been as much of an inspiration as anything else.

CB: On some level. I definitely looked at what businesses are doing, how they're able to reach people. Early on we engaged to find people of different business backgrounds and get their feedback on what we could be doing. As far as influences, I don't know, I just knew we had to do something different from what was being done out there. None of my influences necessarily came from other relief agencies or other non-profit organizations, I looked more towards, "what's Nike doing?" or what's good on a list of MTV, or you know, all these different groups are able to reach a large number of people and engage them.

TVP: I've heard that the big problem with hunger is distribution.

CB: Looking at the corruption issues in those countries?

TVP: Not just corruption, but the food is in one part of the world and people are in another.

CB: It really varies. It's not uncommon for there to be a famine crisis in a country, or not necessarily a famine crisis, but a food shortage in the country. There may be enough food in the country to feed the population; a lot of it comes down to just flat-out poverty. They can't buy it. When I was in Kosovo, which got me started in all this, in the refugee camps there, people in camps are barely surviving, but right next to the camps there's a village where you can go and buy food. There are grocery stores and whatever. So it really comes down to an issue of poverty. If people can't afford it, they're not going to be able to get the food. In situations of famine, which are a small percentage of world hunger, most hunger is related to poverty; in those situations it's a little more complicated. But the big picture with hunger is that most of it is just a lack of money to be able to afford food.

TVP: How much do you think the fall of communism itself had to do with changing perceptions about what will fix world hunger?

CB: It's hard to say. I don't know. We're not encountering that anymore, which has been very refreshing. It's less and less of an issue. People are realizing that there are reasons we should be addressing it.

TVP: The big thing is incentive as far as I can tell. You're encouraging people to do something about it. What goes in to creating that kind of motivation?

CB: A big part of it that works for us is, I was kind of an average Joe who got involved in this, and political leaders, so I have fresh eyes on what works on getting them engaged and getting them to address these issues. The big shocking thing to me is how receptive they are to public opinion, particularly when people are calling the offices or e-mailing the offices. All those forum e-mails that go around that everyone is skeptical about whether they really matter, but it turns out it's shocking how much it does. Specifically most senators and congressional leaders get a weekly report which outlines every issue people have contacted their offices on. So if five people reading this contact their senator and say "please address the global poverty act," that goes into the weekly report that is viewed by the senator. So pretty much any single person out there can get an issue noticed in front of a senator. It's particularly more affective when it's specific bills, which we have a section on our website that encourages people to contact on specific poverty bills or push them. But it's shocking how much impact the average citizen can have by making a thirty second phone call to their congressional leader.

TVP: Are you working with any presidential campaigns?

CB: No. We're not partisan; we try to stay out of that side of it.

TVP: I'm going to work on intuition and say it's probably easier to sell to Democrats?

CB: That's very correct, yeah.

TVP: So how do you sell it to the Right?

CB: We've had success, actually. There's huge national security reasons why the US should be addressing global poverty right now, and that's coming into light. The 9/11 Commission, when they came out with their report, cited the importance of addressing global poverty. You can't have all these regions of people where everyone is barely surviving and not expect that it's going to cause some problems. You look at some of the areas where al Qaeda has been able to operate freely; they're some of the poorest countries on earth. Sudan, Afghanistan, Somalia, these are places where the bad guys come to power, where they take over, and you end up with these governments that are problematic for the US. There's been a great deal of awareness for that. Secretary Gates, the Secretary of Defense, came out recently with a speech that said the US needs to increase funding to US aid, which is pretty interesting for the head of the Pentagon to be saying, "we need to be doing more to address global poverty." That's a big part of what we talk about when we go and meet with the right side.

TVP: How do you sell this to the evil empires- I mean, large, multi-national corporations.

CB: Interestingly enough, out here in Seattle there's been a big boom of CEOs who want global poverty addressed. They're looking at it purely from a financial incentive standpoint. You look at countries like China and India where all of a sudden their populations are coming out of poverty more and more, it's creating more business opportunities for US businesses. A magazine came out not to long ago, Farm Policy Magazine, it said that the world's poor is the largest untapped market on earth. As people transition from barely surviving to becoming potential consumers the US gets some profits and it creates new markets for businesses. So right now there's some kid in Africa who can't afford a little Colgate toothbrush or Colgate toothpaste, and then, oddly enough, they are able to lift themselves out of poverty; those individuals are buying Colgate toothpaste and toothbrushes. There's been a huge awakening in the business community. They obviously have different motivations than you or I for addressing it, but at the end, the more people we have behind the cause, it's a good thing.

TVP: It looks to me like education is ground zero for ending global poverty in your book?

CB: It's a huge component of it, yeah. No question. Especially teaching farmers how to get maximum productivity from their crops, or how to farm, and getting kids in school, and trying to break that poverty cycle.

TVP: Have you looked at organizing labor in third world countries or is that completely not viable?

CB: That would definitely be an option. For us as an organization, we are really specific, we look at different bills going through congress and we build support for those bills and we engage the US public to kind of get behind the issue of poverty. So for us as an organization it wouldn't be a good direction, but it's definitely relevant. It's out there to look at.

TVP: What's the biggest success story you see out there right now?

CB: China. During the 1990s, they cut hunger in half. So like eighty million people who previously were barely surviving are now functioning, productive members of society. So they're definitely like one of the great examples. It's happened all over the world though. There are different pockets of success in different regions. Basically where there's a political commitment, where there's funding and assistance, and government is engaged, good things happen.

TVP: Do you look at poverty in post-industrial countries or is that just on a completely different order of magnitude?

CB: We're pretty much looking at those living on less than a dollar a day. So most of that is geared towards Africa. Although obviously it's a huge issue in China and Asia, and Latin America, but we're pretty specific on those living on less than a dollar a day.

TVP: What is the best thing a college student could throw their energy into to end global poverty now?

CB: The big thing is we need people making those phone calls, those thirty second phone calls, if they go to the

Borgen Projects website we have a section called "poverty alarms." You click on that, it will tell you key bills that are in congress right now that will address the issue of poverty. If they make a thirty second call to their senators on that issue asking them to support it, it will actually have a huge impact for us. We actually just launched this campaign last week that's called the "Five in Fifty campaign." To goal is have five people in each state make a simple call asking their congressional leaders to co-sponsor the Global Poverty Act, which is a big bill we're working on at Senator Obama's office. It calls on the White House to develop and implement a strategy for addressing severe poverty. Congressional leaders, on their weekly report, see that five people have contacted them on a given bill; the chances of them co-sponsoring that bill will go up drastically. It's kind of amazing that it only take five people in each state, but ideally that's the number we're shooting for.

TVP: There's going to be people who want to do something of an ongoing nature. What's your best advice?

CB: The Borgen Project offers internships. There's online volunteering opportunities for individuals also. It can be anything from editing or writing to translating, so I would encourage them to check out the website if there's anything they are particularly wondering.

TVP: What plans for the future that are forming up right now?

CB: Ideally we're getting more and more into the direct lobbying side. That's progressing forward. Ideally the more funding we have, the more bills we can be pushing, so we have a lot of success. We have a pretty amazing level of access to political leaders for organizations working to address global poverty. So we can be taking advantage of that. So the more funding we have, the more bills we'll be able to push through.

TVP: Are you working in concert with organizations that are pushing other big budget governments?

CB: Correct. We work with different non-profit organizations in getting bills through congress. We'll team up with them and work in unison, making sure we're using our power to make a combined impact.

TVP: It strikes me that the big awareness issue is the relative ease with which you can end global hunger.

CB: Yeah. That's the message. There's a huge gap between what the public thinks can be done to address these issues and what can actually be done. There's a lot of cynicism about addressing poverty. World leaders got together in 2000 and agreed to a plan for cutting hunger in half and then abolishing it by 2025. Every world leader on the planet agreed to this issue on some end. There's universal knowledge among the poverty reduction community that this is an issue that can be addressed. But yes, most people are very cynical; they don't realize that it can really be addressed. The public awareness aspect of what we do is huge. Mobilizing, making people aware that these issues can be addressed, encouraging them to pressure their leaders into addressing them.

TVP: You actually have paparazzi, don't you?

CB: I don't know about paparazzi. I'm out here in Seattle.

TVP: I was astounded that I found Borgen fan sites and celebrity portals and things like that. That has to be grating for someone with the drive that you have working on this, but it's also something that you can really leverage.

CB: Obviously it helps the cause. If there's that kind of interest in it, it helps mobilize and engage the public and reach people who typically might not be interested in this kind of stuff. I'm out here in Seattle so I'm tucked away from that kind of stuff. I'm hidden from the typical problems that might come with that. But yeah, ultimately there's a correlation between public interest and what I'm doing, and then those people getting engaged and joining the cause. So it can be leveraged without question.

TVP: I can almost guarantee that one gig on Dancing with the Stars would get you the eighteen billion a year.

CB: If you've got connections, you can make that happen. But I don't think you want to see my dancing skills.

Brazilian Girls: Something to Get Naked About

July 2006
by T. Virgil Parker

I've come to the conclusion that every member of this band is an event as well as an individual. This is why people take off their clothes at Brazilian Girls concerts. The combined kinetic friction of so many avatars on one stage turns up the heat unbearably. Sabina Sciubba, if she were a little less edgy, would make the ideal Bond girl. Mysterious, painfully sexy, and intellectually provocative, all she would have to do is stand there to create an uproar, but she does much more than that.

Bassist Jesse Murphy and drummer Aaron Johnston could easily be mainstream modeling icons, if they could stand still long enough-and a bigger if- if they could lose their contempt for all things vacuous. Keyboardist Didi Gutman is redefining suavity for the 21st Century, in a jubilantly Postmodern way. These are the immediate impressions, before you hear a note.

I know what you're thinking. Four attractive musicians, strong synthesizer foundation: Euro Cheese. Not at all. If you put Nine Inch Nails and the B-52s in a bag and shook it up, you would get a tiny bit of what this sound is about. But it will not stay in one place long enough to be defined. Anarchy and eloquence jockey for position in this music. It will be danceable, but that is the only clue about where it will go next.

Didi Gutman is all about twisting Pop into a high art form, and is obviously more interested in the act of creating than he is by any of the trappings of success.

T. Virgil Parker: The Brazilian Girls appear to be taking off in a rather significant way. How does that feel?

Didi Gutman: I don't feel that, I don't see it like that; we're just playing music like we always did. I don't think it'll change. To me everything has been great and everything that has happened to us has been cool.

TVP: You have such a continental sound, in terms of aesthetic, are you surprised America is embracing it so thoroughly?

DG: This country has been great; we've been digging it. Everywhere we go has been open to us, it's been refreshing. It's been nice in all kinds of places.

TVP: You have the underground people falling all over you, and you have the Manhattan trendsetters, and the Jam crowd. They're all seeing something different, what do you do to attract that kind of diversity?

DG: Well, you know, that's who we are and we like all these different kinds of things; we listen to all kinds of music. We get invited to all different kinds of events and we get to play all different kinds of scenes. We can play at the club, we can play with the jam bands, we can play concellos. It's nice.

We like to be with all the participants of all these different things.

TVP: Most Electronica out there is pretty canned.

DG: We are not exactly Electronica. We have an electronic element to our music, but it's mixed with real playing. They don't know how to categorize us. Someone threw us into Oprah Magazine, which is certainly not our audience. I don't know how we ended up there.

TVP: Are you laying a lot of loops or are you playing everything pretty much live?

DG: Both, it's a hybrid. The thing about the loops is that when we play them live we can bring them in and out and mix them and tweak- we're not playing to a record, is what I'm trying to say. We can be dynamic with an intention, so we can keep it all spontaneous and improvise with the loops.

TVP: The sound is so organic that it is surprising that its so synthesizer driven.

DG: It makes sense when you see us live, how it's integrated, and all the elements. Certainly, Aaron the drummer, he can play too, he's got such good timing and that helps. It's not that easy playing with such a complex thing.

TVP: Most bands that do what you're doing don't have a real drummer.

DG: Right, we're a band, we're not a DJ.

TVP: All of the different elements that come into what you're playing, is it hard to extract exactly what you're looking for?

DG: I don't know exactly what I'm looking for; a lot of it is like spontaneous intuition. There's some work in finding the organic elements that make the sound, programming and stuff but when it starts, you have what you want, each time. It's like preparing a colorful painting. We don't conceptualize or have an exact idea of the painting and how we're going to make it. Start with one brush and then we'll see what happens. I don't know exactly what I want.

TVP: I heard that you just walked into Electric Ladyland Recording Studio and just started composing.

DG: Well, its something we did, also we brought in the ideas that everyone was working on and we developed them there. So a few songs were playing from before and songs that came into fruition as well, they came from a tincture or a groove. But then everybody contributes something to the completion by just playing together, and the way we do it in the studio is the same way we do it live.

We went to Electric Ladyland to record 12 songs and we ended up recording 25.

TVP: You're playing out constantly. Are you writing while you tour?

DG: No, I wish.

TVP: But the live experience obviously feeds into what you write, with that immediate feel.

DG: We try to keep it fresh. We really try to make it something of the moment. It isn't a Broadway musical where everything is rehearsed. Certain songs just work, and chasing the ideas won't make them any better, but there are a lot of areas where we'll just see what happens.

TVP: You band is made up entirely of iconoclasts, very

138

intense individualists. Does that make it easier, or harder to deal with?

DG: I don't know. Everyone is cool, and we're trying to understand each other. We have this thing called the rotating asshole, an entity, a ghost that will take over your body. Every one of us carries it at one point or another. When you're on the road, you can hide somewhere on the bus. Sooner or later everyone is going to show their color. Everyone is being themselves, and that's no big deal. You can recognize yourself in that. I love my band mates.

TVP: Is the industry trying to define you, or are you getting a lot of free reign?

DG: Starting with Verve was a good thing. Verve is off-center, to the left. They don't have to show numbers like other labels. They aren't pushing for the radio thing. They're still marketing us, just like you have to market anything. As far as creative freedom, we really have it with them. If they have anything to say to us, it is usually a welcome contribution.

TVP: Do you think you'll be getting the same kind of reception in Europe?

DG: We're as popular in Europe as we were a year ago in the States, so we're playing smaller venues. A lot of our popularity is by word-of-mouth. The first time we played Los Angeles we played for 100 people. Then next time, 200, 400, 1,000 and so on. We're starting in Germany this week. There's always some kind of reaction when we play. I think we're going to have fun.

TVP: Your sound has a very European feel.

DG: I always thought Europe was going to eat us alive. It was unexpected that we found so much success in the U.S. But I think we're going to have fun in Europe.

TVP: How did you end up playing Jam festivals?

DG: Some of the bands in that scene called us to do that. I wasn't too aware of the scene. I was quite surprised by how big it is, this huge venue for live music, music that as you say, isn't canned. That's a thing we can work with, because we do jam.

The industry is getting a backlash from all that crap out there.

TVP: ...And high time. You're being very true to your inspirations.

DG: That has a lot to do with our home base in New York, which is the club Nublu. It was so free there, and we didn't have any expectation of taking this anywhere else. It wasn't a big deal if Sabina wanted to sing one song in Spanish and one in German. If you look at it from a marketing standpoint you'd be thinking that you had to cater to the scene here. But we had this space and it was Sunday night, and it was kind of like going to church. We did whatever we wanted. It ended up one of our strengths.

Afroman: Higher and Higher

March 2007
By Jessica Hopsicker

I was gonna write an intro to this interview but then I got high...

The excuse has worked for Afroman, because of his popular summer song and stoner anthem of 2001 "Because I Got High." The debut full length CD, The Good Times, went gold on the strength of that tune. Jay and Silent Bob even moonlighted in the video. The lyrics decry the pitfalls of pot smoking with lines such as "I was gonna pay my child support but then I got high" This kind of success nearly saddled him with the terrible title of one hit wonder. Six years later however, he's still plugging away.

His newest album, *Waiting to Inhale*, reams everyone from Beyoncé Knowles to the Black Eyes Peas. "Dicc Hang Low" proves to be a low blow spoofing the ever-so popular "Chain Hang Low" by Jibbs. Though the disk may not have hit the shelves yet, tracks of this hit-and run masterpiece are going positively viral on the internet.

Jessica Hopsicker: How's the new CD coming together?

Afroman: It's underground right now; it hasn't been released yet, still working on a distributor. The tracks that have been released are making people laugh, and that's the whole purpose of it. Tracks are available at afromanmedia. com.

JH: A lot of people are anxious to get the whole thing.

A: A lot of my problems come from getting people to get it on the shelf.

JH: It's extremely rude and funny, especially Dicc Hang Low, and the one where you're ripping on Beyoncé. Do people ever get offended by that stuff?

A: I'm sure, but I don't see them. I see people who come out to the shows. They take it with a grain of salt if it is funny, if it isn't they wait for something that is. For the most part, I see people getting it.

JH: It is a lot more melodic than the stuff you're dissing. How do you feel about hip hop as a medium now?

A: I'm not ripping on the music really, I'm having fun. Dicc Hang Low is R & B, which is perfect for what I'm going after with that one. You go out to a bar, you try to dance with a chick, and this song comes on, and this girl becomes the stimulating partner you're looking for- she turns into that chick. It just isn't conducive, good, for unity. So I thought I'd pick up a mirror and aim it at that. That was fun. I'm Afroman, so I can get away with that. If I was Brian McKnight I couldn't do that. I've got to enjoy being Afroman. Nobody can tell Beyoncé off, but I can take sip of Colt 45 and tell her off.

JH: You pointed out in "Because I Got High" that everybody sings about smoking marijuana, nobody sings about the effects of marijuana?

A: Marijuana is ok if you have nothing to do with your life. If you're out in the country underneath the apple tree, waiting for one to fall, great man. If you're an on-the-go type person, it can be an obstacle.

JH: You've said that you wanted to be the world's best alcoholic woman-chasing Christian?

A: Yes.

JH: Is it hard to be different in this line of work?

A: No, you just be yourself. If you try to play some role, people will sniff out that you're trying to be this guy or that guy.

JH: Your Myspace was deleted because they thought that you weren't the real Afroman?

A: A lot of people are putting Afroman all over everything.

JH: How's your tour so far?

A: Everybody's coming out, having a great time. I'm doing stuff they know, and bringing out new material they don't know. I'm writing new stuff all the time. I stay in the game.

JH: Does it ever seem like work to you?

A: It does. I picked rap so I wouldn't have to work that hard, but I don't care what you do for a living, it is going to be hard. Even if you sell drugs, you have to watch out for the FBI. There's no escaping hard work. We're all cursed to work. If you don't work, you have to work hard to figure out a way not to work. If I have to work, I'd rather work this way.

JH: You're hitting Syracuse and Ithaca?

A: Yeah! I'm Afroman; I go wherever I'm accepted.

JH: It looks like a lot of people are accepting you.

A: I've got a following. It's not like a Bon Jovi concert, but not bad at all. I stay busy every day, so I'm thankful for that.

Al Barr of the Dropkick Murphys: Songs of Solidarity

February 2008
By Jessica Hopsicker

It was August, late afternoon at the Saranac Brewery in Utica, NY and there was an expectant pause after The Tossers left the stage. A cloud descended and the air grew static as the audience fell silent. We craned our necks forward, waiting for the Dropkick Murphys to emerge. Moments prior, I had departed for a beer run only to find that my friends were nowhere in sight. I perilously double fisted four flimsy plastic cups of lager and inched closer. The crowd grew eminently thicker. After a moment's hesitation I glanced stage-ward and then beer-ward. There was no choice but to drink them all, it was only a matter of seconds before my neighbors would erupt into a frenzy of swinging fists and feet, inevitably dousing me in a shower of cold beer. With barely enough time to destroy the evidence, I let out a sudsy cheer as the throng thrust forward, sweeping me along. The Dropkick Murphys took the stage.

Months later, I fought to understand what I witnessed, it wasn't anything tangible or even visible but it made my skin tingle, vibrations beating like waves upon the hot pavement. Then again, it could have been imaginary, the rowdy combination of sweaty fans, loud music, and a belly full of lager. We left that night, soaked, battered, and stinking of beer. Staggering down the sidewalk, we leaned on each other for support, belting out lyrics as we went.

In any case, like the bagpiper's kilt, there is more to the group than the externals imply. The music charges past the places you suspect it can go, and takes you with it. The Dropkick sound cranks out almost independently of the members of the band. Despite occasional lineup changes, this band is perpetually becoming more melodic, heavier. It was a crucial moment to secure an interview, as guitarist Marc Orrell just announced his departure from the band, ushering in the beginning of Jeff DeRosa's career with DKM.

The latest album of this seven-piece outfit *The Meanest of Times*, rocketed to the top 20 on the billboard charts. Lyrically, the album carries themes of solidarity, friends, family, and working class heroes. Much like their live performances, the fireworks begin with their very first track.

It would have been great to catch them again in Boston for St. Patrick's Day weekend, but alas, tickets sold out in a matter of hours.

Jessica Hopsicker: How are you doing?

Al Barr: I'm doing well, doing well. Just riding around, you know?

JH: So, you broke the top 20 on the billboard charts with *The Meanest of Times*. Was it scary, gratifying?

AB: It wasn't scary, but it was definitely a surprise. Especially with where the record market is right now, and has been for a while. With CD sales being in the garbage across the board it was a total surprise to us to have that success with our first release on our new label; we were flabbergasted, as it were.

JH: I can imagine. How are you going to outdo that one?

AB: Yeah! You don't think like that, you know what I mean? If you start thinking like that, you will fail. With every record, we do what we do. If it isn't interesting for us, we know it isn't going to be interesting for the fans. We've got to keep it interesting, you know, and just pour our heart and soul into it, and just do what we do. You know what I mean? But if you get into the game of thinking, "Oh, I've got to outdo this and outdo that," you're not going to. It's got to be an organic thing. It's got to come from a different spot.

JH: So you're heading to Europe?

AB: We're heading to the UK. We call that, "Europe Lite."

JH: What are your experiences with the "Europe Lite" audiences?

AB: England's great. We're going to Ireland first and then Belfast and then Scotland. England is a good time. And we enjoy the continent as well. The mainland, as they call it. It's all good.

JH: Do you still perceive yourself as a Boston band or more of an international act now?

AB: We're a New England band. That's where everybody's from. That's what we call home, that's where our families are and everything, that's where we were born, but we definitely are very blessed to be able to travel the world and have people want to come see us from all over. In a country where English isn't a first or even second language, to have people come and sing our lyrics back at us. It doesn't get much better than that.

JH: Devoting so many years to the music, how do you stay true to your sound?

AB: We are who we are. We always say, "You can't polish a turd." We're like the AC/DC of what we do. You're going to get your American and Celtic folk infused music along with your variety of punk rock and rock 'n roll. That's always what we've done and what we'll continue to do as the Dropkick Murphys. I think as we went from being a four-piece band to a seven-piece band, we always incorporated the Celtic instruments a little bit on our earlier releases. As we got members that were in the punk scene that played those instruments, we could bring the whole thing on the road, and in the studio there's more of that going on. With our older releases I think it was more kind of separated from song to song with the punk and the folk. I think with time it's more fused to together. You're getting everything together, you know?

JH: You've had a lot of changes in your lineup.

AB: Yeah. In a band that's been together for twelve years, you're going to have people come and go. That's the nature of touring. It takes its toll on people, people change, but the main makeup of the band and the heart and soul of the band has always been the same.

JH: How do you feel about Marc leaving?

AB: We knew Marc was going to leave. About a year ago he said he wanted to go and explore other musical directions and he felt like he couldn't do that with us because we are what we are and we're not going to want to all of a sudden change our sound because one member wants to write different music. But it wasn't a poor parting of the ways. You've got to understand, Marc was seventeen when he joined Dropkick Murphys and he's twenty-five now. The only analogy I can use is, if you're an older man or woman and you married a teenager, that person goes through so many growth changes by the time they're twenty-five that you can't expect that that person is going to feel the same as they did when they were a kid. Now he's a young adult and he's got to, as he put it, "spread his musical wings" and try to do some other stuff. We wish him all the best. Obviously we're sad about it too, but it's not going to stop us from going on. The wheels keep spinning. It just kind of speaks to what the band is all about. No one member is the Dropkick Murphys. We, as a collection, make up the band, and the spirit of the band is also kept with the fans as well. So we will continue.

JH: That's quite a way to grow up, with Dropkick Murphys.

AB: I don't think it was a bad deal.

JH: Have you done any work with Jeff DaRosa?

AB: We've known him for a long time. I haven't personally done work with him but we've toured with his old band The Vigilantes years ago. We've known him in the scene for some time, and respected him as a musician. He's a great guy and he knows his shit, so it's going to be great.

JH: So you think he'll be able to handle the purely Dropkick pandemonium that takes place in the audience?

AB: There's no replacing going on the road and seeing how it works, but he's no stranger to the road and he's got the job for sure. So I think he'll be fine, you know?

JH: What was the idea behind Born and Bred Records?

AB: We had been with our old label for ten years. We wanted to shake things up and write a new chapter in the book that is the Dropkick Murphys. It's an extension of what we've always been about, which is DIY. We've always been a do-it-yourself band. Being with Epitaph, they were a great label, but we've always been very self-sufficient. We weren't one to go, "oh, what do you guys think of this idea?" to the label. Obviously when you're working with a label you've got to clear with them, but we were always, if they didn't like an idea we'd do it anyway. We'll just pay for it ourselves or whatever. We've always been of the mind that we've got to run the ship ourselves so this is just an extension of that. So it works out good.

JH: Was it gratifying to bring your song *Tessie* to the World Series?

AB: Yeah, yeah, that and *Shipping Up to Boston*. *Tessie*, and old number that was sung by a group called the Royal Rooters back in the day when the Sox used to win World Series. They broke the eighty-six year curse. The year that that broke, we had brought *Tessie* early on in that year. It was kind of cool legend and returned kind of. It was definitely an amazing experience to do that song and now *Shipping's* kind of eclipsed that song by being adopted by Papelbon and it's just crazy. It's pretty wild.

JH: Did you find it hard to break in to the high end of the music world?

AB: The sports world and the music world are completely different, so that's what made it so uncharacteristic, so you don't really find that. I mean you'll have songs get used and you'll have big huge superstars come and play Fenway or play a sporting event, but a small band like ours to be included in these huge things now, it's wild. It's brought us to a whole different group of listeners. There's a whole bunch of people out there; I mean, I'm sure there's a bunch of people that hate us too, but there's a bunch of new fans who have gotten into the band through *Tessie* and *Shipping up to Boston*.

JH: What are you planning for the future?

AB: Just touring to support "Meanest of Times" is all we're planning now, and continuing to do what we do. Tour and put out the best music we can. That's all we've done and that's what we'll continue to do. All the wonderful and great things that have happened to this band never were preconceived or put together, they just all kind of happened to us. We don't really know what the future holds but it's been great so far. We're loving it.

JH: The audience is insane.

AB: The fans are great. As we always say, they're the other fifty percent that make up the Dropkick Murphys show. We're the fifty percent on stage and they're the fifty percent that makes up the hundred percent, you know?

JH: It's probably one of the best shows that I've been to.

AB: Where did you see us?

JH: At the Utica Brewery.

AB: Oh, okay. Where the barricade broke, right? The outside show, when we played with The Tossers?

JH: Yeah.

AB: Yeah, yeah, I remember that one. The barricade broke at that one. That was a good night, that was a fun show.

JH: I got trampled, but you're only on the ground for like five seconds before they pick up and brush you off, "are you okay?" and then they shove you right back in the crowd.

AB: That's the thing about it. From the outsiders' view, people look at that. I remember being a kid when it was really small, you'd see like twenty kids slamming or whatever you want to call it and people would be like "it looks like it is so painful, it's crazy." You fall down and people pick you right up. And with the larger crowds it still happens. People take care of each other out there. It's a good thing. That's the camaraderie that is a punk rock show as opposed to when you have these huge concerts. You look at what happened years ago at The Who concert where people got trampled, and the Pearl Jam concert in Europe where people don't take care of each other. It's a festival mentality and people just kind of go crazy. Where I see people getting knocked over and everybody keeps a cool head and they pick each other up and dust each other off and they keep going, you know? Knock on wood, in all the years we've been doing it, people get hurt, but it's never in malice, it's always somebody breaks an arm in the pit by accident. It happens. But in general everybody takes care of everybody else. And that to me is Punk Rock.

JH: Yeah. You get punched in the head and they're like "hey, how you doing?"

AB: Yeah.

JH: I woke up in my friend's bathtub.

AB: Hopefully with no water?

JH: No water, thankfully everyone was too drunk to turn on the faucet.

AB: Sounds like a hot night.

JH: Oh yeah. My friend Danni, she's a great fan. I asked her what she wanted for her birthday and she said "Al, from the Dropkick Murphys."

AB: I'm sorry that I can't fulfill that birthday wish but I think my wife would have a little problem with that.

JH: Probably. But at least I mentioned it to you. Is there anything else we haven't covered?

AB: I think that about covers it. We've been in New York, we've done a lot of shows in New York in the past few months so I don't think we'll be back for a while, but we will be back. Thanks for the interview, and we'll see you out there on the road.

Phil Lesh: All in the Music

October 2007
By T. Virgil Parker

We live in a time that experiences historical water-
sheds with startling rapidity. For instance, it is not
quite half a century ago when the shackles of American
Puritanism were, if not broken, loosened. Don't believe me?
I invite any inter-racial couple to walk down any street in
the 1950's. There are parts of our nation where the Consti-
tution was considered voluntary until the National Guard
stopped by. Teachers had to sign loyalty oaths.

Is it possible to argue that music changed the world?
Maybe not, but it certainly provided the rallying point for
the most significant period of American social evolution
and discourse. In small pockets around the nation, people
began to appear who thought that exercising freedom was
as important as dying for it. The Haight/Ashbury neighborhood of San Francisco was one of these. For whatever
reason, the attention given to that place at that time provided a global audience for the ideas formulating there-
ideas imbedded in music. The Grateful Dead was aware

that an entire psychic landscape could be invoked by music. Indeed, they felt it was their duty to try to sonically blast their way out of the straightjacket of the vacuous post-war era; a time that banned author Henry Miller identified as the "air conditioned nightmare".

Break out they did, with a vengeance. Touring more or less constantly for 30 years, they served as ambassadors of the counter culture even in the hostile territory of the Reagan Years, thereby preserving a world-view that almost certainly would have been crushed otherwise. They also became the most popular touring band in the history of the world.

You get a sense of talking to a participant of history when you talk to Phil Lesh, though he is very much in the present. It is evident from the moment he opens his mouth that his primary goal in life, even to this day, is to share significance and good vibes through music. This is equally obvious in the way he manages his current project, Phil Lesh and Friends. He will find a way to coax people who should be headlining their own tours onto his bus. They will not regret joining his quest for the ultimate sound.

TVP: You've always been a champion of avant-garde music. Was it ironic to find yourself in an immensely popular band?

PL: There was a taste of that, yes. Although the good part was that we were able to incorporate some of our avant-garde technique and approach into rock music, which was one of the most attractive features of what the Grateful Dead were doing. Everybody in the band was open to that.

TVP: You can't say that it was mainstream either, because what it did was suck an entire generation out of the mainstream.

PL: That was our fondest hope. Mainstream is what it is. It can get very predictable because of its broad appeal and there are so many more limitations on it, really, on this so-called "mainstream" art.

TVP: Do you ever see a time when an entire generation is going to get sucked out of the harness again?

PL: That's something that's been on my mind a lot lately because I see a lot of similarities between this period of time that we're living in right now and the early '60s. I don't think there's as much desire to find an alternative as before. People, especially young people, I hate to say it, are resigned to the "business as usual part." I don't think there's really the drive or a demand for any kind of expanded spiritual experience that there was back then.

TVP: Do you see class system enforcement kind of facilitating that?

PL: I suppose you could look at it that way, in the sense that the privileged are interested in maintaining that status and the way to do that is to go to the good school, get the good job, fall right into the mainstream progression of life, which is a little bit rewarding in its own way. It's disappointing that its' like, "let's make a lot of money, and I've got mine."

TVP: Now in your book-and I was impressed the way you did this- you very casually drew a straight line from the romantic poets through the beats and into contemporary counter-culture. There is a contemporary counter-culture, but it almost looks like it's the descendants of the initial member's counter-culture. We're seeing a lot of second-generation hippies these days.

PL: Yes, I see a lot of that at my shows. It's very gratifying to see that there are young people who see the vacuum at the heart of our culture and are searching for an alternative path. But I don't see that as a movement. I see that as individuals who are striking out essentially on their own and they are finding community at concerts and other places, I guess. But it's just not the same. That doesn't seem to embrace a wide consensus. Someone else was asking me, "What happened to the values of that time?" My feeling is that they live on in individual hearts and individual consciousness all over. There's sprinkled all over like pepper and salt. There doesn't seem to be a desire to band together and stick your head up in the line of fire, you know what I mean?

TVP: The Grateful Dead was in large part responsible for keeping as much of that vibe that is still around alive.

PL: I won't deny that. In fact, I'm kind of part of it.

TVP: What do you think went into preserving that aura, that sort of sacred space?

PL: People need community and they need a little bit of danger. They need a little bit of adventure and excitement. The Grateful Dead were able to provide that in a setting which was essentially a closed loop, and it was on the whole a very safe environment to explore certain areas of consciousness and being together in a group that you had never met before, and being taken on a journey, an artistic journey where the outcome is not predictable. Or rather, the details of the journey and the actual points of repose or of access are not predictable, but the outcome is generally positive. Joseph Campbell likened it to a Dionysian ritual. And it also resembles the journey of the hero.

TVP: He also postulated some sort of yin-yang of Apollonian/

Dionysian cultures. It must be strange to be one of the key representatives of the twentieth century genesis of Dionysian thought.

PL: It was kind of like a rebirth in the '60s, wasn't it?

TVP: Exactly.

PL: Because there wasn't really a lot of it, at least not in the west. Before '65, say. So yeah, it's definitely the minority viewpoint in this time. I don't know if there's ever been balance, culturally. It's usually either one way or the other the pendulum usually swings back and forth.

TVP: It's almost like the Dionysian influence only emerges when fascism reaches a critical mass.

PL: Exactly. I really feel that strongly. In other words, the cold, clear-eyed rationality; look where it's got us? The polar bears are becoming extinct. The planet is starting to boil. Humans are not going to survive this if we don't turn it around. That kind of thinking has painted us into a corner, and the thing about it is, that's really served to isolate us not only from nature and from our roots in the cosmos, but from each other, which is the worst thing that could possibly happen. If we can't work together to change things, we're well and truly screwed. That's one of the things about the Grateful Dead, and generally the rock music phenomenon no matter who was playing it. This was the message: "Look what you can do when you cooperate on a very high creative level without worrying about who gets the credit or who makes the money."

TVP: That's the key, right there.

PL: I agree, yeah.

TVP: I think the Grateful Dead is the only band who ever consciously attempted to induce altered states of consciousness through sound.

PL: Yes, it's true that we did do that deliberately. I can't say that no one else ever did it, but whether it was subconscious or accidental; I mean, for sure there have been lots of great musicians who have altered consciousness through the ages. You can look back and look at Bach, say, and his church music. His music was very consciously designed to alter consciousness in very specific ways relating to the sermon of the week.

TVP: All the way back there appears to be a tradition that ended in the nineteenth century, I'm guessing, of using music for almost Gnostic purposes.

PL: Well, what is its purpose, you know? That's the question. For me, it's a way of knowledge. It's a way to communicate with the infinite. To me, music is my religion.

TVP: The act of creation itself emulates divinity.

PL: Yes, it does, but only if it's produced in a selfless way.

TVP: The ego is not necessarily a good companion for creativity.

PL: Not necessarily, I agree. That's why I've always felt that the highest achievement that we were able to be part of, and still can do today, is when the magic is really happening on stage or even in the studio, there's nobody there. There are no humans, no personalities or egos involved, it's only the music.

TVP: The lineup changes on Phil and Friends periodically. Does it get harder or easier at times to induce the collective consciousness?

PL: It varies. It varied in the Grateful Dead, even with the same personnel. Basically when I change a lineup, it sort of involves going back to the beginning. Stripping it down just to the songs. "Okay, this is the song; this is how the song goes. This is like the abstract template for the song. Now what are we going to do with it? How are we going to elaborate this abstraction and bring it into collective consciousness in a new way?" That's one of the reasons I do mix it up, it's so that I can bring different perspectives into this music. That being said, however, the plan is to keep this band together for at least a year so that we can develop this thing.

TVP: Your fans, you've always been a lot closer to them than perhaps the vast majority of people who become really ubiquitous. Most immensely popular bands start to see their fan as "other." That didn't happen with you.

PL: No, no, the audience and the community, that's us. That came out of out of that first flush of wonder and amazement, that realizing that there were so many people who were essentially us. They were just like us, they had the same dreams and hopes and desires, and it turned out we were all living together in the same small area of San Francisco. When we would go out to play for free in the park, and for dancing in the middle of a beautiful sunny day, it was so organic; it was just what we did. We weren't playing a concert; we weren't playing a "gig." We were going to church. And with the Grateful Dead, and now my band, traveling around and going to various places and setting up and playing music, it's like the old camp meetings that used to happen in the nineteenth century where people from a town or a city would go out into the country and camp together, and they would cook together, and they would leave all of their class stratifications behind, they would leave all of their wealth and poverty behind and they would be together in a different situation. They would leave their lives behind in order to be together and seek some kind of community. Basically it had a religious component to it. To us, to me, every place we play is church, is what I said.

TVP: Wow, that is awesome. You're doing some work on 60's culture.

PL: I was teaching a class about the '60s in San Francisco at my son's high school. That was last year. I'm involved in producing and creating a, get this, a TV show about a fictional band that I'm creating with collaborators. I'm going to create the whole back catalogue of the band and their whole history and take them into our times in a kind of dramatic, comedic situation. There's going to be lots of music and I'm going to write all the soundtrack music for the show. It's actually starting to come together. That's a really exciting way for me to put more music out in the world that doesn't have to go through the recording industry.

TVP: That's an exciting project.

Your specific method of playing bass, you're one of the three bass players that actually took the bass as an authentic instrument back when rock 'n roll was still being codified. You must see a lot of your influence around you.

PL: Yes and no. I think the influence I see is more general. It stems more from the Grateful Dead than from me particularly, in the whole jam band scene. It's kind of funny; it started really flowering after Jerry's death. It's really gratifying to see. You can't really imitate or derive things from the actual music that's played but what is so satisfying to me is that the whole jam-band phenomenon has evolved beyond musicians, picking up on the concept and the approach, the way of improvised music that was brought to rock 'n roll by the Grateful Dead and applying that to their own music. I see that everywhere from the newest jam bands to major artists actually applying this in their performances. That being said, the Grateful Dead did not originate this. We simply took what jazz musicians did and applied to rock 'n roll.

TVP: True enough, but I see a certain elliptical style of bass playing that was not introduced into contemporary music until you did that.

PL: Yeah, I have to agree with that, but that's more a function of my consciousness or my way of looking at music than almost anything else. I never want to do anything in the standard way because that's already been done. So when I started playing with the band, at first of course it was very stratified and very rigid and kind of wooden because I was just sort of feeling my way. But musicians have a way of getting into the nuts and bolts of how music is made and refreshing it from time to time. I wanted to play the bass in a melodic way, in a contrapuntal way, which derives ultimately from Bach.

TVP: I was going to say, Bach, Telemann.

PL: I had been a trumpet player before and a violin player before that and I just didn't want to plan. The only thing you could do would be to imitate McCartney or James Jamerson at that time. But of course, that being said, I was inspired greatly by masters like Scott LaFaro, and also Mingus.

TVP: That's a completely different world.

PL: Yes, it is, but it's just the approach, you know? Mingus had that down-home, gutsy approach, and Scotty LaFaro had that high-flying melodic, oblongata approach. To hear him keep the groove going when he was playing some amazing melody behind the soloist, that was a revelation and so, like I said, we owe it all to jazz musicians.

TVP: What are you hearing right now that's commanding your attention?

PL: I listen to a lot of jazz and classical music still. My man Jackie Greene is still rocking me out, and he's part of the band now.

TVP: That's one thing I've noticed about Phil and Friends is that you go out and find people that really blow you away.

PL: What else is there?

TVP: A lot of people, when they're putting their band together don't want to be blown away.

PL: Yeah, I know, because it's all about them. But in this case it's all about the music. Who can come in and serve the music, make it new? Make it something that had never been before?

TVP: What kind of material do you have for this tour that will be particularly exciting for people who are checking you out?

PL: Well, we build everything on the Grateful Dead classics. First of all because that's what people want to hear. We can pull them in by doing the classic Grateful Dead material. Jackie's songs, for instance, are so beautiful and melodic and they fit so well in sequences with Grateful Dead material that we're going to be doing a lot of Jackie solos. We'll be doing a lot of covers. You know, some Dylans, the usual suspects, stuff that we like. We're doing a lot of band songs. And also, we're writing new material that we're hoping to bring into the repertoire as soon as we can. That's a new departure for PLF is that we're actually working on new material.

TVP: In traditional style you're going to fine-tune it on the road, I'm assuming?

PL: Absolutely. I mean there's never enough rehearsal time. Everybody has a schedule and a life and a career of their own, so it's just gratifying that these great musicians are interested in playing this music and interested in playing this music and interested in taking it further. That's always what I've wanted to try to do was take it to another level each time. It's interesting because it's like branches on a tree. Every time we start up a new band, like I was saying earlier, we kind of go back to the trunk, then we grow some new branches. The new branches can go in any direction and that's mostly determined by the people who are now in the band.

TVP: One thing I've noticed about Phil and Friends is that there are a lot of people out there covering the Dead. Some of them are amazing. But specifically, Phil and Friends has a way of retaining that authentic looseness that was hallmark to the way the Dead did things. Not sloppiness, but a sort of consistent looseness that let the sound flow outward rather than line up like ducks.

PL: That's a good way to describe it. That gets right to the core of what we want to do because the most significant magic happens in the moment when we'll be playing along and somebody throws out a little idea. It doesn't have to be a big shredding solo or anything. More often it's just some little rhythmic or melodic or textual idea. When that happens and the stars are in the right position, the whole band can pounce on this all of sudden it's like these doors open. It's like you're blasted into orbit and you see everything in a new perspective. The whole music just takes a left turn and goes off in another direction. To me that's exhilarating, and it's really the reason for living are those moments. What we try to do is create an atmosphere where those moments can happen. That's the core of what the Grateful Dead were doing and that's the thing that I took from the Grateful Dead and I try to expand really.

TVP: You're certainly doing it. I expect there's going to be a lot of very happy people from this tour.

PL: I hope so because I'm looking forward to it. I'm going to have a great time.

Warren Haynes and the Improvisational Lifeboat

By Jessica Hopsicker

Warren Haynes has gotta lotta chops. How else could he have ranked among Rolling Stone's list of Greatest Guitar Players of all time? Well, chops, and perseverance to the point of obsession are ways to become a virtuoso of the axe. Another is to find the nearest crossroads and pull a Robert Johnson. Therefore, to become a Rock God, practice makes perfect, or maybe a pact with the devil. Either way it takes more than just a few color-coated plastic buttons on a fret board and a TV screen.

Landing anywhere in the top 100 guitar players on the planet takes a liberal dose of elbow grease, but to be in the top 25 requires the ability to plant your name just about anywhere. He has fronted notable and prolific bands such as Gov't Mule, The Allman Brothers Band, and The Dead. He's played countless shows, headlined numerous festivals, and taken the stage with just about everybody.

Not everyone can pick up a guitar for the first time and crank out Purple Haze, or beat an electronic drum pad and be the next John Bonham. Everyone can become a Rock Star when talent is subtracted from the equation. In the case of the notable Mr. Haynes, I suspect he borders on having talent to spare.

Jess Hopsicker: You're considered one of the top 100 guitar players of all time, what goes into garnering that sort of appreciation?

Warren Haynes: That's a good question, I guess a question for Rolling Stone, I was very flattered, honored, to be on that list. I had no idea; our office got the call saying I made it but they don't tell you what number you are, until the article came out. I just assumed I was number 100.

Warren Haynes: I felt lucky to be on it all. I was very honored had made it, there's a lot of great people that made the list and a lot of great people that didn't make it, let alone making 23, that is pretty impressive.

WH: I was very shocked yeah.

JH: It seems you give every once of yourself while you're playing, do you feel that's your obligation as an artist?

WH: I don't know if it is the responsibility as much it just seems to happen. People that are completely immersed in their art and hooked on what they do, just tend to do it, whether you owe it to the public or not. It just seems to happen.

JH: You're also one of the hardest working performers today, is it hard to be a creative person and an A Type personality at the same time?

WH: I think creativity goes in cycles so you have to maintain some sort of focus and drive. But knowing that you're going to have spurts of creativity, and segments of time when you don't feel so inspired, you continue to do what you do and try to draw inspiration from somewhere. It's funny because I can use songwriting as an example. I'll go sometimes two or three months without writing anything. I'm not one of those people that write every day or every week. Every time I start second guessing myself and going, "when am I ever going to write another song, have I written my last song?" Then eventually the wave will come back around, and then I'll write two or three in a row that I'm really into. I'll feel excited again. After all this time, you would think I'd be used to it. But it still scares me every time it happens.

JH: That you think you'll never be able to write anymore?

WH: You wonder. I'm hoping that it will never happen but whenever I go through a slump I always get those feelings, you know.

JH: I guess it's better than getting too comfortable.

WH: It's not good to be complacent, and artistically speaking you have constantly try and break new ground. Hopefully you can draw inspiration from different places, you never know exactly where to draw it from.

JH: What went into the creative process of becoming the person and musician you are today?

WH: When I was around six years old I heard black gospel music on the radio in North Carolina, and that was the first sound that made the hair on my arms stand up. I think from that moment foreword I had some sort of obsession with music. Then I discovered Soul music like James Brown, The Temptations, Four Tops, Otis Redding and Wilson Pickett. I started singing in the bedroom and spent hours and hours every day listening to music and singing along. Then I eventually discovered rock music like Hendrix, Cream and stuff like that, that's when I wanted to play guitar. I never lost that desire to keep learning and keep getting better and better. Whereas, a lot of the time you look around at the people who are playing music. You get tired of it and something else takes the place of that hobby, so to speak. It never felt like a hobby to me. It always felt like an obsession. As far as my career is concerned, I have been extremely lucky to have a career from the time I was sixteen. There have been lean years and there have been good years. But I have always maintained some sort of career. I think that's mostly from just doing what I think is in my heart. Never second-guess the marketplace. I don't want to say don't compromise, life is full of compromises, but as far as compromising your integrity I have always tried not to do that and to just play music that I would go and pay to hear and make records that I would buy. That has always been my rule of thumb. Not worrying about chasing the trends or jumping on whatever trend that's happening at the moment. If you want longevity you've just got to do what you do and know that things move in cycles and waves and that your time will come. We've always just built an audience based on the type of music we love to play. Do what you do and whoever likes that approach will become part of it, you know.

JH: Does music today tend to lack that sort of wholeness that you have to offer?

WH: I think that there is a young generation of musicians and artists and people that just want to be celebrities that are willing to sell out at the drop of a hat. They just want to be famous and don't care what it takes, whereas the generation that I grew up in, people were more concerned at being really good at what they do, than with being famous, not everyone, but a larger percentage. Now there are a really high percentage of people that just want to be famous and don't care what they have to do to get there. That compromises the overall picture.

JH: You have been working rather closely will the Jam environment, how is that working for you?

WH: That's a scene that kind of just appeared one day and garnered some sort of staying power and grew and grew and grew. I'm glad that it did because even though Gov't Mule is predominately a Rock and Roll band, there are a lot of things we have in common with the Jam scene, mostly that we play a different set list every night and take a different approach to the songs night after night. Improvisation is the lifeboat of our music. We take a lot of roots music, as far as rock, blues, jazz, reggae, soul, country, folk; all these things and mix it together to create whatever it is that Gov't Mule does. But we're very different than the average Jam band. And I think that's okay because I think the scene should include all types of root-oriented and improvisational music There's no reason you can't hear an improvisational rock band on the same stage as a jazz, bluegrass, or reggae band. People who love music love all types of music and I think the thing that has made the jam scene so successful is the open-mindedness and the unwillingness to sell out to the corporate MTV force-fed type music world.

JH: Non-denominational.

WH: Pretty much, that's a big concern. Nobody wants to be told what to listen to. People are entirely too intelligent to be told this is what they should listen to.

JH: Though it does seem we're getting a lot of that lately-

WH: Yeah, all the way around though, not just music, but in everyday life, politics, and art. I think in some ways arts is at an all time low, as far as how important it is in our society. It's a scary indication of where we are as a society.

JH: Are you getting sick of Phil Lesh questions?

WH: No

JH: Are there any surprises in store for the Mountain Jam?

WH: Yeah there are some surprises that we're going to announce eventually but we have to wait a little bit longer before we can legally announce them. There are some really good surprises coming up at the Mountain Jam.

JH: I believe that is just about it.

WH: You mean no Phil Lesh questions?

JH: Actually, no, I don't have any.

WH: You just wanted to know if I was sick of it?

JH: Yeah.

WH: No. I'm not.

JH: Is there anything else we haven't covered?

WH: Gov't Mule is almost finished with a new CD that we're hoping to have out in August, and were very excited about playing all of the new material, which we kinda started to do, I don't know how much we'll play between now and when the CD comes out, because we still want there to be some surprises. We're very excited about that and I think it's the best thing we've done, musically speaking, and from that point foreword we're going to be doing a lot of touring.

JH: Excellent.

Suicide Girls:
Missy Suicide Got the Ball Rolling, Nixon Suicide Took It on the Road

January 2007
By T. Virgil Parker

Mark Twain pointed out that Americans are passionate about preserving freedom of speech, but wise enough never to actually exercise the right. It is possible that this wisdom comes at a high price. As sophisticated as we like to think we are, the American Id is firmly planted beneath the super ego. Self-repression is a boiling pot and the top will fly off eventually, in the worst way. I think this is what causes midlife crises. And I find it interesting that there are more murders in the U.S than in any country in the world. We need more broken noses, less broken homes. The popular idea that following your natural impulses leads to chaos and destruction is possibly the most misguided notion in our culture.

What does this have to do with the Suicide Girls? Everything.

What we are really denying, after all, when we repress, is our full selfhood. There is an evolution of the definition of expression, of beauty, of acceptance, of selfhood flowering

172

under the guise of good, mildly unclean fun on the ever popular website.

T. Virgil Parker: It strikes me that a third of all women below 25 are trying to become Suicide Girls.

Missy Suicide: I don't think the numbers are quite that high, but we do get an incredible amount of requests, around a thousand a month.

TVP: This is like a cultural sea change. There have always been, still are, a lot of taboos associated with this kind of expression. Do you feel you've contributed to that evolution?

MS: What we've done is create a platform for girls to express their individuality. Having a place where people can congregate together has probably impacted perception by mainstream media. I certainly can't take full credit.

TVP: But you have contributed to the trend.

MS: With 1,200 Suicide girls all sharing their lives online and the attention that's drawn, it has definitely affected the trend.

TVP: Do you get more, say, requests to become a Suicide Girl, than death threats from Fundamentalists?

MS: Fundamentalists tend to leave me alone. It's because this is pin-up style nudity and the girls are being themselves, sharing their thoughts and ideas. We have doctors and lawyers and researchers who are Suicide Girls, and they have intelligent things to say and share with the community and the world.

TVP: Suddenly it is acceptable to express sexuality and be eloquent and intelligent.

MS: I certainly saw a void and wondered why they had to be mutually exclusive.

TVP: In the past this might have been seen as gender-driven exploitation.

MS: Everybody has a body, and everybody's body is beautiful. It is confidence that conveys beauty. That is empowerment, not exploitation, and that is why this doesn't contradict Feminist values.

TVP: Is it possible that people are beginning to understand that denying this kind of expression is itself misogynistic?

MS: Yes.

TVP: That seems to be an inherent assumption of Suicide Girls.

MS: We are not Feminist Central. We don't claim to waive the flag for all Feminists. We do represent an important component of human expression.

TVP: When you launched Suicide Girls you were looking for a creative project that excited you. What planted that particular seed?

MS: I was connecting with all these amazing women that I had been friends with before I started the project, and it just grew from seeing them as beautiful, but not in a way that had been accepted.

TVP: The project is huge now, and not getting any smaller. How do you sustain your original vision?

MS: We choose venues that express that vision. Suicide Girls Live is all about that. It's touring right now. It is sort of an old style burlesque, but with a difference.

TVP: I understand that it is raising a few eyebrows.

MS: It seems like natural fun to me. We're taking a tradition and updating it. It is edgy, but in a Punk way. We're taking it to venues where a lot of punk bands play. It's very exciting.

TVP: You're getting a lot of crossover from intellectuals at the shows, a lot of people you wouldn't normally see at exotic dance places.

MS: Suicide Girls fans are like that. They're not exactly your typical crowd. One of the unique phenomena about Suicide Girls is the high level of dialogue on the site. The girls are smart, they express themselves. Suicide Girls Live is just another medium of expression.

TVP: In addition to one of the most popular websites in the world, you have a book under your belt, the DVD, and the tour. Do you see this becoming an empire like Playboy?

MS: If that happens, it is certainly going to be a few years down the road. We're just doing what we like to do.

TVP: It looks like Suicide Girls, especially with the books, is making an effort to produce serious art.

MS: It's all my photography in the books. I do. I do perceive it as being art.

TVP: The art world is still a bit more conservative than it would like to think it is.

MS: The definitions are broadening slowly but surely. People are becoming more open-minded, accepting.

TVP: Do you perceive yourself as being a social engineer?

MS: I'm not sitting down designing a plot to take over the world, not at this point.

TVP: Suicide Girls bond rather than compete, which is very unusual where anything like fame and publicity are concerned.

MS: It's about expressing yourself in an authentic way. That requires trust.

TVP: What else is coming up?

MS: We're taking this tour all over Europe. The second DVD is coming out. We're also going to be on *CSI New York* on October 18th. The creator of the show is a big fan.

TVP: Where do you want to see all this going?

MS: I would love for all women to feel beautiful about themselves. If I can help that happen I'll be happy.

In the interest of pure journalistic objectivity, I thought it would be important to connect with an authentic Suicide Girl and find out what it's like from the ground floor. Nixon Suicide is touring with Suicide Girls Live, and if she is any indication of what the tour is going to be like when it hits New York, they should change the name to Suicide Girls Sets the Town on Fire. She's utterly energetic, vivacious, and eloquent at the same time.

TVP: Have you been performing publicly for a long time, or is this your first experience with this kind of thing?

Nixon Suicide: I've been in burlesque for about five years now.

TVP: The Counterculture worldview is introspective in a lot of ways. Does that side of you ever clash with the more explosive, public side of you?

NS: I'd imagine that's universal, but I feel that the various parts of my personality work very well together. My only problem is that both sides are over-achievers. I do this for a couple months out of the year, I travel, and I come home to my regular job. I feel like the lucky one who gets to do all of those things.

TVP: There must be a lot of affection coming at you from the audience. What does that feel like?

NS: Though the show is sort of sexual in nature, I feel that the energy we get from the audience is very similar to what you'd get from a Rock concert. You get a definite stage rush, absolutely, but it isn't personal, it's everybody having a really good time.

TVP: The show is energy-driven.

NS: A lot of the places we're going, especially in the Midwest, have never seen anything like this before. They go insane.

TVP: Suicide Girls has a very arty reputation. Are you seeing a sort of non-typical crowd for a burlesque show?

NS: It's an interesting crossover. There are people who'd usually be home on their computers or reading a book actually coming out to the show. We have a lot of bits that are full of pop culture references. We did a Hunter S. Thompson sketch. We get really good feedback when we do things like that.

TVP: Burlesque has a long history and set of traditions; you're keeping that intact and revving it up for the 21st Century.

NS: We're trying to uphold the elements that make it different from what you see in a typical strip club. Humor certainly plays a role. There's more concentration on the tease up to the reveal than on the reveal itself. We're certainly jazzing up the moves and the music and making it truly contemporary.

TVP: Where do you think you're going to go with this?

NS: I'm always amazed it has gone this far. It's like this fantastic ride that I've been on. Mostly, I want to take it overseas a bit more. We went to Australia earlier this year. I love to travel, so my hope is Europe, Japan. There are a lot of places I'd like to go.

Guster: At the Intersection of Beer Pong and National Public Radio

January 2007
T. Virgil Parker

Most people who allocate themselves into the category of Nerd do not do so with a great deal of self-satisfaction. As a result, I always thought that if you could go back in time and give R.E.M. Prozac they might have been more like Guster. The unending popularity of this band is that they live, write and perform from the world-view of the kid whose gym locker was always Jell-O-bombed, and then suddenly got hold of Sauron's Ring of Power.

Not that they have it out for anybody much, or at least anybody who doesn't deserve it. There is a confidence in their music that precludes much in the way of bad vibes, and allows them to stake out territory that's pretty much their own. In fact, despite the full support of one of the most powerful record companies on the planet, they still prefer to do everything in the trademark Guster style, which can only be called one of shabby gentility. They take pride in tossing aside the trappings of success.

And there is a lot to toss aside. Critics, and people who

have less than the usual lead exposure, can't get enough of their sound. Each album exceeds the previous one in both subtlety and popularity. This most archetypal of college bands has the best of both worlds: Impeccable Indie credentials and a global audience.

Tim Parker: The distance between Guster and their fans is basically zero.

Ryan Miller: That's a good thing, right?

TVP: Yeah.

RM: We do road journals and things like that and certainly have a reputation for being accessible. I think we even present ourselves on stage in an accessible way. There's not a lot of pretense unless it's tongue-in-cheek. We don't do a lot of Rock Star posing on stage, I hope. We're into the wearing a t-shirt that we wore to bed the night before kind of thing.

TVP: You can't be ironic and a Rock Star at the same time.

RM: What's ironic? Is Ben Folds ironic when he does his thing? I suppose it is irony. We spend a lot of time playing with convention, or calling bullshit on convention. Some of what we do is very conventional at the same time. It isn't our full M.O. to pull back the curtain on what it means to play a Rock show. Sometimes that will rear its head in the middle of a show and we'll try to play with it in a funny or entertaining way.

TVP: Do you think your fans have more in common with you than is usually the case?

RM: There is a sort of arrested development that has gone on in our lives. We'll go to parties after shows on college campuses and play beer pong. We're still kind of nerds, and we download music and watch the same movies. It is hard to say. A lot of times fans tend to emulate the bands that they like, or the other way around. I feel a lot of overlap with our fans, I can say that.

TVP: Your fans seen to share a culture with you in formative ways.

RM: For example?

TVP: With the Alt culture, really Gen. X, authority is automatically suspect, meaning is automatically ambiguous. That's not the entire generation, but a world-view you certainly share with your fans.

RM: Yeah. There is an aesthetic that's consistent in the Onion, and The Daily Show and a lot of films and music that have that sort of meta-ness about it.

TVP: Now that you've been doing this for a while, how does adulthood and being in a band mix?

RM: That goes back to the arrested development statement I made. Going around in a bus for eight months a year is not necessarily an enterprise, but it can be. We don't sleep on couches anymore and we have a lot of really talented people help us on the road. That does help to alleviate the adolescent nature of touring.

I don't necessarily feel like an adult. All my friends in NY are younger than me. We're married and we have mortgages and responsibilities, but I still play in a Rock band, and playing beer pong is part of my job sometimes.

TVP: I think many people now perceive adulthood as a kind of surrender.

RM: Adulthood is necessary. There are many wonderful things about adulthood. I see no reason to rush it needlessly.

At least in my own personal life, it's always gotten better. I appreciate the wisdom that comes every year, and learning from mistakes, and having more empathy. I don't think adulthood is a bad word. Giving yourself completely over to adulthood is a bad thing for me, and not necessarily a quality I like in others around me.

A certain wonder, and carelessness, and unabashed creativity is a really compelling feature in people. I have friends who are Capital A adults, and they're great. I don't think that will ever be me.

TVP: How have the colleges been responding to your promotion of bio-diesel?

RM: Last year was our inaugural run with Adam's non-profit, Reverb. The response was mostly good. I don't know how many kids really give a shit about what we're doing. That's to be expected. We're a band first, and messengers of good will, second or third.

We're just trying to get behind things that we care about, that are relatively apolitical like bio-diesel and cleaner energy. Most kids don't walk away from our concerts thinking that that's an important part of it, but if ten percent of them walk away with a pamphlet in their hands, that's great.

TVP: Most bands don't get better with time, but everything Guster puts out is stronger than the previous album.

RM: There are people who don't share that opinion; we lose people every record. I don't know if popularity is a good measure, but we just had our most successful year ever. That feels good because we did it on our own terms, we didn't do something we didn't want to do. We keep pushing ourselves to make better records. That progression you're referring to is the driving force in the band.

TVP: Critics are almost unanimous about *Ganging up on the Sun*, even critics who don't have anything to do with the genre. Is that kind of respect important to you?

RM: I want to say it isn't, but it is important to me. I don't rely on critics but I consult them in my media decisions, music especially. I read Pitchfork and Metacritic and Pop Matters. That's my filtering system of how I discover new music. That's actually a credible way of getting turned on to music. While critical respect isn't the most important thing, if it comes along with the other things we want, that's great.

TVP: Is it kind of scary getting praise from National Public Radio?

RM: No. I really appreciate it because of the intelligence. We just had a sort of interesting run. I was reading the New Yorker- I know that sounds pretentious- it's a rich enough story that it almost belongs in there. We've started out as this not-that-awesome college band, and we've been very successful in a lot of ways. We pre-dated this whole internet marketing thing. We have one foot in this DIY grassroots touring world and another foot firmly planted in major label land. When NPR does a story on us we can get navel-gazing for a minute and talk about the journey.

TVP: You had to be one of the first bands to do the whole street team/internet thing to get where you are.

RM: I feel like we were. We took that whole street team thing and made it our own before even the internet or email was big. It was out of necessity. We had made a record that we really believed in. We'd given it to a big Boston manager who managed all the big super-hit Boston bands and he gave it to his three friends and they didn't like it. He told us to make another one in a year. We really felt that if we went out there and busted our ass, that it would find an audience. We sent it to kids who were interested and we busked in Harvard Square, and played all the colleges. That's how we got a leg up. When the internet came up we made the most of it, in large part because we're all immersed in it and all nerds. That's a natural extension of our band. All those ideas on the site come from us.

TVP: Are you surprised that the Jam people are giving the band such a warm welcome?

RM: I wouldn't characterize them as being super into it. We don't get invited to the super noodle-fests. It sort of makes sense; we're not really an improvisational band at all. There is an ethos in the band that's consistent with the Jam Band scene. There's an emphasis on the live performance. We tour a lot and we know it is important and try to make it special. I can see how we would cross over to an extent, but for Jam Band purists, where anything can happen musically from night to night, we're not that. When I see that I think it's just crazy. I'd never be able to pull that off.

TVP: You are masters at innovating, and your fans expect something unusual from you on a consistent basis. Anything like that in the works now?

RM: We're just gearing up for a tour now so we're trying to come up with things that look home-made but are effective. We've been touring on this album for almost a year, so we're going to come up with new songs, new arrangements. We always tweak the set list. That comes to fruition when we're on the road. We tried to do a video installation but it got too expensive. We don't have mega millions to play with, but if we did, we'd throw more of it into the show. In the mean time we're just trying to find cheap ways to make the show special.

Killer Keller: Keller Williams

October 2004
By T. Virgil Parker

Keller Williams' brain works the way I expect kitchen appliances to work in about 300 years. You might put kelp in there and a wedding cake might come out the other end. The tiniest shred of musical ideation will be permutated infinitely and transplanted in a number of realms before coming to rest. There are many sophisticated musicians capable of this kind of thing, but usually in a bloodless intellectual way that is somehow impressive but ultimately boring. Not for Keller. There's a sense of death-defying adventure in his music. If there were a big sign on his guitar that said "DON'T HIT THE RED BUTTON" he would hit the red button.

Many four-piece bands cannot come close to erecting the towers of sound he cranks out in live performances. Trapping loops and jamming against them in layer after layer, he somehow manages to combine the mix into a truly authoritative sound.

If you haven't been to one of the shows you probably

assume people are there to gape at the prodigious nature of the performance. In fact, as unusual and amazing as the delivery of the music is, the sound coming out of the speakers is an invocation of amusement and partying. Though he is literally turning himself inside out to get this music out without accomplices, the sensation of the music is funky, fun.

Keller's new live disk *Stage* is awash with a sense of jollity and playfulness. It is obvious that he wants to get the biggest recreation possible from these performances. It is equally clear that the audiences feel the same way.

TVP: In your new live double CD "Stage", the first disk is the West Coast gigs and the second is East Coast. Was I projecting or does it seem that the second disk is more expressive and the first is more technical?

KW: That's the way the energies of the two coasts seem to work. The energy of the East Coast is more of a party vibe and out west it's more of a sit-back and listen/pay attention kind of energy, though there's a lot of similarity between both coasts.

TVP: I've been noticing that an entire One Man Band genre has evolved over the last few years. If you go to an Open Mic you can usually find one or two people who demonstrate the ability to get lost in a sea of loops. You really pile the loops on and you never seem to get lost.

KW: I have a little theatre training and a background in drama. It has happened, a lot in fact, but I've gotten very good at covering it up. People who see me a lot can probably tell. The longer I've been doing this, the less it happens. The machine can mess up and keep recording, so I end up with a Millie Vanilie scenario. That gets frustrating but dealing with that kind of thing strengthens you up for anything that can happen. When you're doing something like this it is like walking a tightrope. There's very little room for mistakes, but sometimes mistakes can be turned into Jazz!

TVP: You ever see a band where every musician is trying to blow each other off the stage?

KW: Yeah?

TVP: It's like you're trying to do that to yourself.

KW: There are never any rules. I can do anything I want. Technology is so cool these days that I if I don't like what I'm doing I hit the 'suck' button and that layer is gone. I can lay a really cool improv and bring that to the front.

TVP: It strikes me that you are the kind of person who never runs out of ideas.

KW: I like to stay busy thinking about what I'm doing and I always try to put myself in the place of the audience. If I go and see someone several times I would hope that they would incorporate different ideas. So I try to keep it fresh for the people who keep coming back.

TVP: Nine out of ten musicians are banging their heads against the wall trying to come up with any idea. You seem to be the kind of person who has to weed through a plethora of concepts to find the right one.

KW: There's no shortage of ideas. Maybe it's just my thinking process and how I go about thinking about things in a different way. There's a comfort level to sticking with one idea if it works. There's a selfish element to what I do. I learned a long time ago that you can't please everyone all the time. So I have to focus on pleasing myself, at least on stage.

TVP: I think that's communicated to the audience, if you're having a sincerely good time up there.

KW: It's very self-indulgent.

TVP: Do you think that having been a festival goer has drawn you to a unique way of understanding your audience?

KW: I think so. It is all about your own way of thinking. People have different opinions about everything. I always try to put the music loving side of me up there- what would I want to hear if I was in the audience? I've been to enough shows and enough festivals that I have I pretty good idea of what I would want to see if I was in the audience.

TVP: You're playing some really elaborate stuff, and no one is accusing you of playing Jazz.

KW: The real Jazz guys know I'm a poser, and the people who don't know what Jazz is- well that speaks for itself. I love Jazz and I love to imitate it. I don't actually think I'm playing Jazz.

TVP: I'd say that you play with idioms but you don't buy them lock, stock and barrel.

KW: What do you mean?

TVP: You might play some Jazz but you wouldn't be saying to yourself "I'm a Jazz man."- that sort of non-verbal way that Jazz people have of letting the world know that they're Jazz people.

KW: Yes.

TVP: It's the 'serious' index in Jazz. There's a balancing act going on. You're playing serious music, but you're not playing it seriously.

KW: I'm accepted in some circles as an entertainer. People like all kinds of music, just like me. I hope that they come for my interpretations of various genres.

TVP: If you work in a context where people aren't required to take you with absolute seriousness, they have more fun and you have the latitude to so anything you want.

KW: Absolutely true.

TVP: Now on to the 'anything you want'- is there anything that would not consider using as a musical instrument?

KW: I don't think I've ever succeeded at using a violin, or a reed instrument. The reeds are really tough, the saxophone, the clarinet, flutes. The violin is something I can't seem to comprehend.

TVP: If you expect anything like instant gratification, then the violin is out of the picture.

KW: Maybe a one stringed violin.

TVP: Ever since I started listening to you I'll see something like a bamboo saxophone on the Internet and think 'Gee, I wonder if Keller Williams knows about it."

KW: I recently got into the theramin- that's a fun instrument. I first came across it in the Beach Boys' song "Good Vibrations" and I've seen them in documentaries. Phish broke one out a couple years ago. The more I use it the closer I get to being in key. It's a very visual instrument and a lot of people don't understand this- it is fun to watch.

TVP: When you write, do you use the same body of skills you use when you're jamming?

KW: When I write it's a little more mental than when I'm jamming. A jam session comes in with a little bit of structure when I set up the loop. The improvisation comes when I'm soloing over the loop. When I'm writing there's more of a direction to go, certainly at least with the lyrics. You have a meaning, tell some kind of story, sum it up. Then I have characters, conflict. A jam has a little structure in the beginning and then improv.

TVP: You always start with a lyric when you're writing?

KW: That's normally what inspires me to come up with a song, kind of a hook chorus. I might put that to a melody without even picking up a guitar. Other times the song might be entirely written on the guitar, from mindlessly doodling. When there's words involved usually the words come first.

TVP: When you play a cover live you Kellerize it. When you take your own studio material on the road do you create a Kellerization of a Kellerization?

KW: A lot of my songs get road tested before they get recorded. When I go to the studio I have a pretty good idea of how that song is going to be laid out on tape. A cover song I kind of absorb and my own little things go into it without my even trying.

TVP: It strikes me that you were very dedicated to the Dead at a point in your history. There's a whole new generation of people who are doing the same thing. It has become a tradition. Did you ever feel that you would become part of that same process?

KW: It's always been all about the music. I got into the scene and the community and making friends and going to shows. Then the shows stopped. They're different now. It's definitely not the same without Jerry. It's not better or worse, it's just different. But when Jerry died I just stayed with the music but the scene was basically over.

This was a time when my career started picking up. I started out as the 'ambiance' guy in the corner in places where there wasn't even a cover charge and I slowly started opening shows and performing in shows where people actually bought tickets. My career was picking up right about when Jerry died, which was a huge hit to everyone on the scene.

I have a couple of Dead lyric books and I can just go through page by page and play the songs, I love the songs so much.

TVP: I had thought at the time that a lot of people were being diverted from creating in their own right by being in Dead cover bands, but then all this incredibly diverse music started coming out of that.

KW: The Grateful Dead opened up a lot of people's eyes in a lot of different ways. Whether it be the jumping around from genre to genre or just improvisation that took place. A whole method and way that they went about life touring.

TVP: You have a huge, devoted following. That's a phenomenon that usually happens to bands rather than solo performers. Listening to Stage I can see why. You had to be literally turning yourself inside out to be producing that much sound live.

KW: Well, thanks.

TVP: Who would you consider to be your influences?

KW: The main influences would be Michael Hedges, Jerry Garcia, and Bobby McFarin, Victor Wooten, Michael Hedges being and inspiration as a solo artist who took it as far as he could go. Victor Wooten is enormous on the bass, before the technology, but I picked up on his looping ideas, Bobby McFarin as a vocal master, and Jerry, for his soul and the energy he put into his singing, his certain specific noodly style that he would lead with just rings out in my head. If you put all that together you've got where I'm coming from.

TVP: Every instrument you use you also use as a percussive instrument.

KW: There's something going on with me hitting any instrument to create a percussive quality.

TVP: You ever look out and see a few thousand people looking back and wonder what you're going to do next?

KW: Oh yeah. I used to thrive off of not performing with a set list. I was very proud of that for a very long time. The more I go back to the same cities the more I want to make sure I'm doing something new, so I pay more attention to what I played the time before with that particular set list. I'll run that through the request list on my web site and try to make sure I have a unique show.

TVP: Can you tell me about Keller's Cellar?

KW: It's a self-indulgent narrated mix tape that goes on for an hour. The stations it plays on are mostly college stations and secondary markets. I'm not dealing with commercial radio where I'd have to plug in ad windows every seven minutes. I get to work with stations where there's creative control instead of massive central programming from some computer somewhere. It's called "Keller's Cellar Somewhat Rule-less Radio." It's all music from my own collection. I'm recording it in a recording studio and not a radio station. Since I've started the show a year ago I get lots of CD's in the mail, which is really cool. I listen to every disk that comes to me.

TVP: What do you see happening in the next few years?

KW: I can only hope and wish that it continues to go the way it is now. I'm very comfortable at this stage now playing 1,000 and 1,500 seats. It's large enough to have a certain kind of energy, but small enough to feel somewhat intimate. Once you go higher the rooms get bigger and the sound gets lost. Bigger than that and I'd need a lot more staff and sound equipment and the show becomes very expensive. Life's too short for that kind of stress. If it does goes bigger, I could accept it. It could realistically get smaller. I'd gladly drop back into the smaller rooms. I don't really have a backup plan, nor do I want one.

TVP: Anything else that you want to talk about?

KW: The best way to understand what I'm talking about is to come to a show. It's very difficult to read about it. If you come check it out you'll get a good idea of what it's all about.

Chuck Palahniuk: Angels, Anarchy and Atavism

October 2008
By Jessica Hopsicker

It is impossible not to bring up Chuck Palahniuk's cult masterpiece *Fight Club*, when a few devout followers legally changed their name to Tyler Durden, and fight clubs multiply like mushroom spores worldwide. One can't help but begrudgingly recall the stomach- churning "Guts" that seminal first short story in *Haunted* about masturbation disasters that made all those people faint at his readings. There's so much more to it than that.

He doesn't speak to the angry, jaded, and disenfranchised youth, his novels; hijack their minds, launching them on a ride from the very first line. Readers throttle though the black terrain of what he likes to call Satirical Horror and Transgressional Fiction fraught with sexual deviance, gore, and violence. His words shock and nauseate but also somehow incite and inspire in significant ways. Cast into labyrinthine plot lines, text and subtext strewn with arcane trivia and useless information, Chuck subjects the readers to poignant themes tackling consumerism, social stigmas, and sexuality. He pummels the "gentle reader" to the point of whiplash with the grotesque and subversive. Through the course of *Fight Club*, *Survivor*, *Invisible Monsters*, *Choke*, *Lullaby*, *Diary*, *Haunted*, *Rant*, and *Snuff* the reader emerges a different person.

The second novel adapted for film is *Choke*, released September 26 2008, will also be considered as definitive Chuck. Just days away from its release, I finally snagged an interview with the man.

Jessica Hopsicker: When you develop a character, does it start out as a personality or a set of ideas?

Chuck Palahniuk: It starts out as a physical action.

JH: Really?

CP: Yeah. All of my characters start out as a gesture or a repeated course of action that creates them physically on the page. People, I think interpret verbs in a much more involuntary way, less sort of intellectual way. Verbs sort of come in under their radar and have a more subconscious effect on the reader.

JH: Is there any place that you wouldn't go as an author?

CP: Not really. I've kind of accepted that regret is a short-term reaction. In the long term, regret is kind of a sure sign that I've done something that is worth doing.

JH: Do your ideas meet your expectations on film?

CP: Maybe, only because I don't have very much as far as expectations. I really don't want to try to control somebody else's work and so I don't bring any expectations to their product.

JH: What is it like to write about a character and see the character cast as an actual person?

CP: It feels like a big completion, because my characters are typically based on real people. It's seeing the character go from being a person, to being a story, and then back to being a person. So, in a way it's kind of full cycle.

JH: What sort of verbs do you have in mind when you're creating these characters?

CP: They're always physical verbs. Like, "shit," or "kiss," or "run." Because there have been a number of studies recently that show that the human brain interprets those words as if the person reading those verbs were actually doing the action. And your brain really doesn't know that difference between a physical verb and the actual action. That's also why I try to avoid passive or intellectual verbs. Abstract verbs, like "think" or "love" or "believe" or "remember," as well as just the word "to be," "is," or "to have;" going through your work and getting rid of all the examples of "is" or "have" is the first the step toward making it much more dynamic and tangible.

JH: Group therapy appears to be a theme in your work. Can you elaborate on what it represents?

CP: It's really only been in a couple things. There were the support groups in *Fight Club* and the twelve step recovery groups in *Choke*. And in a way I've always felt that support groups are taking on a function that churches used to provide. It used to be that people would go to church once a week and present the worst aspects of their behavior and be forgiven by their community and accepted back into community through communion. But more and more churches have become places where people go just to look good. And support groups have really become the place where people can risk looking bad and find forgiveness and find reconnection with their peers. So I'm always looking for those sort of storytelling places where people talk about their worst selves and also kind of hone their storytelling skills out loud.

JH: Do you find that there's anything redemptive about he American culture today?

CP: I really don't think American culture is any better or any worse than it's always been. If you read any kind of history going back, you see that what we're experiencing now is almost identical to what we were experiencing a hundred years ago. In the year 1900, we were involved in the Philippines War, the Spanish-American War. We were trying to occupy the Philippines and we were losing soldiers at a remarkable rate. Really almost everything that's happening now was happening a hundred years ago. That really kind of takes the edge off of what happens here and now.

JH: Is the current political landscape interesting to you as a writer? In the course that we're going now, or is it still pretty much the same old thing?

CP: It really just does feel like the same old thing. It's always pretty much the same conflict and the same sets of ideals and the same issues. Technology makes them a little different generation to generation, but they really are of a pattern.

JH: It also seems kind of like they're rushing towards the end of the world.

CP: It's always rushing toward the end of the world. When you have Y2K and you have SARS and then you have bird flu and then you have swine flu, and I think that the end of the world just sells a lot of newspapers. We're always being sold "The End of the World."

JH: What kinds of impressions have you gotten about your following?

CP: They tend to be people who were passionate about books when they were much younger. A lot of required reading kind of put them off of reading, and they are really rediscovered how much they enjoyed reading as much younger children. They tend to be internet savvy and they tend to be finding community through the internet. Those are the generalizations I can say right now. I'm hoping that long term, that people themselves will start writing. Because it seems like the natural progression from enjoying reading would be to enjoy writing.

JH: That would be good if you could have your hand in that.

CP: It would be nice. It would be sort of the ultimate compliment, that your work excited or gave someone else permission to create their own work.

JH: Did you ever think that *Fight Club* would resonate so deeply with these people?

CP: I had no intention and no expectation that *Fight Club* would even be a book. But it was a lot of fun to write, and I think that's the first sign that something is going to reach an audience.

JH: What other kinds of projects are you working on?

CP: The book for next year is called *Pygmy*, and that's done. I'm working on the book for, I guess it would be 2010.

JH: What is *Pygmy* about?

CP: Pygmy is kind of a dark comedy about terrorism. It's about a twelve-year-old kid who is sent over as an exchange student from an unnamed foreign country. He's supposed to be here to live with a middle class, Christian, suburban family, but his real mission is to build a science fair project that will win at the local competition and be taken to Washington, DC for finals, and there it will explode, killing everyone on the east coast.

JH: Sounds like a good book.

CP: It's a romance.

JH: How so?

CP: Oh, he's got a host sister. I guess the daughter of his host family, whom he becomes infatuated with. And so that's the romance.

JH: Do you think *Choke* the movie will be widely accepted?

CP: You know, again, I really...

JH: No expectations?

CP: Yeah, exactly.

Yellow Thunder Woman: Princess, Provocateur

January 2008
By T. Virgil Parker

The first thing you will notice about Yellow Thunder Woman is her effortless ability to generate unmitigated lust. She could be a poster child for lookism, though people would keep stealing the posters. Before the dust settles however, she will demonstrate a couple of learned skills:

- The ability to offend almost everyone.
- The ability to make almost everyone want to be offended by her again.

These two talents serve her, if possible, better than her extensive musical and artistic talents as she stirs up controversies that dovetail into national incidents. Thunder Woman and her Bastard Fairies band mate Robin Davey cooked up a little YouTube bomb called *The Coolest 8 Year Old in the World Talks About O'Reilly*. The narrative of a young girl ripping on religion, and of course, Bill O'Reilly, certainly created controversy, but at the O'Reilly Factor, it created an earthquake. The revered (and reviled) outer of CIA agents took a little umbrage at the video, accusing the band of endangering the welfare of the child actress by feeding her 'foul' ideas. Naturally, millions of people boogied on over to YouTube to have a peek, making the clip the most viewed YouTube video of all time at that moment.

Given the lack of courage in national media these days, I doubt there would have been a smoother path to the national spotlight for the Bastard Fairies' *somewhat* unique material.

Their CD, *Memento Mori,* despite the layers of mockery and cynicism, sounds like Mom and Dad accidentally left out the keys to the studio. There is perpetual vertigo resulting from exaggerated innocence crashing against the headlong debauchery of these songs. These tracks are compelling and addictive, catchy in a surreal Pop way, and meaningful as well.

I wasn't surprised that when I discovered Yellow Thunder Woman's celebrated paintings online; they struck me as an aesthetic assault against Frida Kahlo; the same delicacy, but greater violence. What did surprise me was an award-winning documentary to her credit. The *Canary Effect* is an unrelenting depiction of the history and conditions of Native Americans. The truth marches forward like an occupying force. If you really want to understand the legacy of American Cultural Imperialism, you must watch this film.

As edgy and original as Yellow Thunder Woman assuredly is, I think in some way that she is following a tradition as it would have evolved if the natural progression of her native culture hadn't been systematically erased. Directly drawing her descent from celebrated Ponca Chief Standing Bear, she perfectly fits the job description for a Postmodern Indian Princess.

T. Virgil Parker: I had been having trouble deciding if it was still possible to be both relevant and controversial, before I encountered your work.

Yellow Thunder Woman: It's actually quite easy. You just have to have a good argument and know what you're talking about. And it's okay to be controversial and still be relevant because it's important to do research and know what you're talking about. That's what being a good lawyer is, you make a case. Every time you talk about something you make a good case.

TVP: It's kind of a testament to how much we haven't evolved that you need to do a movie like *The Canary Effect*.

YTW: If anything, because of the way culture is, people are actually devolving. I think it's important- regardless of all the destroying our brains we may do when we drink- to exercise your brain. And because of the brain's plasticity, we can always grow new neurons the more we learn. It's important to learn new things.

I wanted to do *The Canary Effect* because I wanted people to just learn about it. There's even a lot of my own people who, because of the way schools are, haven't been taught a lot about history, the true history. And I think it's just important for people to know about history because without having any knowledge about history, then you'll just end up making the same mistakes over and over again.

TVP: I thought it was cool that you made quick work of Columbus, because kids are still being brainwashed into, you know, here's this hero who comes over.

YTW: And he wasn't a hero, he was a complete asshole. And he was also a stupid asshole as well and everyone likes giving him credit for, you know, "discovering America." America was already discovered and it was already occupied by a lot of people who were quite happy and peaceful, actually. People say, "oh, they were savages, and they started scalping," and stuff like that. And no, we didn't. The truth is that we were really sorted people in our way of lives. The pilgrims came over and didn't know what to do; they would have died without us. We ended up helping them, and then they killed us off because we were savages. It's all that religious bullshit. It's the same thing in England where they thought cats were evil. And so they ended up killing all their cats and then the rat population went up and everyone got the plague because of all that religious bullshit which makes life really hard when it shouldn't be.

TVP: What blew my mind about the whole O'Reilly thing is that essentially, he was accusing you of imperialism.

YTW: I actually think what Bill O'Reilly did was cool because it got us more attention. He did us a service by being a little stupid baby: "They put me down, I'm going to make them seem like idiots," but actually he made himself look like an idiot. He conveniently edited out all things that we said about him

TVP: Right.

YTW: How convenient; how Fox News. I've been called a chauvinist and everything. There's lots of people that love to hate me, and lots of people that hate to love me.

TVP: Right, but they do.

YTW: Like I always say, I want to go out with death threats and love letters.

TVP: It seems like there's an imperative in our culture to literally sit down and shut up.

YTW: The problem is that people need to have a voice and they need to know that they have the right to have a voice. And they need to have the right to complain and also speak out when something is completely and utterly unfair and wrong. You have to know when to speak out.

Sometimes it doesn't make sense to speak out because you'll get fired, but when it comes to basic human rights, someone needs to stand up for it, and people also need to be told to stand up for their rights.

TVP: How aware were you of the media frenzy you would kick in.

YTW: I was pretty aware of it. I mean it was quite surprising how big is got but when we did *The Coolest 8 Year Old* video we knew that it would get a lot of attention because it was so controversial. It's something that a lot of people have been talking about but a lot of people have actually been afraid to voice their views on the subject. And because we're really brave people and don't care what people think about us, we thought "we need to do this, we need to do this one, for ourselves, and second, for other people, so they feel that it is okay, it's okay to have your own views."

TVP: You must have known the full extent of cultural provincialism out there. Christianity itself can be a form of imperialism when you force it on someone who already has a religion or a philosophy.

YTW: I'm not discriminating when I talk about religion, I don't like any of it. And even sometimes religion can be veganism, if you're a Vegan, that is a religion and people don't like to look at it that way. Even love can be a religion. You have to be careful when you believe in something. You have to be able to question everything about it. And the thing is that I like vegan food, but to be honest, I love eating meat. I'll eat vegan food and I'll eat meat, I'll eat vegetarian or whatever, but I'm not going to buy into it. I'm not going to say "oh, I'm a Vegan, I'm a vegetarian." And even with that, I won't say I'm an atheist. I'm more of an anti-theist.

TVP: Any idea that comes straight out of the box isn't going to be good for your development.

YTW: Yeah, exactly, it's not. Because like I said, because of the brain's plasticity, you have to, in order for your brain to grow, you have to learn new things. You have to learn about new ideas and consider new ideas. That's evolution, baby.

TVP: When you were putting Memento Mori together, did you go out of your way to find toy instruments?

YTW: No, actually, I'm an extremely lazy person when it comes to stuff like that, and I'm a cheap person as well. I don't want to spend any money on anything. We lived right next to this town called Ventura in California, Ventura County. They had a shit load of thrift stores. We found what we needed and we came back and started work on the album because I wanted to get it done in five days. And Robin was just like "Yeah, you're fucking insane," but I'm very impatient and also very lazy, so I like to get things done quick and easy.

TVP: It's an immensely empowering message in and of itself that you spent next to nothing on the project.

YTW: Yeah, but I don't think you need to. And the benefit of that, of having obstacles and stuff like that is that you have to have talent. Not just anybody can do it. You do have to know what your talent is, for one, and have faith in the fact you can do it.

TVP: It's very easy to get lost in the bells and whistles at a real studio sometimes.

YTW: Yeah, it is for a lot of people, but you do have to be certain about what you want to do. When you go into anything, even if it's making a movie, you have to know what you want to say. And you have to know what you want the end result to be. It's important to have a plan, but not an extreme dictation. But you have to have some sort of a plan and also be able to go with the flow as well.

I put myself in the audience's point of view: "what do I want to see and what do I want to hear?" And at the end of the day I want to satisfy myself.

TVP: Now you've probably thought about this, but it occurred to me that you're using a lot of the same strategies that your ancestor Standing Bear used.

YTW: Yeah, I think I do. I'm also Yankton Sioux and my people have been looked at in history as being the worst, because we actually fought for our rights.

TVP: You defended yourselves.

YTW: Yeah, we actually defended ourselves and the other tribes thought that it would be easier just to try to work with the government, but they ended up getting screwed. They ended up getting killed either way. With the Sioux mentality, we were warriors; we were going to fight for our basic human rights. Standing Bear got it legally recognized in America that Native Americans were humans. Because of religion, we were thought to be savages. Even to this day I'm thought of as savage. Not because I'm Indian, just because of the way I am. Because I love my body and I don't mind showing it and I don't mind people looking at my tits and stuff like that because tits are wonderful. I mean come on, you'd have to be a frigid asshole to think they're not, or asexual.

TVP: That's a component of Western Civilization. It

obsesses about sex and denies it at the same time. It's created more neurosis, more psychosis than any factor in western civilization.

YTW: Yeah, exactly, and I completely agree there. I think there's nothing wrong with sexuality. I think it's a part of being human. And you know, I don't believe in a god. I believe that life is quite chaotic, but it's beautifully chaotic. It's interesting, it's mind building, and it is constantly evolving and everything. I recently did a radio show and just got off tour, so that's another reason why I'm really fucked. I had quite the rock 'n roll week, lots of partying. But yeah, I did an interview. The guy, he didn't believe in global warming, he thought it was bullshit and we talked about climate change. And I said well, this Earth started out as molten lava. And what about the ice age? People forget about the ice age. They think it is all man made, but that's quite arrogant to think that it is, because this world is bigger than us. In five million years, the sun is going to turn into a dwarf star, and we're all going to be gone anyway. So it's all about giving people here and now a good life until they die because none of us is forever. It's all about being able to have basic rights, and have a good life, and be happy before you die.

TVP: Are you ever concerned about the gender issues?

YTW: I'm quite a happy person, I don't really worry about most stuff, but I think with the gender issue, it's not really a big problem for me. I don't think about it a lot. I mean it does come up, people do have prejudices, people are discriminating in a lot of ways, but I don't let it bother me, and I think that's the best way to look at it. Don't let things bother you. Lots of people like attention no matter how they get it, whether it's negative attention or positive attention, and if someone is really coming at you wanting a lot of negative attention, the best thing you can do is just ignore them.

TVP: This is the one thing that nobody says. It's very empowering to be good to look at.

YTW: Yes, of course it is. I learned from my dad because he used to dress like a peacock every time he went out and I remember I asked him once, why he did that, and he said it's out of respect for other people. You have to make an effort for other people. And to dress up, to dress well for other people, you show them that you respect them and that you care enough to want to look good for them. I think it's important. I mean I'm Native American, we always wore costumes and we always dressed up. I think every human did it. I think it's an important thing. Animals do it. Birds have beautiful feathers for a reason. You have to make yourself enticing to people.

TVP: What you have is a system of thought that is not an ideology.

YTW: Tell me why that is. I don't understand.

TVP: I'm going to guess it's because you have a lot of fluid intelligence.

YTW: I think I'm tits with a brain, but I think it's important! And I think also when you're stupid it's important to realize when you're stupid and to use what you've got and everything. But if you have a lot of that stuff, it's important to use it. It's how you get through life a lot easier.

TVP: Basically a lot of our ideas and a lot of our traditions were actually thought-saving devices.

YTW: Yes, and also very antiquated.

TVP: Yes, and they literally get written into your DNA in my opinion.

YTW: Yeah, I think they sometimes do, I think it does happen and it's important for people like me, for people who don't mind being in the limelight, but it's not, to be honest; I don't care about other people's applause. Like I said, I was loved by my parents, both of my parents loved me so I don't need other peoples' approval, but in a way that kind of makes people like me more, because I don't give a shit. I can't change the world, but I can change your mind.

TVP: I think a lot of people haven't given themselves the opportunity to find out who they are.

YTW: That is a problem. You do have to first figure out who you are and once you know who you are, it's a lot easier to figure out other people. Because people are sometimes just puzzled by life and I think because it's all these complicated things like, you know, you look at religion. Religion is nothing but a giant contradiction. That's why people are confused by it. That's why people go through life confused. Because, oh, I have to be this way, but then I can't be this way because the Bible tells me to do this, but then it also tells me to do this, which is a great big contradiction. I think it's important to have your own ideas, and to also experiment with your own ideas. Sometimes your own ideas might be right, but sometimes they're spot on. And that's the thing; there's nothing wrong with experimentation.

TVP: Do you ever find yourself, aware of places where your own thinking has been impeded by inherited cultural modes of thought.

YTW: I think that's kind of like with anybody. I know when

I was younger I was really smart for my age, but I was also quite naive and quite stupid. But I also knew that I needed parents for a reason. If us humans were made to be like spiders and we knew everything we were going to need to know for the rest of our lives then we wouldn't need parents, but the fact is that we do and I did and I know when I was younger I made loads of mistakes. Some of the mistakes, it would have been better if my parents told me right away, "that's a mistake and you're going to suffer for that." To be honest, I don't know if I'd listen, but still, it's good to have that. I think sometimes even adults still need that. I know I don't, but I know a lot of adults still need a sort of parenting in a way because growing up is a hard thing, and it's hard to realize that you do have to grow up. And some people just don't want to.

TVP: How much hostility do you have to process?

YTW: I do get a lot of hostility but to be honest, for every one person that doesn't like me, there are always ten that do.

TVP: Yeah, I was going to assume as much.

YTW: Yeah. You know, and I'm a likeable person. Come on, I'm charming and I have nice tits. I always have. The thing is I've always gotten into arguments with men, with like Christian men or people who are very political, and at the end of the argument they ended up wanting to screw me. So that says a lot about people's views, at the end of the day we're all human and we love fucking.

TVP: That's the one thing that transcends politics, as far as I can tell.

YTW: Yeah, sex is definitely a wonderful thing for me, and I think for every man. Not for every woman it isn't. I was surprised to find out, by doing research, that only fifty per-cent of women can have orgasm during sex. And I think that's really sad because it says how evolution hasn't really quite caught up yet.

TVP: No, that's cultural imprinting. I guarantee if you went to a native culture that did not have the same cultural mes-sages, you would not find that.

YTW: Maybe, but it's about the human body as well. For women, we evolved in such a way where sex was mainly for procreation. You look at a lot of animals, females, like look at cheetahs, they have to be raped in order to procreate, they don't like having sex. It's not a nice thing for them. It's more that procreation was the main focus for a lot of women to have sex; that was main thing. But I think people like me are quite lucky. I get a lot of enjoyment out of sex and I think it's quite wonderful and it should be done more often. It just takes stress off, it's a lot of stress relief.

TVP: I think that when people build up a lot of barriers around sex, they suffer in other ways, too.

YTW: Yeah, they do, that's true. It is difficult for women because women's brains, like I've been called a chauvinist saying I hate women, it's not that I hate women, I love women a lot, but I find women really hard to be around because of the way their brain works, because they're so complicated and they have so many hormones. And I like the simplicity of men. I really do. I like the fact that they can just say "fuck it, let's have some fun." It's not like I don't like women, I love women. My mother was a woman, come on!

TVP: I'm still convinced that the whole chauvinistic thrust of culture has basically positioned the majority of women to be defined.

YTW: It has, because women have been treated really poorly for a lot of years, and so you get women who now absolutely hate men because of it. But I think you shouldn't. You should be more correcting of them. You should say, "It's not good that you do this, but what you do here, here, and here, is wonderful." And that's the thing. Men's brains actually stop growing around twenty-one, while women's brains can stop growing a lot earlier. That's a neurological fact. But the problem with women is that we have all these fucking hormones, so it drives us absolutely crazy, and we only get crazier as we get older. So by the time we're like in our fifties and we've gone through menopause or something like that, we're completely insane. But you have to be able to adore it though.

TVP: Men do have hormonal issues too.

YTW: Yes, they do, they do as well, but women have a lot more. Because we have to have kids and we get periods and stuff like that so being intelligent can drive you crazy as well.

TVP: It's always amazed me that intelligence is not one of the things that give most men wood, you know?

YTW: I don't know, I think it is, actually. I think a lot of men prefer me over stupid women because stupid women often make life a lot more complicated. I think it does give men wood, I think men do appreciate intelligence, but they, you know, appreciate open intelligence. You know, people who are open with their sexuality, are okay with guys checking them out, and who like it and think it's cool. It's a part of human nature and there's nothing wrong with it. I think we've been told we're savages because of the way we are, but I don't think so. I think we're animals and I think it's natural. I think the Bible and religion is unnatural, I think that's the unnatural thing.

TVP: In terms of what it's done to humanity, I have to agree.

YTW: You also get a lot of men who still get hard-ones but you get a lot of frigid men. There's no coincidence that certain cultures, like with serial killers, there's no coincidence that a lot of serial killers are white. And they're men. And a lot of serial killers have a hard time getting a hard-on. They're impotent, and so they get their sick kick out of mutilating women or young boys or something like that. See that's the bad thing. That's where religion and being brought up in such strict kind of ways can really screw you up. But also being spoiled can do it as well as well.

TVP: William Blake was all over that idea two centuries ago.

YTW: I find a lot of famous people that I have met are really no different from serial killers, because they come to expect things, and not respect things.

TVP: In your current situation, you could easily end up with a kind of fame that you wouldn't be comfortable with.

YTW: Yeah. I like attention just like anyone else but I don't like too much of it. And I don't want people looking up to me as though I'm a god. I want people to look up to me as though I'm just a human with intelligence.

TVP: You've got companies offering you big checks.

YTW: It's kind of a bad decision to go with a record label at the moment and it's a lot better to do things yourself. And also with the music side of things, I grew up not liking a lot of music. I grew up around musicians and I was always around musicians my whole life, so I absolutely fucking hated them. So I never wanted to be a musician. Kind of like when I did do my album, I did it purely for myself, because I paint as well. I paint for myself because I enjoy it. When I did my album I wanted to make my favorite album. I wanted to do something I would enjoy listening to, but also enjoy doing. So that's why I did give it away for free. I wasn't planning on making any money out of it. It would be nice if I did, but to be honest, I am all for having a nine-to-five job as well.

TVP: Your album, Memento Mori, the undercurrent that goes all the way through it, is basically depraved innocence.

YTW: Yeah, well, I think like with my lyrics, I think they're quite unusual. You listen to a song like Apple Pie; a lot of people don't get the irony of it. I'm not talking about myself. I always put myself in the first person when it comes to writing lyrics. So I'm not talking about myself, I'm making fun of somebody. Somebody who I know who is like that. And there's some songs that I do write about myself. You know, like Habitual Inmate, that's about me. I am a systematic victim. I did have OCD really bad as a kid and I don't anymore because basically I've learned to laugh at myself and tell myself, "yeah, you're being fucking crazy! And you shouldn't be, because it's not fun!"

TVP: I think the message of OCD is to find a good channel to plug it into. Or good channels, really.

YTW: Yeah, you have to. Because, like I said, at the end of the day, we're animals. You look at hamsters, you look at most animals, they don't have OCD. You put them in a cage, then that's when you see it. You see them doing things that just aren't necessary. But because their brain works in a certain way where it's all about survival, you know if they were in the wild, all the things that they would be doing would be necessary for survival. You put them in a cage; they end up acting like crazy little creatures. Which is fun, but still.

TVP: I think that's true of a lot of us humans.

YTW: Yeah, it is, it is true of a lot of people. I think that's just nature's way.

TVP: Another theme that's in Memento Mori, and I don't want to get all arty on you, but, the theme of the disempowered woman.

YTW: I don't see it there, but I know what you're saying. I do know what you're saying about it. I think a lot of people choose their place. They choose to be weak. They do choose that place because I think a lot of people are comfortable with being told what to do because it means they don't have to think.

TVP: Seeing it that thread is intensely ironic because anyone who listens to the album understands that they're dealing with someone who is as self-empowered as you can get, pretty much.

YTW: I think I could probably get a little bit more. I can always evolve.

TVP: Well, you're in the place you need to be to get more empowered, right?

YTW: Yeah. I'm never done, I'm only done when I die.

TVP: Right.

YTW: Time enough for sleep in the grave.

TVP: When we put on the disc here in the office, for

example, people crowd around the speakers, because it is so different.

YTW: It's not that I wanted it to be different; it's just that I'm different. I'm different to a lot of people. Which is fine, but I think life would be a lot easier for me if a lot of people were more like me. Like, threw caution to the wind. And just had fun, genuine fun, not someone else's perception of fun.

TVP: Right, well, you know though, our America is a place where everyone is happy on the spreadsheet, but not really happy.

YTW: I think a lot of people suffer from denial. People tell me I'm not very patriotic and the fact is, that I'm not. But I do love America. I love the country because when I go to other places, yeah there's other places that are more open and a lot of fun, but I go to a place like England where they're quite snobby and they do believe that they're smarter than other people there, and they don't like the French even though the French are the same way. You go to England and they're so miserable. The only cool thing about England is the bar scene. It's wonderful! Because the people are so standoffish there and so proper, and then once they start drinking, they're fabulous! They're fabulous people! The bar scene in LA is actually horrible because everyone does cocaine and smokes pot and stuff like that. And I hate that shit! I don't like cokeheads and I don't like potheads. And, you know, I smoke pot once in a while. I haven't in a long time, but I like people who drink. I think they're a lot of fun!

TVP: It gets the super-ego out of the way.

YTW: Yeah. People are so pretentious here. And that's what I love about the bar scene in England.

TVP: It's like taking a soda bottle and shaking it up and then taking the cap off.

YTW: Yeah, exactly! That's a perfect analogy, actually.

TVP: There's so much of an imperative in the UK to be not just okay, but almost nonexistent, you know?

YTW: It kind of seems like English people go out of their way to be uncomfortable. And I think having comfort is really nice. I don't think it makes you lazy at all. A lot of people say it makes you lazy. I think it makes life easier, and it makes it easier for you just to get on work, because you don't have to work for all those little simple things that should just come easy. When it comes down to just doing real work, you're more willing to do it, and you're more willing to work your ass off.

TVP: That's probable. I think the reason that the class is so rigid in England is because individual achievement is not necessarily encouraged.

YTW: Yeah, but also, it's the type of place where people are miserable because people are told not to complain. Restaurants on the whole are pretty crap in England. Service is pretty crap in England. The other day I was at this restaurant because for one thing, no one sat us and so I went and sat down and there were all these waiters walking around. I was like waving my hands and yelling at people and there was this one waiter who saw me, looked at me, and then purposely walked away. And I was okay, it would have been so fucking easy for you to come, and nobody tips there. Here, people work for their tips. And they should. If you have a good attitude, be nice to people, they're going to feel good about tipping you. I gave a bartender a tip in England. It was only like ten pence, something like that, and he like said, "are you sure?! Are you sure?" And I was like, "Yeah, it's like ten p, that's nothing." He was like so surprised. And, you know, I always tip my bartender here because if they're good and they give you drinks and stuff like that on time, then you know, why not?

TVP: It is sort of a double-edged sword, though, because people are so programmed toward money here that it's almost the only impulse left.

YTW: I think there's nothing wrong with money. I think money is a good thing. It helps keep the economy and everything going. But I think people do get obsessed with things just as people get obsessed with other people. That's why it's not that I don't believe in love, it's just that I know that love, it's not what people think it is, it's not that romantic thing. Love, basically, when you look at most people's perception of it, it doesn't exist. So a lot of times I say I don't believe in love because it doesn't exist. I like people, and this is the thing is that with humans, you look someone in the eye and you can tell if that person is attracted to you. You get endorphins. Dopamine gets released in your brain, and you like that person, you're attracted to them. But what happens after that basic infatuation goes, is that if that person isn't cool and you don't get on with them, it's not going to last. It's really not. And you have to like someone; you have to genuinely like them, like who they are, like hanging around them. Get a kick out of the type of person that they are. Because if you don't, it's pointless, it's not going to last at all.

TVP: I suspect that monogamy was really enforced by religion.

YTW: That's why a lot of people who weren't happy stayed in marriages for so long even though they fucking hated that person that they were with. Which, you know, I mean for me, I'm not a monogamous person. I have more, kind of, I like companionship and stuff like that, but I'm not faithful. Like, when I get drunk and want to have sex, I'm just going to have sex.

TVP: You know, I would rather someone cheat on me than have them sit in the corner grinding their teeth when I walk by.

YTW: Yeah, exactly. I don't see it as cheating.

TVP: Well no, it doesn't have to be.

YTW: Yeah, and you know, as a kid growing up, I'm the youngest of fifteen brother's and sisters and my parents, they were both really cool people, but they fought a lot and my mom wasn't that happy with her relationship with him, but they were both awesome people. But you know, they stayed together for a long time and everything, but I always thought, "I'm not going to do that" as a kid. I don't really want a relationship. I don't want a relationship until I'm old and I'm ready to give up. Then I'll just give up and say fuck it, I'll just deal with you, it's too much work to do whatever, but as of right now, I'm not that into relationships. They make my life too complicated and I kind of want to focus on other things.

TVP: So you're saying that you're going to get married as soon as you have no energy left at all?

YTW: Yeah, exactly. Whenever I'm just ready to let my brain die. Then I'll go, okay, I give up, I'll fucking deal with you, whoever it is. Right now I'm a bit too feisty.

TVP: What is your favorite art form to create in?

YTW: My favorite art form has to be film.

TVP: Are you looking at anything that's not a documentary?

YTW: Oh, yeah! I love all films. I love documentaries, I love fiction films, I want to make a slasher movie. But I want to make a slasher movie on the reservation, which would be really cool.

TVP: That hasn't been done.

YTW: Yeah, and it'd be really cheap, which would be awesome, because I'm a cheap asshole.

TVP: And you wouldn't have a white police officer come in and save the day at the end, which is the theme in a lot of those.

YTW: I think it would be so much fun to make a slasher movie. When I was a kid, because I was rebelling from, you know, my family, I wanted to be a writer, and so I used to write short stories all the time. And that's probably why my lyrics are so weird, because I do them from a writer's point of view. They're not poetry, they're more perspective.

TVP: Right. There isn't even necessarily a plot in there. It's a series of statements.

YTW: Kind of, almost a social commentary.

TVP: Oh, absolutely. You would think because everyone has a medium of expression these days, be it message boards, Myspace, and email groups, that there would be a plethora of viewpoints out there.

YTW: But people are so afraid of expressing their own views because everyone wants approval of other people. Well not everyone, there's people are there that don't, but most people want other people's approval, so they are afraid to have their own point of view.

I encourage people to have their own point of view. Even if I don't agree with it, I still encourage it, because at least it's them. It's like really popular in England for American bands to go up on stage and say "George Bush is a cunt!" And everyone claps automatically. But to be honest, I don't think he's a country. I think he shouldn't be running the country, but he actually seems like a cool guy to go out and have a beer with. But he shouldn't be the leader of the free world.

TVP: The scariest people are always the people who think that they're doing the right thing.

YTW: Yeah, and then there's the stupid people. He's adorably stupid, but he just shouldn't have the power that he has. And the problem with that, with politics and everything, is that it's almost like choosing the lesser of two evils.

TVP: It's always like choosing the lesser of two evils.

YTW: The thing is, is that everyone wants to jump on Bush. And they want to jump on him. But the thing is, you look at all the past presidents, none of them were really that good. And so, you look at all them, they all made huge mistakes and they all did really fucked up things. And you look at Abraham Lincoln with the way he was and yeah, he freed a lot of slaves, but he also killed a lot of Native Americans. And also his wife was a crazy money-hungry asshole who used to charge, the people who worked for him to see him. They'd have to see Abraham Lincoln, even though they worked for him and they should be able to see him. And so no president was perfect and I don't believe in perfection and I think you're not going to get a perfect president. I'd quite like to see Hillary Clinton win, even though I don't vote, I'd like to see her win because I always wanted to know what it would be like to have a frigid bitch as a president. I don't vote though, I don't believe in it. I know that's probably a bad message.

TVP: You know what though? I don't think there's any moral to voting, per say, if all of the choices are pointless. It's more of a habit for me than anything else.

YTW: But the thing is that I can't really complain because I know I'd be an awful president. I'd be worse than George Bush!

TVP: I don't think anyone is supposed to lead the free world.

YTW: I think there does need to be order and stuff like that. There do need to be rules; otherwise it would be fucking absolute chaos. And like I said, if I ruled the world, it would be chaos. You'd have more deaths than anything.

TVP: I'd vote for you.

YTW: Good!

TVP: I voted for Perot because I thought that he would make it all grind to a halt. And then we'd end up painting ourselves blue and sharpening sticks. That's my idea of a good time.

YTW: Yeah! The one person I really don't like is Al Gore. I think he's a fame-hungry prick.

TVP: A poser?

YTW: Yeah. He wants fame, that's all he wants. And people have asked him, "Are you going to run for president?" And he's like, "no, no I'm not." And of course he's not, because all he wanted was fame. And so he made up this whole Global Warming bullshit and, you know, now they play that fucking, I don't know what it's called, The Inconvenient Truth or whatever, fucking horrible documentary. I tried to watch it at Michael Moore's film festival when I was there. I ended up falling asleep! The first half is him just fucking talking about himself. And he's such a boring guy. It's just like, I don't fucking care! I don't want to know anything about you. Get your fucking point out and get on with it.

TVP: It must have been fun for him to sit around for years after the election and watch America go to hell in a hand basket.

YTW: Yeah, well I don't think he could have done anything better, that's the thing. But that's just my opinion. Opinions are like assholes, everyone has one, but not everyone has a hemorrhaging asshole.

TVP: I have more than one.

YTW: I think Al Gore's opinion is a hemorrhaging asshole.

TVP: How were the shows in England?

YTW: Oh, they were awesome! The thing about England is that people don't clap, really. And so when you get a response, even if it's a slight one, you're happy. I made a point of saying to people when I was on stage, "none of you need to like me, and I don't need you to like me, because I like me." And that's all that matters. So you know, fuck off, drink a lot of booze, and enjoy yourself.

TVP: That's a great moral to the story.

YTW: Yeah!

TVP: You know, George Bush grew up as a hedonist.

YTW: Yeah, and now he's a born again Christian, who are the most boring assholes in the world.

TVP: His parents were loaded, it should have been okay for him to just party his brains out for the rest of his life.

YTW: Yeah, it should have been! Like I said, he seems like a nice guy.

TVP: Given all your different careers, what is next on your agenda?

YTW: There's a lot of things going on, but at the moment we just want to go out and do more gigs, because we had so much fun this time. That's the plan, to get out and play and stuff. Because it was a fucking blast. Like I said, we had a true Rock 'n Roll week. We were just doing gigs and then going out and getting hammered and waking up the next day completely fucked. And then doing it all over again. It was pretty awesome.

TVP: In a way, you've inherited Rock 'n Roll.

YTW: Yeah, I definitely did. My dad was a musician and everyone always told me I was my father's daughter because, you know, I'm just like him. I'm just like my dad. Or the way he was. He's dead now, he died in '98. But yeah, he was a fucking cool, cool guy. He was a really intelligent guy. He always pissed people off but at the end of the day he was charming and you couldn't help but love him.

TVP: Again, I want to say that people are drawn to your ideas because they're not taken right off the shelf.

YTW: No, they're not. I do think about things. I always make a point of thinking about what I say because it's important. It's kind of pointless to have views if you don't think about them and if they don't make a lot of sense. I sometimes think a lot of people that want to argue with me want to argue with me because they just desperately want to have a point of view. But when you pick apart what they're saying, they don't have a good case.

TVP: I think everyone who's arguing with you is almost asking to have their ass handed back to them.

YTW: That's the thing. When I made my documentary, *The Canary Effect*, I really did go after it because as a kid, I wanted to be lawyer when I grew up. My dad was a bit of a lawyer. People always say, "Oh, lawyers are the sleaziest people," I always thought they were the most honest people. Because, you know, I'd talk to a lawyer and if he was all about money he'd say, "I'm all about money. I like getting paid; I work for the mob, because I like the money." And you know, they were just the cool people that I always enjoyed hanging around because they were always bastards.

TVP: I don't think pretending to have values helps anyone.

YTW: Yeah. It's about your argument. Arguments are kind of like a tree, you can always find a branch, and you can always find a way to win an argument. But for me, I think you have to actually believe in what you have to say. And as hard as it may be for some people, you have to practice it. You have to practice what you preach. And the thing is, is that I preach very simplistic things. And I do practice them because it's easy to.

TVP: There was nothing in *The Canary Effect* that was the tiniest bit of a stretch, you know? There are a lot of sensationalized appeals for white people to stop raping cultures.

Allowing things to just march forward like you did is far more devastating.

YTW: Right. Yeah. I think, like with the Native American culture, it suffers from being bashed in the head, basically, and you get a lot of Post-Traumatic Stress Disorder there. And a lot of people are really suffering from that, from five hundred years of abuse, basically. And being treated like you're basically less than a dog. You know, people treat their dogs better than they treat Native Americans basically. We all like to have that romantic view that, "oh, they're spiritual!" and bullshit like that. But the thing is, is that they were really cool people and to be honest, they still are really cool people. But they are suffering a lot. And that's what pisses me off. Because there was no need to destroy that culture and the way it was destroyed. I think it was done out of pure hatefulness and jealousy. A lot of people came over to this country with entitlement issues, I can tell you that.

TVP: Right. Really, the people who were left out of the aristocratic tree, as it were, the disenfranchised were the people who came here.

YTW: The victims become the victimizers.

TVP: Right, and that's true over and over again. The oppressed always become the oppressors. So what it was, really, was a class train wreck.

YTW: Yeah, exactly. A lot of people want answers when they watch *The Canary Effect* because we don't sugar coat it. It's just basically, these are the facts, this is how it is. And if you don't like it, I'm sorry, the truth hurts, but it is the truth. At some point we all need to hear the basic truth. And that's the only way you can change things: by educating yourself and by knowing the truth. A lot of people I know can't watch surgery. They have to look away. But the thing is that there has to be people that can watch it and there has to be people that can do it. Otherwise we're all fucked.

TVP: One thing I've noticed about America is that we are in complete denial about what we're not good at.

YTW: Yeah, exactly. It's really important to know what you're good at and what you're not good at. And you have to know. And you have to have respect for other people as well. There are certain things I know I'm not good at. I know I'm not good at being a musician. I'm not good at playing instruments. Why? Because I'm usually too drunk most of the time, and I'm also too fucking lazy. But I appreciate good musicians. I appreciate people who can play their instruments well. Without them, I wouldn't have a band. But that's the thing: That the reason I didn't like a lot of musicians is that they're all attention hungry people and they needed so many people to approve of them. A lot of them are actually quite frigid and had a lot of messed up problems. But you'll find most artists have a lot of problems. Like you look at a clam. There needs to be a disturbance to create a pearl.

TVP: Right. Yeah, for sure.

YTW: And that's the thing with artists. Actors, musicians, all of them, they're all pretty fucked up, you'll find. But it kind of makes them create good things and it makes them create entertaining things, which I think is really important.

TVP: It is. You're an artist, by the way.

YTW: Yeah. And I'm pretty fucked up, as you can tell. I don't deny that. Like people that I drink with, they always go "I'm not a drunk, I know my limit." Well I am. I'm a drunk, and I don't know my limit. I admit to everything. The truth will set you free.

Elsewhere With Umphrey's

February 2006
By T. Virgil Parker

When I got the advance copy of Umphrey's new disk I knew my day was pretty much shot. Based on my previous experience of the band, nothing was going to get done while I was listening to this. Defusing that much sound is almost an ordeal, but in the sense of an extreme sport or a rite of passage. Listening to *Anchor Drops,* their last album, built up a highly distracting metaphor in my mind: A nuclear music box from another dimension. Raw notes are dumped in by the truckload; spidery mechanical octopus arms sort them. Impossible music comes out the other end. I'd like to get my hands on one, but sadly, metaphors take a long time to get on the market.

Meanwhile, their new disk: *Safety in Numbers*, would have to suffice. One thing which I had forgotten about Umphrey's McGee, is that your expectations about them have very little to do with their musical objectives. They managed to create a sound without much of a precedent in their body of work. This new music is so smooth you can almost hear ice tinkling in Black Velvet. You detect a distant nod to Steely Dan, a flashlight shown down some dusty corridors of Jazz, but hanging like a net over the entire set of songs is an essence that seems to serve both as the contour that contains the music, and the music itself: The essence of silk. They will no doubt continue to devastate audiences with their penetrating live music, but no one could have easily predicted this pocket of serenity hiding behind Umphrey's elaborate contortions.

You can imagine that I was rather anxious to have a few words with Umphrey's formidable keyboard player, Joel Cummings.

T. Virgil Parker: The first thing that was evident when I got my hands on your new disk is that Umphrey's has high expectations of their fans.

Joel Cummings: I think that's what people really want. I don't think they just want to hear a verse, chorus, verse chorus kind of song. We do have a couple songs on there that are closer to that format. I think it's much better to listen to something that you don't process the first couple times your hear it; you don't necessarily know where it's headed.

TVP: Your last disk was like the seventies had just continued without the intervention of the 80's. This one is coming from a completely different headspace. That takes a certain amount of bravado.

JC: It's more a matter of us following our own muses. Where we're at and what we feel is our sound in that particular time. It's not like we put things out and call that our sound, how it has to be.

Right now we're at the stage of working on new material. That stuff will probably be out in a year and a half. I don't think we consciously choose to go in one direction. We wrote about 24 tracks for this disk. When we chose what went on it wasn't just a matter of finding the strongest material, but finding the strongest material that goes together. I see an analogy being that you have a basketball team and some players are really strong. Maybe your strongest player isn't your starter, but you have to find a combination that works well.

TVP: You have a completely different set of expectations in the studio than you do from a life performance.

JC: When we're in the studio we focus on songs. When we're re in a live setting, we're doing something that includes the audience. The improvisation is a huge part of the live show. That's what we like to do. We use the songs as springboards for that. Sometimes, but not as much, it works the other way around.

TVP: Progressive music is so precision-based; it's almost completely antithetical to jam. What how do you maintain that?

JC: They can happen together; it's just that in the Jam world you're not used to hearing the two things together. One of the things that keep things tighter live is that we have a lot of visual cues we use back and forth to indicate where somebody sees an idea going and we can use that as a group. That creates a lot of the tightness that you're talking about. Those are two things that we work on: The idea of creativity within improvisation and the idea of tightness. Always working on both of those and sometimes they work together. Sometimes there's a situation where we're playing something a little bit tighter as an exercise and working on that and we come across an improvisational aspect.

TVP: Umphrey's is showing signs of being the next big thing in the genre. How does that feel?

JC: We're sort of grateful to be where we're at. At the same time, we've kept doing what we've always been doing. We communicate together and play whatever we think is our best material.

TVP: When it comes to building a song, do you take it from the ground up, or do you start passing ideas around. What's the compositional process like?

JC: For the most part we try to get everybody's take on something different in there and to be inclusive about how we do things.

Songs start lots of different ways. People will bring ideas from home, and we'll try to put ideas together. We'll have an entire song written by one person, or a couple people will get together and write something, or even in the live setting where we're creating something on the spot and it ends up a composed tune that we use.

That's one of our goals in improvisation, to come up with something that seems previously composed as opposed to a loose improvisation that's more noodly.

One really funny review of a show that we saw said that we didn't improvise at all, and it was a night where there was a ton of improvisation. We were able to trick somebody into believing that our jams were previously composed.

TVP: I went to an Umphrey's fan site and told them I was going to do this interview, and got a ton of questions, so I decided to pull a few of them out.

This is from PKSConrad: Are any of the new songs going to be played on the road in February?

JC: New material will be played in February, but I'm not sure what, because we're still in the process of working that out. We'll have two to four new pieces of music that we've been working on over the past six months. That stuff is not on the new album. The stuff that's on the new album, I would guess, is going to get played in April, when the album comes out. We want that stuff to be fresh and a surprise when people start hearing it. There are five or six songs that people never heard before that are on the album.

TVP: Willtotte wants to know-this is rather cryptic for me-Who was in the Gorilla suit?

JC: I don't know if I should give that one away, I know who that is. Well, OK. It was a couple of our good friends, Barry and Chris. They were excellent Gorillas.

TVP: TheOtrane wants to know: How do you pick your set lists?

JC: It's a combination of what we want to play, and we look back and make sure we haven't played a song in a given area the last three of four times we were there. We have a big enough catalog of songs that we also make sure we don't play the same stuff the night before. We all get into working the set lists on different days, so we each have our own preferences for different songs. There'll be songs that I like to play that nobody else likes to play and I'll try to get them in there. It doesn't always happen, but I can always try.

TVP: Gunnes842- this is a good question-asks: Do you want to be as huge as possible? If so, are you worried about the baggage and the drama that comes with the territory?

JC: That's not something that's really too much in our control. We don't really make decisions like: What's going to make us as huge as possible? To get to where we are now was definitely a goal and I think as long as we can continue to produce music and be happy with it and support ourselves, that's something that was ultimately our goal. We're almost there right now, which is pretty cool. At this point it takes on a life of its own. We're just going to keep doing what we've been doing and we'll see where it goes. We're very happy to be where we're at.

TVP: And, from JimmySnucka, When the [Insert expletive] are we going to get the G song?

JC: 1998. That's when you're going to get it. You're going to have to do a little Back to the Future action to get there.

TVP: The average Umphrey's song has about as much content as you find in a typical album these days.

JC: Thank you!

TVP: You go to a lot of different places to gather that content, how do you bring it all together and make it Umphrey's?

JC: One of the things that is essential to making disparate sections of music sound related is how you get from point A to point B and how you get back there. That's something that's permeated our songwriting and makes it a lot easier to create things you'd think were impossible to relate to one another. Sometimes, those things are poly-rhythms and have to do more with rhythmic aspects, sometimes things are thematic. You can manipulate a theme or a melody to traverse both sides of that. I think that's something that we've worked on, and maybe that contributes to the idea that you are relating to as our sound. That's a huge part of that and without that things could sound a little disjointed. I think occasionally we do fall into that trap. We try to avoid that as much as possible and make things work that are going to change things up and be interesting to the listener yet somehow find a thread to tie them together.

TVP: With a bunch of really aggressive musicians on stage, do you ever find yourselves trying to blow each other off the stage, or is it just total cooperation?

JC: Some nights are better than others, but I think for the most part we have the feeling that any one of us can take the lead in any set or any night. When somebody's having a good night we can feel that and we give that person the ball. That's one good thing about all the visual cues that we have. And, if someone's having a bad night they can pass the ball. That's the kind of teamwork that helps us build each other up. It builds a kind of trust in how we create things on state.

TVP: Do you think you're going to lose any other members to the medical profession? That's becoming an epidemic in the Jam scene.

JC: We started the trend. Now it's the thing to do, but I don't foresee it happening to us again. But then, you never know.

TVP: Is there anything under the radar that you know about that I don't know about yet?

JC: At this point we're gearing up for the album release and how we're going to do that. We're looking at another year of touring, and hopefully making good music.

William Gibson: Sci-Fi Icon Becomes Prophet of the Present

July 2007
By T. Virgil Parker

Science Fiction writers are expected to give the envelope a little nudge. Usually this means dreaming up a new gizmo and running it through an adventure plot. Once in a while though, someone comes along with a whole new envelope, and William Gibson's envelope is bursting at the seams; bursting out of Sci-Fi, at present.

Gibson pretty much invented the genre of Cyberpunk and scooped up every available award with his first novel, *Neuromancer*. Then he painstaking developed his storytelling power, firing out a hefty number of novels that are still picked over vigorously in chat rooms and message boards. He carved out tools that when turned at the present day, deftly expose the surrealism we have no choice but to call reality.

Gibson's elaborate vision of the internet- before it existed- and Reality TV- before it existed- has led many to call his work prophetic. Now that his fiction is set squarely in 'this' world, the results are downright scary. His first

237

effort to bring his Sci-Fi prowess to the present day, *Pattern Recognition*, was hailed as one of the first significant novels of the 21st Century, and earned him a cozy place on the New York Times Best Seller List.

His most recent novel, Spook Country, builds upon the sinister post 9/11 atmosphere of *Pattern Recognition. Spook Country* partakes of the cloak-and-dagger stuff that is in all likelihood pervasive these days. The story of a smuggler, a former Rock Star, and two rival intelligence groups could easily have veered into the realm of Cheap Spy Novel were it not woven with the postmodern irony that may turn out to be the only sane perspective left to us. The secret cargo from Iraq on which the plot hinges is not the only mystery in this book. The biggest mystery is how this story manages to resonate with the our most menacing headlines without losing the archetypal power and playfulness that William Gibson seems to summon at will.

T. Virgil Parker: Your early Sci-Fi commented obliquely on contemporary issues, but it gave you a very unique set of strategies that you're using to explicate the present.

William Gibson: Well, I don't actually think they're unique because I acquired them through the course of working in the genre of science-fiction, but I also acquired a conviction that what they're actually good for, maybe the only thing that they're really good for, is trying to get a handle on our sort of increasingly confused and confusing present.

TVP: Do you think that from your perspective, reality caught up to science fiction in certain ways- just by cre-ating so surreal a contemporary landscape that it parallels Sci-Fi?

WG: Well, in a sense, although I think when I started, one of the assumptions that I had was that science fiction is necessarily always about the day in which it was written. That was my conviction from having read a lot of old science fiction. 19th century science fiction obviously expresses all of the concerns and the neuroses of the 19th century and science fiction from the 1940's is the 1940's. George Orwell's *1984* is really about 1948, the year in which he wrote it. It can't be about the future. It's about where the person who wrote it thought their present was, because you can't envision a future without having some sort of conviction, whether you express it or not in the text, about where your present is.

I also started with the assumption that all fiction is speculative. That all fiction is an attempt to make a model of reality, and any model of reality is necessarily speculative because it's generated by an individual writer. It can't be absolute. Fiction is never reality. I know I had those ideas to handle when I started writing because I was an English major and I was studying things like Comparative Literary Criticism. I came into it with a kind of mild, post-modern spin, and I think I was a little more self-conscious about what I was doing than someone who would have started writing science fiction forty years before. I think that as I've gone along, somehow that's all geared up with the result that I now find myself writing speculative fiction about last February, rather than the middle of the coming century.

There's a character in my previous novel, *Pattern Recognition*, who argues that we can't culturally have futures the way that we used to have futures because we don't have a present in the sense that we used to have a present. Things are moving too quickly for us to have a present to stand on from which we can say, "oh, the future, it's over there and it looks like this."

TVP: The present is contingent upon a kind of objectivity that no longer exists.

WG: Yeah, exactly.

TVP: But having said that, isn't it a bit uncanny that all of the dystopian texts of science-fiction appear to be aiming at the present that we're experiencing right now?

WG: Well, I would find that spookier if I had been believing all along that those sort of dystopian themes in science fiction were about some sort of vision of the future. I think they were actually like being perceived in the past when that stuff was being written. *1984* is a powerful book precisely because Orwell didn't have to make a lot of shit up. He had Nazi Germany and the Soviet Union under Stalin as models for what he was doing. He only had to dress it up a little bit; sort of pile it up in a certain way to say, "This is the future." But the reason it's powerful is that it resonates of history. It doesn't resonate back from the future; it resonates out of modern history. And the power with which it resonates is directly contingent on the sort of point-for-point mimesis, like sort of point-for-point realism, in terms of what we know happened.

TVP: With that in mind, is it harder for you to write about the present, *as* the present?

WG: Yeah, it actually is. There are ways in which I find it a lot more demanding. It makes it harder to make shit up, if I get to something like what in Hollywood they call a "story point," something that's not working, like a plot point that's not working for me. When I was writing a novel like *Count Zero* I would just invent some other level of imaginary technology or invent some part of the back story of my future history that would account for me having a way to scoot past that bit of illogic in the story. I hope I didn't do that *too* much when I was doing that, but it's just something you can do when you're writing about an imaginary future.

When you're writing about a present, whether it's imaginary or not, and there's some major imaginary elements in *Spook Country,* the rules are different. It isn't the same. I have to come up with something that allows me to suspend my disbelief in my fantastic narrative and which I hope will allow the reader to suspend their disbelief. So actually, it is more work. It requires a different sort of examination of my own sense of the world outside myself.

TVP: Does working through a female protagonist help provide that kind of distance?

WG: I don't know why I do that except that they're better company for me. In the months that it takes me, I have to live with these characters for really a long time, in considerable depth. I find it's really a lot more pleasant for me if at least half of them are female. I don't know why that is, but I certainly found it fairly odd. It probably had something to do with some sort of unexamined model I have of what constitutes humanity. Come to think of it, some of it might be that traditionally, the science fiction I grew up with, a lot of which had been written in the 1940's and before, was arguably very much a male universe. And a lot of people assumed science fiction to be a fundamentally male genre.

TVP: That's still largely the case, isn't it?

WG: Well, I'm not sure, actually. Someone made a very convincing argument to me last year that Science Fiction today has become a young adult sub-genre, and as such is marketed to some extent to girls, in a way that it wasn't previously. I probably shouldn't comment on that so much because I read so little genre SF at this point that I don't really know what's going on.

When I started writing science fiction, the most radical thing that was going on was Feminist SF, and a lot of which seemed to be coming out of the Pacific Northwest, which is close to where I live and where I lived when I started writing. So that got my attention just because it was a sort of radical faction within what I saw as a kind of dead-ended genre. I think my golden age of science fiction was when I was about fifteen-years-old and the British wave was going on. There was a lot of sort of radical SF happening. When I came back to it in my twenties after having ignored it for years, I was shocked at how orthodox and dull it had become. When I started writing science fiction, what I had in mind was to go counter to that. People like, you know, Ursula Le Guin and Joanna Russ had an effect on me because they were kicking ass, you know? They were doing something really radical with science fiction and that may have something to do with my having started out. I might have assumed at the beginning that I couldn't write SF and be hip if I didn't have convincing female characters.

TVP: Something unusual in science fiction, your work has always been character-driven.

WG: Yeah, well, it has. I wish I had figured some of this stuff out like ten years ago. I could still remember what my original motivations were. I've been doing it for so long that it's just second nature. But I know that when I started writing science fiction, in the last two years of a BA in English Literature at UBC, I had acquired ideas about what novels could do. And of course in getting that degree I had to read a lot of stuff. I had to read fiction more widely than I would have done otherwise, so when I came to writing science fiction I had some ideas that I know I never would have acquired within the culture of writing SF. Like E. M. Forester's idea that if you're in control of what you're characters are doing then you're not really doing your job. And I think that I started with idea that the character-driven thing

242

had to be major and that this would necessarily decrease my control over the material. Since it seemed in my reading of a lot of SF that it's had this kind of creepily didactic function where someone was saying, "I've worked all this out in my head, and the world is like this. Look, I've created a model world which proves my idea of how the world works." And I just thought that that was like worse than useless. It certainly was for me, it certainly wasn't what I wanted to read.

TVP: The freaky thing about what you're doing now, to me, is that you're using metaphors that help to reveal things that are going on now. We kind of live in an era where people should be hysterical, but aren't.

WG: Yeah.

TVP: And I think it's because they're not *imagining* what is going on. I think they're just getting bits of data.

WG: Yeah, I know what you mean; I think that we have a way of living in the past. I think that our sense of reality, at any given time, particularly in the modern era, lags behind our sense of what's really going on. I think that we need that in order to function, in order to be comfortable in our own skin. I doubt that need even existed before, although it may well have. The fourteenth century was not an easy time, either. Humanity has gone through some very strange periods and I think that we're going through a very strange one now. A decade ago I was saying that we live sort of back from the moment; we live well back from the windshield of the present moment as it's encountering the wind of the future. I said then that occasionally you would turn on the television and have what my friend Bruce Sterling called a "CNN moment," and in that moment we would be really in the present moment. And it would be like the Frederick

Jamison experience, you know? Simultaneously we would be like over the moon about it and scared shitless and experiencing extreme vertigo, but then we would snap back into that position that we always have. After 9/11 I'm not sure if we have that anymore. For me, 9/11 sort of blew that particular metaphor of mind out of the water. But that may be because it literally changed something. I don't know now what would constitute a "CNN moment." It seems like a dated term.

TVP: That's because every moment is a CNN moment?

WG: Now, what constitutes a "YouTube moment?" You know, something has changed.

TVP: I have a feeling that your sense of social responsibility is leading you to pick up certain themes.

WG: I don't know. In a way I hope not. I don't believe that didactic writing can be really good. If I'm figuring out what I think is going on the world, and creating a fiction to illustrate that. I don't feel like that's really what I'm supposed to be doing. When I'm doing what I'm supposed to be doing, I feel like I'm sort of inviting those characters in for a cup of coffee. And if I surrendered control over the process sufficiently, I won't know what will be there until the narrative closes. And then it will take me a while to figure it out. So when, in *Spook Country*, for instance, I was in that narrative for a long time. Months and months, with no idea what was in the box. I had no idea. I was hundreds of pages into it and had no idea what was in that container. Or rather, I had like a dozen different ideas of what was in the container. I had to let the narrative inform me of what it was. It's a very uncomfortable way of working, but it's the only way I know to write a book. In the beginning all I had was that scene that became the second chapter with Tito and the old man and I didn't really know anything about them and I just kind of stuck with that for months. Then I got some early version of the Hollis stuff and somehow it built a bridge between the two things and this narrative started to emerge. That sense of "this is how things are" that I think you're talking about is secondary. It may be there, but it's secondary to the process of pulling that narrative out and finding where it's going. Like if I *know* where it's going, it's dead for me. I can't do it.

TVP: I think one of the reasons that you have so much immediacy is because of that. You're cliffhanging at the same time that reader is cliffhanging.

WG: Yeah, yeah I guess I am. And if I'm not it just sort of dies for me. And sometimes I catch myself writing the novel and when I do that, I have to destroy all of that material. I have to erase the part that I wrote. I mean when the character who goes to the 7/11 to buy a jug of milk is written into the novel, it's not a good novel. It's just not satisfactory. Whatever part of me can write a novel, I don't have conscious access to. And I ideally don't have any control over it. The stress of doing it for me is trying to force myself to get out of the way of the novel writing guy who refuses to talk me, and who I can't count on to turn up, and who I can't count on to pay the rent, although God bless him, he has now for a long time, but like, I'm never sure that he's going to turn up and I never trust what he's doing. One of the things that I found really quite satisfying about *Spook Country* is that I have less faith in what the novel-writing guy was doing than I ever had and somehow, because of that, I'm more satisfied with the result. I wouldn't just get on with it, even though it scared me to death, because I didn't understand where it was going.

TVP: So that's organicity.

WG: Yeah, you're right, but it doesn't come naturally to me. It generates a lot of anxiety.

TVP: That's the truth of all the seemingly trite things that were being said about Zen in the 70's.

WG: Yeah, probably, it probably is, I just wish there was some easier way to get to it for me but there doesn't seem to be.

TVP: I always get the sense that music is as much of an inspiration to your writing as other writing is.

WG: I think it used to be. I don't think it is in the same way. I know I'm not absorbing as much contemporary music as I did when I was younger. I've got like a lifetime of processing everything I can remember about everybody I've ever known who was a professional musician. In *Spook Country* it's more about music business and the culture of the music business than the music that us guys were listening to or the music, you know the people they mention. I have no idea what Hollis' band would have sounded like but at some point I had it worked out in my head what labels they would have been on, and that was what mattered to me rather than what they sounded like. I haven't got a clue about that part of it. It just never gelled for me and I think that's something that's different. If I'd been trying to do something like that twenty years ago, I would have had some idea about what they sounded like. This time I had some idea of what the *packaging* would have been like on their recordings but not what the music was.

TVP: I get the sense that some of your chapters start with a power chord and end with a kick drum.

WG: I'm astonishingly non-musical for someone who really enjoys listening to music.

There were people who argued in the 60's that the way the individual song was the paradigm of rock or pop, the short story was the paradigmatic form of science fiction. I don't know whether I actually *believe* that but it was somewhere in the back of my mind. I became a writer who was not much interested in writing short fiction. There's way in which any one of those chapters, can be treated the same as a story. The chapters become sort of the units, movements or something, of the piece.

TVP: Yeah, in your earlier work, almost in the sense of a montage.

WG: I was always interested in how some novels didn't use montage. Chapter closes, chapter starts, but there was an interesting thing that you could do that joined things, where you choose to join the chapters. I think that was one of the things that led to that whole cyberspace stuff in my early fiction, in that it allowed me to do all this cinematic editing and I could do the equivalent without being William Burroughs arty. The imaginary cyberspace depicted in the narrative let me do things like the equivalent of splicing two pieces of unrelated film. I could change characters in mid-sentence doing that and I think I actually came to the technology more out of the desire to be able to do that than any interest in where virtual reality was going.

TVP: So much of your work is cinematic that I've always been astounded that more of it doesn't end up in film.

WG: I've come to the conclusion that it actually makes it harder, paradoxically. It makes it harder to film because so much of it is about cinema. It may be that *any* fiction that's too informed by cinema isn't going to make good cinema. You think it's cinematic because it gives you a cinematic experience in your *head,* but when a director or screenwriter sits down with it, they're like, "there's not much for us here, really."

TVP: The whole thing would be CGI.

WG: Yeah, and you know, maybe that's what it needs. Maybe I just have weird film karma, which is possible. Some novelists do.

TVP: I think you've used metaphysics at times in the same way that you use cyberspace as a medium to explore narrative.

WG: At some point it become apparent to me that if I became too carried away with ideas of technological novelty, all I needed to do was look at the history of metaphysics to sort of get that back into perspective. I think that's sort of another semi-conscious technique of mine. Like if I get too wrapped up in virtual reality I sort of go to, like, "what would the 14th Century have made of this?" Would it have wowed them the way it wows us? And often, the answer is no. They had their own stuff going on.

TVP: You don't see people really *embrace* as much as they do *adapt*.

WG: Yeah, most people just adapt.

TVP: Celebrity is essential to a lot your novels. Where do you think that comes from?

WG: It comes from a sense of that being so much of what we *do*, or so much what we *did*. I think we've gone into another stage of that in the last ten or fifteen years. Back in the early 80's when I started writing, one of the things I noticed was that we were making increasingly less of the tennis shoes and automobiles. What we were doing was outsourcing the manufacturing of that stuff. What we really were doing was making celebrities. And that was like "the biz," it was what this culture could do.

TVP: In a way that's happening on a whole different level now. I mean almost self-generated.

WG: Yeah, well, I'm not sure where it is now. I sort of suggested, in *Virtual Light*, there's that reality show "Cops in Trouble," which was, when *Virtual Light* was published, quite funny. It wouldn't be the same for fifteen-year-olds reading that, they would just go "okay." It's like kind of beyond, the irony has evaporated. It doesn't have the kick it had when the book was published because we've gone so much further than that. I mean the evil celebrity-destroying show Slitscan in *Virtual Light* just seems like, you know, it's all here now.

TVP: Yeah, and I think these shows are somehow less insidious now when they're obviously evil.

WG: Yeah, absolutely. Whenever anything is obviously evil in that way, these days it's got to have quote marks around it anyway. It's like, 'the glamour.' I always remember Hannah Arendt's idea of the inherent bogusness of the glamour of evil. She said that evil is always like "the now." We just don't want to see it that way, but she argued that was like the adult view and I think she was probably right. It's not glamorous. And so the real world version of the Science Fiction conceit of Slitscan is just kind of the tone of a lot of our media now. There's no evil genius behind it.

TVP: Right. That's why, I think when you import something into fiction, it's easier to understand than when it glares at you from the front page.

WG: It's easier to get a handle on. It's possible to use fiction in a way that lets people directly access the thought without being threatened by it. You turn it into a sort of fun house.

Angelica: The Kerosene Queen

By Jessica Hopsicker

Sometimes, freaks are the nicest people you meet, whereas, it's the overtly normal folks that tend to be the freakiest. More often than not, the upstanding citizens are the ones you should look out for. They may very well be the ones with children buried in the basement dirt.

Angelica carries herself as if there is something perfectly natural about drinking fuel and spitting flame, or scaling a ladder assembled out of swords - sharp edge up. Her appearance is immediately identifiable, dread locked, heavily tattooed, 5" 4' Amazonian performer with feet like granite. She cultivates her freakiness and wears it like a coat of arms.

As legend would have it, or shall I say her biography on the Coney Island web site, she was stranded, orphaned, in the Island of Fiji for 10 years. It was there she was forced to adapt, surviving eating insects and strengthening her feet by walking barefoot on the razor sharp rocks. Lonely nights around campfires turned out to be her venue for fire eating.

Her sideshow persona known as "Insectavora" would be a bit of a misnomer as of late. Just like any other human being becoming conscientious of self-preservation, she quit smoking and became a Vegan, which inevitably included giving up the bug munching as well. After changing her way of life, she was once again left with the task of adapting.

So, what does a reformed Insectivore do next? Launch a music career, of course. Despite everything, she remains one of the last great performers in America's fading playground, Coney Island.

Jessica Hopsicker: So, how is the new season treating you so far?

Angelica: Pretty good. We're just open on the weekends right now, but the regular show isn't running this weekend or next weekend, it's different shows. So I'll be here working on the building, like construction stuff, helping out with the bar.

JH: I heard this year was a pretty transitional year for you.

A: Yeah, I'm working on these different projects right now because I've got to start working on other things too in case my body can't handle the fire-eating anymore. It's kind of poisonous, as often as they do it. I've been working on this awesome music project, so that's cool, I've been doing that all winter. Hopefully, this weekend the first two videos I want to release will be online. That's exciting.

JH: I heard you also quit smoking too?

A: Yes and no. I cheat sometimes. It's hard, I've been smoking for a while. I really want to quit, but stress gets me crazy.

JH: You also turned Vegan?

A: Yes I did. That I've been really good at. It just bums me out. I hope I become successful with my music. You know how famous people put out their own clothing lines? So that's my thing. I want to put out Vegan, green, that doesn't look granola. Like cool stuff. I'm going to make awesome motorcycle jackets made out of canvas that look cool, not like PVC stuff. I want everything to be green.

JH: That sounds cool. So what kind of music is it that you're launching?

A: I don't really know how to describe it. It's kind of I guess like independent, alternative. Not so much Goth, but it's mellow.

JH: And you're getting videos out for that?

A: Yeah. I recorded six songs so far so I'll be having an EP coming out, and next week the first videos I want to release will be up on YouTube and my Myspace thingy and all of that stuff.

JH: Awesome. So you rarely use the name Insectavora anymore?

A: No. Because when I went Vegan I even gave up eating bugs.

JH: I was actually going to ask you that, too.

A: Yeah, I haven't eaten bugs in a while. I've given that up. And then it was like well, Insectavora kind of means devouring insects, so it's like well, give that up. I get bummed that I can't change my Myspace URL. But so many people know me as that so it's all right. They'll get it eventually.

JH: Now that you've cut down on breathing fire, what else do you have in your repertoire?

A: As far as sideshow or everything in general? In the side-show, the fire eating is still my main act. I do other stuff. I have a ladder of swords I walk on with my bare feet.

JH: How do you condition your body to do that?

A: If you walk around barefoot and don't moisturize your feet for a long time it builds up really tough skin on the bottoms of your feet. Kind of like dog's paws, you know? And even if you don't, you can walk up it like twice and it won't mark if your feet aren't conditioned. But if your feet are conditioned, then you can do it like ten to fifteen times a day and it doesn't bother you.

JH: Wow.

A: Then I lie on a bed of nails and have someone smash a cinder block over me. I do other fire stuff besides fire eating. I do this big fire fan dance. I do a fire poi; spin it around with a little false fire at the end of a chain.

JH: Dare I ask about the X-Rated Fire Down Below?

A: I don't really do that anymore either. I already get enough attention just looking the way I do, and then with that, people who see my show, like these weird guys, are like, "oh yeah, I saw your fire below act the other night," and it just kind of bothered me. Like when I did and put the whole act together, I thought "oh, it's so funny! It's so goofy!" But then, I don't know, people just see it differently from the way I think about it. I don't like this kind of thing.

JH: You must attract some pretty unique fans too.

A: I do! Anywhere from really nice people all the way to really psycho cyber-stalkers.

JH: I heard you have stalkers.

A: Yeah. It's funny, I have two restraining orders. Thankfully, that's it though, because some people have more. The Internet is something. It's weird being out, like when we're here at work at the sideshow and I'm up front for a minute getting water or something. And it's usually male. I get these guys that come and they know all this stuff about me. They read my Myspace religiously, they Google me all the time, and complete strangers are like, "so how was that show the other night?" And I'm like what? What are you talking about? And they're like "oh, I'm sorry to hear you had a bad day." I'm like, "what are you talking about?" And they're like, "I read your blog." I'm not writing to you, per se, but yeah. It makes me feel awkward. But in a way maybe it's a good thing because hopefully they'll watch my videos like a million times.

JH: Right. And when you get your LPs out too.

A: Yeah. I've got to take the good with the bad. Well I guess it's not too bad. Nobody's ever actually gotten physically violent with me. But I don't know, it makes me feel awkward sometimes.

JH: You could probably kick their asses, too.

A: I don't know. I'm little; I'm only like 5'4". That's another funny thing when people meet me in person. It's like, "wow, you're short!" But I'm the same way when I meet movie stars. I met Woody Harrelson and he was shorter than I thought he was. When you think of people on the Internet or on TV or movies it's like this larger than life image you have a preconceived idea of.

JH: What was it like meeting Woody Harrelson?

A: It was awesome! It was one of my birthdays when I was living in Minneapolis. This guy I was dating at the time, his sister got us all these awesome tickets for stuff. So he took me to the opening night of Tom Waits, who is one of my favorite music people. It was awesome, and Wood Harrelson and Steve Guttenberg. I didn't know Steve Guttenberg was Steve Guttenberg, I only recognized Woody Harrelson. So I went up to the bar and was like, "you are so awesome!" Then I got my drink and just ran away, I was star struck. Then later in the night they were like, "how was it standing next to Woody Harrelson and Steve Guttenberg?" And I was like, "Steve Guttenberg was there?" And they were like, "yeah, that was the guy right next to him." It was like, wow! He's funny too. Later that week I got to see this play that they were in.

JH: On that note, what has it been like to be on CNN, the Learning Channel, and all those other media giants? Did they treat you any differently?

A: Working with the big dogs of TLC, CNN, NBC, FOX etc. I've always been treated quite nicely and with much respect. So far, I'm happy to say that all of my experiences with mass media have been pleasant, fun, and exciting. And I think that has a lot do with how you present yourself. If you come off as a big jerk face then you'll be treated as such but I'm pretty down to earth, I don't take myself too seriously, and I'm a pretty happy person and that comes across with all the great people I get to work with.

JH: So you actually have to go to school now for the sideshow?

A: I never went to the school, but they've had that program for years and years for people who want to learn the safe way how to train your body to do the stuff that we do here at the sideshow. You can pay something like six or seven hundred dollars and you too can learn how to wow your friends. I don't know anybody would want to do that, it's hard. You either beat yourself up physically in some of the acts, or it's just poisonous for you. Like the fire eating because you ingest fuel. It gets into your system through the blood vessels in your mouth so you've got to watch your liver, you can't drink too much alcohol, it's not good for you. It's a dirty job but somebody's got to do it.

JH: I was actually thinking about quitting my job here and going back to school... sideshow school.

A: Yeah, I recommend it for learning how to do stuff the safe way. Instead of me, who's self-taught.

JH: Wait... you were self-taught?

A: Yeah, everybody yells at me, "Angelica, you were self-taught, that's terrible." But, I can't recommend it to every-body. Like most people, I believe I have very good common sense. So some people, their common sense skills aren't that great, so they may not teach themselves well. So, that's why we recommend they get proper training. I've been around sideshow so long. When you see it every day; you kind of know what to do and what not to do by watching other people and their mistake, too. So, that helps.

JH: I think I've covered everything. Is there anything else you want to add?

A: Can I be shameless?

JH: Go ahead.

A: You can write maybe, "look for her new music videos. www.myspace.com/paintthewallsred." My videos are up on YouTube. All you gotta do is go to YouTube and search PaintTheWallsRed. Yep, all one word or other wacky stuff comes up.

JH: Awesome. Oh, I forgot to mention, my friend Duckie loves you.

A: Hey there, Duckie!

JH: He's even got your picture in his wallet.

A: Aww! Well tell Duckie I said hi... oh wait we're recording. "Hi Duckie!"

Mickey Hart: The Rhythm of the Infinite

September 2006
By T. Virgil Parker

Anyone who has absorbed an authentic Grateful Dead show back in the day has spent a little time in spaces where the laws of what we like to call reality appear to be at one remove. This is a phenomenon that was produced by sound, and it was no accident. It is particularly evident when talking to Mickey Hart that he has spent a good part of his life in places that can't be found on any map, psychic territories carved out with rhythm. His quest has brought him to every corner of the planet, traversing jungles and deserts, recorder in hand, to track down the ur-sound. He has sent teams of researchers out to delve into the ancient wisdom and the latest discoveries about sound and rhythm. It is not hard to think of him as the Carl Jung of drums. Speaking to him is like traveling to an outpost in the collective unconscious.

From this outpost he has managed to achieve things in a rather hefty way, like bringing the healing powers of music and rhythm to the forefront of modern science, or participating in the foundation of not one, but two massive genres of music. In addition to the ubiquitous world of Jam, he played an essential role in bringing World Music to a global audience.

T. Virgil Parker: I had a poetry professor in the UK who said that he could not understand William Carlos Williams' cadences until he literally stood on an American street and heard the distinct rhythmical patterns here. You more than anyone else seem qualified to answer this question: How much of a culture comes with its rhythms?

Mickey Hart: All of it. Rhythm is life, and all about life. Each culture's rhythms are both culturally specific and cosmically specific. Our universe was born of rhythm: the Big Bang. It is a vibratory universe that we live in. Anything that vibrates has a rhythm. Music is a great metaphor in that respect, and it is a great connector to the origin; the seed sound of the universe; the big bang, the primal connector. As a result, music connects you to the infinite. Rhythm is certainly culturally specific, but more a planetary or cosmic connection that we're dealing with. We're embedded in a world rhythm. We're creatures of rhythm scanning for other rhythms, everywhere.

TVP: People have noted that Rock and Roll, consciousness expansion, and the occult evolved together, pretty much at the same time. Did bringing non-Western rhythms into mainstream Western Culture play a role in that?

MH: It is great for understanding another culture. Bo Diddley brought Quali rhythms into American popular music in the 50's. Suddenly you have the most potent rhythm of another culture. You discover the sensibilities of that culture from the ground up. That's where it all comes from; thousands of years of the evolution of that culture.

Then with the new sound you have an entrainment, a flowing together that becomes greater than the individual parts when it merges. What you're talking about here is music and trance.

TVP: Yes-

MH: -Trance and altered states of consciousness, whether it be psychoactive or driven by auditory experiences. Rhythm will get you that. That's what it is for. And there is evidence of art depicting altered states of conscious 19,000 years ago, as well as in Mesoamerican cultures. The need for consciousness expansion must have been there since we crawled out of the swamps. And art has always been part of it, there with it, and attributed to the altered state. The Grateful Dead did not invent that, I assure you.

TVP: No, but you brought it into a culture where ecstatic experience was very badly needed.

MH: Some might think that, I do.

TVP: You have done more than anyone to demonstrate the relationship between healing and rhythm.

MH: Yes.

TVP: There must have been a personal experience that got you thinking about researching that.

MH: My grandmother had Alzheimer Disease. She wasn't talking at the time, hadn't for several months. I played the drum for her for a long time, kind of to say goodbye. All the sudden she came back into the light. She shook her finger at me and smiled at me and said my name. I couldn't believe it. I almost stopped playing. She was doing all the things she hadn't done for months. I decided there must have been something to that. Aside from seeing thousands of people go into ecstatic experience at shows, this was personal. It was a very unusual, powerful experience that gave me the idea that rhythm can be used in medicinal ways. That started it. Now, we know that certain parts of the brain light up when certain rhythms are played. And we now know that the motor impaired, including Alzheimer patients, with rhythmic stimuli, can come out of it for a while, at least. And it may have some preventative properties. Rhythmic therapy as well as music therapy, has become real. HMO's in many states are actually underwriting prescriptions for music and sound therapy. It is now recognized by legitimate science, by insurance companies. They're uncovering the neurology of music.

TVP: You've worked directly with congress to spearhead this concept.

MH: I testified in front of the Senate in 1991, and tried to kick start this idea here in the West. We got $1,000,000 in research grants from Harry Reid, on the Subcommittee on Aging. We needed to prove that music is part of the healing process, which is now fact. Harry Reid was a believer, as was Oliver Sacks, the doctor depicted in the Awakenings movie. Harry Reid had read one of my books and called. We went to the Senate and laid it on them, and Harry proved to be a great visionary at the time.

TVP: I have to say that you've made better, more productive use of your time than any Rock Star that comes to mind.

MH: I'm not a Rock Star; I'm a musician, a drummer. That's the way I like it.

TVP: You're transcending the image.

MH: It isn't what you really are; it is just a way that people perceive you. I do what I have to do and what I think is appropriate and what makes for a better world. The world needs as much care as it can possible have. Music is one of the great caretakers. It's real medicine, not only for me personally, but look at all the millions of people who use it as their lifeline. People really do use it as a spiritual tool. It is a sacred dimension. It operates here in the profane world, and yet has that sacredness to it. It's completely invisible. It's so mysterious. It is such a pleasure to be involved with it every day. It is a way of life, not something I go to a concert for. I enjoy playing for myself daily, and having a personal experience as well as a large public performance, which is slightly different.

TVP: There are drum circles in every city in America now.

MH: The prophecy has been realized. It's fascinating to have seen it from the beginning. We just had 4,750 or so drummers up at Wavy Gravy's Place, a world record, all drumming at the same time. It was interesting to watch these rhythms from around the world come together in the hands of these white kids in a field. Almost 5,000 of them trying to get a hold of these trance rhythms, the archaic rising within each of these people. It was fascinating to look at because I know the history of it and how it all came here. Drum circles in every city; it's happening in a lot of neighborhoods too, people sharing drum circles.

TVP: I know you're out of time, but a lot of our readers wanted to know what kind of excitement you had planned for the Gathering of the Vibes.

MH: I have an astonishing lineup for that show. We're really going to push it to the next level.

Gogol Bordello's Great Global Revolution: An Interview With Tommy Gobena

October 2007
By Jessica Hopsicker

The bleach fumes were getting to me. As I went outside for a reprieve from scrubbing my tub and a smoke, my drunken neighbor sat down beside me at the picnic table. It didn't take him long to question my choice of music that cranked through the open window of my apartment. "What the hell is this shit?"

"Celtic I think," another neighbor quipped.

"Nah not this," I grinned as if preparing to preach, "This is Gypsy Punk, Gogol Bordello. The guy's Ukrainian, he-" It was then he cut me off by lifting a cheek and letting one rip in my direction: "I just dropped some ass, that's what I think about your gypsy shit." He nodded, seeming rather pleased with his flatulence.

"Um, yeah, why don't you just go and beat your girl-friend a couple more times," I bit back my retort and smiled snidely, nodding along with him, figuring it was time to take my leave. After all, I had better things to do; like scrubbing the toilet, and cleaning the shower ceiling tiles while dancing around like a maniac. Moments later, I looked out the open window to see him pull his pick-up truck to where they sat drinking. Country music blared in retaliation.

At that moment, it became astoundingly clear that I had grown far too weird, or even cultured, for such a small town. My neighbor's reaction was warranted from such a sonic assault on his minute sensibilities. After all, I was stationed in my old high school district, where any significant change came slowly, if at all. Librarians have never heard of H.P. Lovecraft, and gas station clerks fight to find the word 'costume' if you happen in to buy a cup of tea dressed as a pirate. The great global revolution that blew through civilization bypassed this place entirely. There are entire zip codes where inbreeding seems a far safer route than cultural crossbreeding. Intermingling ideas, the blending of beliefs; simply unheard of.

In 1999, the super eclectic, insanely eccentric Gogol Bordello began crossing borders not just in the physical landscape but in musical terrain as well. The man behind the maelstrom is the Kiev-born Ukrainian madman Eugene Hutz. He takes considerable pride in his Gypsy roots, tracing descent from the Sirva Roma Gypsies in the Carpathian Mountains. After fleeing the Chernobyl meltdown his family had to migrate around refugee camps in Europe, and ultimately ended up here.

The sparks of the revolution began to fly in the Lower East Side of New York. Today the group's membership would have Lou Dobbs scurrying after their green cards; hailing from more countries than you can fit in a trade agreement. They bring their roots and influences into a sound that is truly beyond classification.

Critics worldwide drool over the live performances; and they are reserving the same kind of praise for the band's newest accomplishment: SUPER TARANTA!. Eugene himself dubbed it as 'pure orgasmo hysteria'. The theme of the disk is New Rebel Intelligence, (NRI), a concept that the band developed by combining globalization with string theory, creationism, and political cataclysms with pure melodic anarchy; a far cry from the brainless claptrap that saturates the media today.

Tommy Gobena, the Ethiopian-born bassist, is the newest addition to the calamitous menagerie. He takes this latest accomplishment to a different level entirely. Throwing reggae, funk, R&B, African Groove, and dub into the volatile cocktail. Initially, I doubted there could possibly be enough room for more sound. The more I listened, diving deeper into the circus of kick drums, violins, accordions, and guitars it became apparent that he was the one keeping the chaos together, transforming it into a sound that is tighter than a wound clock.

It was a blessing finally to interview someone in the band. With appearances on late night talk shows, NPR, Henry Rollins, Live Earth, and a new album to compete with, it seemed as if it would never happen. Through cell phone static and an ocean between us, I made the Tribal Connection. He assured me that they weren't going to slow down any time soon.

JH: So, where exactly am I calling right now?

TG: I'm somewhere on the road closer to England.

JH: Sounds like fun.

TG: Yes, it's a long drive.

JH: So, how is it to be a bassist in a band where there are so many other things going on at any given time during a show?

TG: You know, it actually complements the whole sound

because all the other instruments are really high-sounding instruments. The violin, the accordion, the guitar. So they are very high on the frequency side, then the bass comes in really low. So it like in the space in between. It's actually a very well planned out on top. So it's great.

JH: What does your background bring to the sound?

TG: Well, I'm Ethiopian originally, so I come from a lot of African-groove, dub, reggae kind of background. I also played R&B and funk and stuff like that. All my influences are based on grooves that are a little bit heavier on the bass. They were looking for a bass player like that. I never heard of them initially but after I auditioned for them I really loved the originality and the honesty and the energy they have. So I went in for the audition and it worked out really nice. They liked the kind of background I have, they were actually looking for people like me.

JH: That is pretty much my next question: how did you happen along with band?

TG: Our sound engineer is friends with a friend of mine that is a producer in New York. When they were looking for a bass player, they called my friend and they're like, "we need a bass player, do you know anyone?" I had worked with him and he said, "Why don't you call Thomas and see if he is interested?" So they called me, and I listened to it, and it was great. I went in for an audition and ended up jamming for seven hours straight. So it was like a match made in heaven.

JH: What is it like working with someone like Eugene?

TG: It's great. He's a very creative, vibrant person. It's never boring, it's always fun, and the fact that we all come from different places lets us work off of each other's differences in cultures and whatnot, so it's very colorful.

JH: The music itself, I mean gypsy, speed metal, dub, reggae, flamenco, punk; I mean how do you classify such a genre?

TG: You don't classify it as a genre; you classify it as good music.

JH: Clearly, it is.

TG: It is what it is. Like you said, those are the influences that we come from and that are how it works. We bring people like that together and put them in a creative environment and it comes out naturally. It's a natural progression.

JH: And it is refreshing to hear something other than consumer-driven music about status symbols or whining drivel.

TG: Absolutely. That's what I liked about the band when I first heard it. I'd never heard anything like that in my life before. That sort of really attracted me and the rest was for me to actually play with them and find out. We love to find out how other people are, you know? Sometime gigs like that end up just being like you go into an office or something. You don't really like it, but you get paid for it. I wasn't looking for something like that. But when I went in and played for them and met everybody, and these are beautiful people, you know we're like family now. It's good to know that when you join a band.

JH: Exactly, and it isn't like work.

TG: No, it's not work. It's work from the fact that it's known to be demanding; when we're touring and stuff we're driving twenty-four hours at times, like we're doing right now. But when you get on stage everything becomes something else.

JH: The fans are completely different animals themselves. How do you invoke such anarchy?

TG: It's just exchange of energy. They see us do what we do on stage. They ask, "Can you give it back to us?" And we give it back to them and it's like a symbiotic relationship. It just gives you hope that not the whole music industry is driven by money and all that other stuff. That's actually music. You go and play in front of a crowd like that and you know what's good and what's bad right off the bat. Nobody can fake what we have on stage and nobody can fake what the crowd is reacting like. It's not driven by anything else but the good music. It sort of conveys a refreshing kind of environment.

JH: Exactly. I saw the show at Bonnaroo while I was covering it and it was just completely insane.

TG: Absolutely, absolutely.

JH: I was up front swinging around in like ninety plus heat. So much dust.

TG: You forget all those things once the music starts. You complain before and you complain after but during you just lose yourself in the music.

JH: Exactly, even when I nearly busted my toes.

TG: That happens sometimes as well. I hope you're doing well now.

JH: It was amazing.

JH: Do you think you'll ever be able to outdo yourself with this SUPER TARANTA!? I mean clearly it's the best album yet.

TG: Yeah, it keeps getting better. That's the whole thing

about music and musicians. You know once you're in the right path, there's no way to go back. You just keep creating. Especially with bands like us, it's not really commercially driven. It's always about the creativity and taking it to the next level. Bands that are concerned about other stuff might lose track of what they're doing and go a different place, but we really focus on our art and what we do and the creativity and where all that stuff really comes from. I have no doubt that the next one will be even better than this one.

JH: The band has been described as legendary in the global touring circuit.

TG: I believe it.

JH: Did you ever think it would be that way?

TG: Definitely. Of course, there's no reason why we can't be, you know? Like I said, SUPER TARANTA! was taking everything to the next level. So whatever the next album that we have, it's the same people, same creative energy, different experiences and we'll try to reflect on those and take it to the next level once again. We're not about to slow down.

JH: What's next for you, and/or Gogol Bordello?

TG: Well, we just released a new album, so it's going to be basically tour-driven. We just did a summer leg in Europe and we're going to do a little west coast thing for a week and a half next, come back and do a whole US tour, and all European tour after that. So, basically support the album for now. I'm sure side projects will pop up that we might hear about in the future, but that's what we're doing.

JH: You're clearly making waves in the music industry.

TG: I hope so. I mean we don't want to go mainstream just the hell of being commercial, but we want to bring the mainstream to our little corner party. So as long we're bringing people together, that's great.

JH: Is there anything else you want to add to your fans?

TG: Hopefully people will be inspired to be creative and original in whatever they do.

Georgina Cates:
A Woman of Many Parts

September 2006
By T. Virgil Parker

Many people park artistic integrity alongside other quaint American indulgences, such as journalistic objectivity. It may exist in some form, but it doesn't pay the bills. Contemporary film, with budgets like the GDP of small countries, is not a place one would expect to find droves of it. For countless thousands of hopeful actors, getting noticed is the main thing, the only thing. Georgina Cates, nearly as famous for the way she broke into film as she is for her startling performances, wouldn't seem at first glance the most obvious defender of artistic integrity, but it occupies her hierarchy of needs just a tad below food and shelter.

In fact, her impetuous emergence into mainstream film is a testament to what talent can do when it is driven by vision. Rejected for the role of Claire in 1995's *An Awfully Big Adventure*, she disguised herself, went back to auditions under an assumed name, and got the part. This requires a level of talent almost impossible to find even though it may seem like a brazen act. Nevertheless, the more you know about her, the more obvious it becomes that her vision of the character was more compelling than her career goals. Georgina rejects roles she doesn't find challenging or deeply meaningful.

If her entrance into the spotlight seems impetuous, her departure from it seems even more so. No one simply walks away from a burgeoning film career. With former husband, actor 'Skeet' Ulrich, she packed off to rural Virginia to raise their children.

Her fans complained bitterly about her absence, and were more likely to blame the industry than her choice of real estate for child-rearing. As a result, her comeback seems almost like a vindication of the medium itself. She's choosing parts that require a frightening range of talent and intellect, only casually drawing on her profound aesthetic advantages. She's not trying to impress anyone; she's trying to blast them through the wall.

T. Virgil Parker: Does acting feel different this time around?

Georgina Cates: Yes, because I know why I'm doing it now. I started very young, and I loved it, but there came a lot of pressure to do things a certain way. After a certain point you have to choose one path or the other. Are you going to be known, or are you going to keep on doing work that people don't see?

Now I really know when I want to do something, when something really feels exciting and new. It means spending time without my kids, and that's a really good yard post to know how you're really responding to something.

TVP: Has the time off affected the way you approach a character?

GC: Not really. I think I've always worked the same way. I'm a gut-reaction actor. I know inherently what I want to do. I'm always someone who does homework and homework and homework so that I can turn up on the set and play. Then, I can throw it all out because I know instinctually how this person would do something. As soon as someone throws out an idea, I can just go with it. I've never been a pre-planned scene kind of girl. I do that in my homework time and then when I get there it's really about making it better than it can be. I think it's really dangerous to preplan too much.

TVP: How much does your classical training go into the way you work a part now?

GC: I was always the rebel when it came to classical training. I've heard so many actors talk about this. People talk about what class they're going to. When people really dig deep, they know what their strengths are, and if they're born to act, or just learning how to do it well.

I started seriously going to classical training at 15. It gave me a basis from which I can now diversify. I can look at something and know the safe way, and that lets me turn the safe way completely on its head. That's exciting to me.

TVP: Your early acting was in the UK. The way acting is approached there is completely different from the way it is approached in the US.

GC: Yes. In the UK, the good actors are good, and they do it because they love it. They have very little embarrassment levels. They're not pre-planning their careers, they're not playing themselves. You do your training and you take from that what works for you. It is not geared towards anything in particular. When you come to the States, people class themselves in very specific ways. Are you a television actor, are you a theater actor, are you an Indie film actor, or mainstream? That just doesn't happen there. You do what you do and you do it professionally. The other stuff doesn't enter in, the magazines, the interviews. It isn't a part of the lifestyle there.

TVP: The BBC seems to be trying to bridge the gap between theater and film. Has your experience with them encouraged you to be more pliable when you approach a character?

GC: Maybe. This is the way I've always done it. I'd rather have fun with something and go for it, than I would be safe and fit in the middle. When you talk about bridging the gap between theater and mainstream, at the BBC they enjoy letting actors act. It isn't so much about the nifty camera moves, or special effects. They let actors breathe. Directors really direct. If you're an actor in England you're not doing it for the money, you're doing it for a reason. It's what they believe they should be doing, they have a passion for it, and they'd rather be earning very little money doing that than very little money doing something else.

TVP: That is somewhat true of American Independent Film.

GC: American Independent Film doesn't really exist that strongly anymore. That was a change I noticed from the time I left acting to the time I came back. Now the majority of Indie films still require "names" and what it used to be was a great script. You go in, you blow the director away, you get the part and you all make the movie for the right reasons. There were no other requirements, and if people saw the movie, great, and if they didn't, they didn't. Now it seems there's only a handful of truly independent movies. The one I did recently, *Sinner* was truly an independent movie. They chose to do it that way because they didn't want to give up control of that film. I don't believe there's a truly independent film festival anymore. Look at Sundance.

TVP: They have assumed control.

GC: It's a real shame. It will change again, it has to. When the only thing people want to see is Little Miss Sunshine, it's telling people something. I think things are shifting again, where truly creative people are starting to fight back and make their own movies, but there really are so few truly independent movies right now.

TVP: So much of that is economics.

GC: Of course.

TVP: I've noticed that the parts you're taking now require a great deal of psychological commitment. Does having children, that connection, watching them develop; help with that kind of dimensionality?

GC: First, I'm older now; I have more experience to bring to the table, but I'm not doing things with an essentially different approach. A lot of people build up a name and basically start playing a caricature of themselves in every movie. I never did that, and it was something I was really scared of happening. I'm not that interesting to begin with. I'm not Julia Roberts with a smile that can make people that interested.

TVP: I don't know if you can honestly call that acting.

GC: It's not. I think people fall into a trap, very quickly, of playing caricatures of themselves in any given role. Slight variations, maybe you have an accent, or you walk a little differently, but inherently you're being cast as yourself. That was never very interesting to me and it certainly isn't now.

I love what I do and I really care about what I do. If you're not willing to really push the limits then it's kind of pointless. It has to be that kind of thing that keeps people energized and on their toes. When you have kids, it's a blessing. You relive being a kid again. You open up and understand that you can go from one emotion to the other in three minutes. Kids do it all the time. The more life you live that's real, the more you can bring that forth.

That's the joke of L.A. existence. Most of the time you're not living real life, writers aren't writing about real life.

TVP: The industry is almost completely self-reflexive.

GC: Yes. That will have a change too. Actors should admire what other actors do, should respect other actors. Really, the obsession with what actors do outside of acting has become a joke unto itself. That can really restrain you as an actor. You're not allowed to take risks anymore. The actors you truly admire are not the actors you want to read about who they're having sex with.

We're actors, that's what we do; we're only part of an equation. That's the huge difference between being on stage and being on a movie set. When you're on stage you're in complete control of your performance every night. In a movie, you don't have a clue until you're in that ADR room.

TVP: That has to be a little scary.

GC: It is. I was looping the last movie yesterday and I was talking to the director. Aside from what I was saying about actors not acting, directors don't direct. When you're an actor who wants to be fearless, wants to do not a good, but a great job, you have to feel safe. You have to trust who you're working with. I don't know that that happens a lot.

My friends and I play a game in which we recast a movie. There are a lot of films that if you recast with the right actors, would be fascinating to watch.

TVP: You seem unusually adventurous in terms of where you want to bring a character.

GC: I think it's the only reason I want to get up at 5:00 a.m. and get on the set with all that mayhem and cry your heart out in various scenes, be buck naked in other ones. The only reason to do any of that is to make people look at things in new ways.

I think strong, fresh, female characters are rare. It's about time that changed. You can have a woman who's funny and gutsy and ballsy and interesting and diverse. People are shocked by it.

TVP: We have this cultural dichotomy between talent and attractiveness. That has to have affected your career in the past.

GC: In what way?

TVP: Getting casted for beauty when you want to bring your talents to bear on complex roles, perhaps.

GC: This is what's really interesting. And this is why you grow up. In fact, I used to be the girl who wasn't pretty enough, and later I wasn't getting parts because they said I was too attractive. I honestly had to burst out laughing. Without putting myself in a box, I'll never be anything other than a character actor. That's what I am. The whole female physicality thing is staring to evolve slowly, not fast enough. Female characters are under-written anyway.

When I first came here and I was twenty years old, sitting down in these ridiculous general meetings and they'd seen the movie I came here with, they would talk to me in this bizarre way about what I wanted to do. I'd say that I'd never been cast in anything I'm physically right for, or look right for. Movies sometimes simply don't step out of the box enough. The ones that do, that's when people talk about it.

TVP: And many people are afraid to do that.

GC: I'm lucky that no one knows what I look like or knows what I sound like. Every movie has been different. When I came back to acting it was an advantage that nobody knew what I looked like in the first place, or where I was from, or how old I am. When I'm reading a script I always want the part that they're not offering me. I have the balls to tell people I know what I can do.

The way the business is set up these days, actors are limiting themselves. If you're not the gorgeous blond you think you have to be the quirky ex-girlfriend.

TVP: Is that more apparent now than when you first went to Hollywood?

GC: No, because I was never the conventional cookie cutter beauty. I had to convince everyone that I could be American. They wanted a gorgeous blonde for *Clay Pigeons*. I went in with no makeup and my hair pulled up. Luckily there was a director who had some brains and some balls and fought for me. It's been the same with every movie.

I'm better at protecting myself now. It isn't easy for any person to go through the process that this brings up. You're basically all the time trying to please other people. Now I have a firm idea of what I can do and what I want to do. I've never had a game plan or a career plan; I want to do good work. If you can say that you're proud of your work, you're ahead of the game.

TVP: You're not going after the big bucks. As a result you're in a position to go after the roles you want.

GC: Yes. I'm a single mom with two kids. I'm conscious of the fact that I haven't had to do anything else to support myself, I'm really lucky. I'm optioning two books. If I believe in what I've been saying to you I have to make a change. From an actor's viewpoint I'm not optioning so I can have a starring vehicle; it's about making movies that you actually want to see. You can do and say what you really want to say. I'm not saying that anybody should turn down ten million bucks for a movie, then you've got time on your hands to go and do the stuff you really want to do.

When you take a risk and it doesn't work, you're kind of tainted by that, but the bottom line is, sometimes things don't work. In film, I don't believe any one person can be blamed for that.

TVP: Film is, by definition, risk.

GC: It is. I found this tough when I decided to take a break. People had a certain game plan. When *Clay Pigeons* came out, I was getting a lot of those femme fatale offers, and I had just done that, so I didn't want to do it again.

TVP: The fastest way to get typecast.

GC: That film was supposed to be the next big thing. Very few people saw it. That's why I say, if I did a good job, I can walk away. I have no control over what turns up on screen or how people react to it. If my experience was good, then I'm one step ahead. Of course it would be great for a lot of people to see my work, but you can't be reliant on that.

TVP: You're doing it for intrinsic reasons. Your goal is to produce experience, rather than being motivated by so many of the other reasons people are doing it.

GC: I did a movie with John Turturro, and he's one of the most creative people I've ever met. Everyone on that set was there for the right reasons. None of us really understood the script. It was his vision and you were there. You wanted to be a part of his vision. That's what actors do, that's what's fun. That movie, *Illuminata,* had a really good script and a really good heart, so you go for it.

TVP: Given your commitment to executing vision, have you thought about directing?

GC: I write quite a bit, but I don't think I'm there yet. Any actor has to find a project they feel so passionately about -and that they're not in- that they really need to see it to fruition. It's hard. The next movie I'm doing, *Among the Shadows*, is really close to me. I can see it in my head. Then, as an actor, I'll have to let that go. I'm not technically minded as a director. As a director I'd need an entirely different vocabulary. When I quit acting, I photographed for five years. It can't be an ego thing. That's why I think George Clooney had such success. It was very evidently coming from his passion and not from ego.

TVP: He was driven by an agenda, one that has been culturally undernourished lately.

GC: Very surprising. I don't think anybody thought he could do that. Actors are great with other actors, but you have to become very careful about the whole ego thing. I have to guard myself when I'm writing, about the ego thing. As an actor you come from a different viewpoint. That's why it's fun when you do things that are more like collaboration. When they feel like collaboration, you don't feel like you just did your thing and left. Not to the level of directing, but you feel like you've had more of an effect on the outcome.

TVP: When I saw the storyline for *Among the Shadows* I

had to wonder how much of a part like that becomes internalized.

GC: It's an interesting thing. The last movie I did I had two weeks prep time, which I hate. The character was completely and utterly opposite from me, and it was bizarre. The only way I work is by knowing the script inside out, knowing everything. I have every question answered before I get there. And this is stupid, I know, but clothes are really important to me. I have all that down and I can turn up the next day and throw it all away. I already know how the character sounds; I know how they laugh, so that I don't have to consciously think about it while I'm on set. I can walk in and out of a character in every scene. In *Sinner* I'd be sobbing and they'd say "cut" and I'd be out of it. If you can walk in and out, then it's easy. How much is internalized? A lot, but this new movie, *Among the Shadows* is the closest to me of anything I've ever done. It's kind of nice to go from something that was overt in every way to something that's kind of insular.

TVP: I'm guessing that your perspective must have been enriched by developing so many latent aspects of yourself, when you're acting.

GC: A lot of the people I've played were not sympathetic. I don't believe in playing roles that are too pat. I told the director of the last movie that I wasn't going to play a prostitute with a heart of gold. I said that when they offered the part to me. Partly because of this business and partly because of who people are and who they are on the next level, and the next, which don't have to coincide. I'm not judgmental of who I am, and I'm not judgmental of anything I read, or any person I read. There's always an interesting question for actors, do you have to like the character? The answer is no. I don't have to like them; I have to be them for a period of time. You absorb a lot of things when you're playing a part, or getting ready to play one. Everyone has their moments of being obnoxious, or sympathetic, or unsympathetic. That's how I approach everything. Blank page, start from zero, there you go.

I don't appreciate dumbing a character down for the audience.

Where's Poe Going?

September, 2003
By T. Virgil Parker

As the reigning queen of the Alt Rock radio dial in the '90s, Poe was well poised to redefine platinum. Being possessed of more than the beauty required for commercial success, and enough talent to meet the demands of the creative arts, she possess an even rarer gift; the wisdom necessary to evade all the dehumanizing temptations of fame.

From her music, you'd expect a person who is in an ongoing battle to overcome darkness; a person who has not given up, but has every reason to do so. Surprisingly, Poe is overflowing with mirth and intellectual energy. She has looked into the void, and jumped over, not into it. She speaks from the viewpoint of a person who maintained integrity of selfhood, of vision, and is reaping the greater rewards that come with autonomy.

I initially sought this interview to find out what had become of her. After a few words with her, I had to wonder how the world let her slip out of sight for a second.

284

T. Virgil Parker: My first observation about you is that your goal was never to get a giant fan base

Poe: My intention is much more close to home; it is all about communicating. How many people you communicate to isn't part of my equation. You put a record out and a bunch of people go out and pick it up and it means something to them. That is great. If five people go out and get it– and love it or hate it. It's still the same process.

TVP: To put it another way, there are people who shape their music specifically to reach as massive an audience as is humanly possible, and though you achieved the status they look for, you are not one of them.

Poe: I'm the antithesis of that, perhaps in spite of myself. I'm just not wired that way. If your intention is just to craft something that is commercially appealing- that is crafted purely for sales; you may as well be making coat hangers. To me music and art are about reflecting the world that you see and expressing your perceptions as accurately and truthfully as you can. To create a glimpse of order out of chaos, sometimes you have to invent a new language and often that's not appealing commercially, at least not at first. If you start trying to second-guess how the market is going to embrace that, you've really lost your vision. That's just corruption.

TVP: It is a question of whether you're real or not.

Poe: Exactly. The road I've chosen is not the easier one. There are a lot of people who make a really commercial record and get the perfect commercial team behind them. They make it a connect-the-dot kind of thing. "I have a fan base, I have things I could capitalize on, when I'm a hit and get rich then I can do what I want for the rest of my life".

I've seen too many people just lose themselves in that. I believe that if you keep sticking to your own vision and your own sense of truth, ultimately you will arrive. My goal is to continue making records for the rest of my life-- it's not to have one big huge success and then retire and do it as a hobby.

TVP: Some artists try to get unsigned so that they can express themselves more freely.

Poe: I ultimately was not creatively constrained by Atlantic but I did battle with them periodically. When I started making "Haunted" I was under a lot of pressure to just crank out another record like *Hello*, but with smoother, more commercial contours. Atlantic wanted me to work with a big name producer and a bunch of writers. From a commercial standpoint it might have been clever for me to do that but, as I mentioned, I'm not wired that way. I had a certain album in my head and I really wanted to make that record and I knew who I wanted to make it with. I'd seen many artists that I loved succumb to that kind of pressure over the years and I always felt that they ended up losing something that might never be found again. That possibility has always scared me more than poverty and anonymity. I would rather wait for years for an album that really means something to me, than get one out in a year's time in order to please some imaginary corporate machine. I just decided I was not going to do that. In my mind, if I couldn't come up with an album that scraped through every corner of my heart and soul- and taught me something in the process- well, I really wouldn't have a right to put it out. I would be wasting a listener's time.

Atlantic, ultimately did let me make the album I wanted to make, and they let me do it my way- without a big well-known corporate machine around me. When it was finished however, they didn't really know what to do with it. For one thing, the Alternative stations that had supported my music in the past had all changed their formats and were playing only male talent. They openly admitted that they were not allowed to play women! So Atlantic was at a loss for how to market *Haunted*. The only category that really made sense for me was Alternative, but without radio, it might be difficult. Meanwhile, other formats like Pop or Adult Contemporary, weren't likely to respond well to me or to *Haunted*. For quite awhile after *Haunted*'s release, Atlantic stalled and refused to put their support behind the normal promotional things such as a tour, a single or a video.

Frustrated beyond belief, I made a few calls to radio stations that had supported my music in the past. Mark Hamilton, who was the program director of KROK in Seattle, was the first person I called. He is awesome! Mark suggested that I do a re-mix of the song "Hey Pretty" with my brother reading passages from his book over the verses. I loved the idea! My brother's book *House of Leaves* had just been published by Pantheon and was a "sibling" work to *Haunted*. *Haunted* was full of references to *House of Leaves*; and *House of Leaves* was, in turn full of references to *Haunted*. It made perfect sense to include passages from my brother's book in a re-mix. I got straight to work and when it was finished I sent Mark Hamilton the finished remix. He warned me that his listeners were primarily male and into the whole Korn/Blink 182 thing and said he didn't think it would fly, but that he would play it once and we could see what happened. Well, he played it once and it took off! The phones lit up. It went crazy. Then the song started popping up on the playlists of many other stations--even KROCK in L.A. (a station that record companies notoriously pay thousands of dollars to, in order to get air-play). A lot of stations were getting great calls on "Hey Pretty" and it started to break the album. Sales of *Haunted* began to increase steadily, "Hey Pretty" entered the top 10 on the alternative charts, and then Depeche Mode invited me to open up for them on their US arena tour. All this excitement finally earned me Atlantic's support. They agreed to fund my stint on the Depeche Mode tour and more importantly Atlantic decided to pick up their next option on my contract, which meant, quite simply, that they were committing a lot of money to my future. Things seemed good. This weird spooky record I'd made was unexpectedly making waves commercially and I felt very secure and confident that I'd be able to continue making quirky albums for Atlantic on my own terms. But then a strange thing happened: I was dropped...

It made no sense to anyone at first, least of all me- and it was devastating! In the end, the explanation was as tragic as it was simple. I was signed to Atlantic through a boutique label called Modern Records. Modern's distribution deal with Atlantic was 18 years old, and when Atlantic's upper management changed, they re-examined that distribution deal. What Atlantic discovered enraged them. Despite all of the time and money they had invested in my career they were not the owners of any Poe master. In spite of the fact that they had funded my entire career, it turned out that as soon as I delivered to them the third album they had agreed to fund, a guy named Paul Fishkin, would walk away with all the masters. In essence, Atlantic was kind of screwed- and I was definitely out of luck. Atlantic at that point, having no hope of long-term financial rewards, settled with Fishkin- paying him a percentage of what they had committed to my future in order to wash their hands of the whole thing. And that was the end of *Haunted*. It was surreal.

Had I then been free to move on, things might have been okay. Sadly, that was only the beginning of my troubles. You would really have to devote your entire book to my story if I got started on all of that now! And frankly, now that it's over, I'm happy to think of other things. Suffice it to say that after Atlantic severed ties with myself and Modern Records, bits of my future were bought out by an evil Texas Oil man (Not kidding!) and a war began. It took roughly 5 years for me to win my freedom and my future back. During that time I could not release any new material, or tour.

I have spent many years now making music in a vacuum, but as always that process still keeps me going everyday-- with or without a commercial release! That being said, I do look forward to being able to share some of this music again. Those who supported my music in past have remained supportive. The difference between what I do and what a Pop act does is that if a person gets where I'm coming from and likes my record, that's going to be someone I want to be friends with because if they relate to my songs, chances are we have a lot in common.

TVP: They have the same aesthetic, the same worldview.

Poe: More like they have the same questions- about life, death, love, art, humor, sex, memories, technology; how to get through a day and why. The way that I've related to people who listen to my music has been as complete equals. I have gone to booths across the country to sign autographs and ended up listening to stories that were twenty times more interesting than my own. That is the beauty of what art can do. If you can't find a way to describe something, you sequester yourself in a room, and whether it's a painting or a photograph you bring it out and say, "Now do you see what I mean?" When someone really gets what you mean, then something magical has happened and a very real relationship has been created.

TVP: Art really transcends normal communication.

Poe: It does, and it's the opposite of that old celebrity archetype. The one that tells you: you're a young girl and you're walking through a shopping mall and somebody's going to "discover" you and then your life will be made. But made into what? That's kind of "luck" is the worst thing that could ever happen to you, do you know why?

TVP: You become someone else's vision.

Poe: And it preempts self-discovery. On the surface it seems like a beautiful fantasy- someone will see your worth and then show everyone else how wonderful and special you are. But ultimately no one can do that for you- you have to do it yourself and art is a good way to go about it. Art at its very best is a process of self-discovery. Who are we? Why are we here on this planet? Why do we die? Why does love hurt? Why do I get road rage? From the mundane, to the epic.

TVP: This ties into something that I wanted to ask you. Each of your albums has a unifying theme that holds the songs together. I see a persona in *Hello*, of a beautiful, gifted, intelligent woman...

Poe: Thank you!

TVP: Exploited and victimized by a repressive culture.

Poe: Yeah.

TVP: Overlaid with images of objectification, and a voice that rises up and fights it.

Poe: Yes.

TVP: *Haunted*. A sense of resolution comes to the foreground.

Poe: Definitely.

TVP: There's an internal dialogue that ultimately isn't internal. It transcends our reality to bring about closure. Do you feel a new theme rising within yourself while you're in the studio now?

Poe: More than you can ever imagine. The process for any-body, not just me, of overcoming inertia and continuing to evolve as a human being is something that doesn't take place on a corporate clock. The way the industry translates art into commodity is not friendly to that process. Ulti-mately that's very destructive.

There used to be people in music companies who had musical backgrounds and were committed to protecting the growth of artists with an eye toward the long term. Now the process is about creating formulas that will hit the market quickly and make a lot of money in one shot. They don't care about a second album. They're not building art-ists; they're turning out disposable hits. It's the difference between wallpaper and a beautiful piece of art.

That's not what I'm trying to do. An artist tries to make sense of things that didn't make sense before. It could be just a feeling, an attitude and a sound you get when you put musicians together, and you feel like you could take on a world when you hear it- when you didn't feel that way before.

Life is worth living for the sole purpose of reaching for those things. It won't always make you money but what you get back is so much more valuable. And you do get to take it with you.

TVP: I believe that the industry is beginning to understand that there's a greater value in a long-term relationship.

Poe: The whole breakdown is caused by a misunderstanding of what an artist's relationship is to their listeners.

The issue of piracy always interests me. There's a part of

me- I can't help it- that just giggles. Pirates on the Internet are everything that's Rock and Roll: They're against the status quo, they're sexy. Corporate America can't handle it. I should be saying, "Don't steal my shit," but as far as I'm concerned, I'm glad if anyone listens to it. If they want to support me, they should go buy the record, listen to it, burn it for your friends if they don't have any money.

At the end of the day I'll let you know if I'm starving to death and I'll take donations. The more people who can get their hands on good music and information and ideas, the better.

TVP: Your real fans will buy it anyway.

Poe: Yes, to support the cause. I can't tour if I don't sell records, and they understand that. I'm very seriously considering staying independent. I think that my community is as powerful as a major label. They revel in my saying, "Let me and my little community of fans take you guys on."

TVP: You've demonstrated what you can do with *Haunted*; you know that you can pull it off if you have to.

Poe: The more artists who have the balls to go independent, and trust their listeners to follow them, the better the music will get.

TVP: Independent doesn't have to mean a guy in a basement with a CD Burner anyway.

Poe: Yes! There are other kinds of alliances that you can make with corporations that don't want to control your art: A software company who makes your editing software, a video game company. You're selling out less by doing that than by signing to a record company who will own you, try to control you, and potentially put your record on a shelf where it will collect dust eternally!

This is the most exciting time in music. The corporate world has become so solidified–and yet is it in such turmoil. This opens up an avenue where everything that's living on the fringe has so much freedom.

I've never felt more freedom or had more fun making a CD than I am having right now. The future is totally unknown.

TVP: Nobody staring over your shoulder.

Poe: I have no idea if it's ever going to come out. I might just put it up on the Internet. I'll try to put it out in some more organized way. This album is coming along very organically. There's no A and R guy checking up on me, and my relationship with other musicians has changed as well. People behave differently when you have an Atlantic budget. Now I call someone and say, "I have no money, if you want to come over and jam, come down." That has attracted the kind of people who really are in it for the music.

TVP: What kind of feelings do you associate with that creative process while you're working?

Poe: All of them.

TVP: Like, maybe you're trying to get something over and over and finally something kicks in to put it over the top, or is it a more methodical process?

Poe: It's not methodical at all. Every song has its own process. To me it's more like finding something. This window opens and you get this sense. Like when you wake up from a dream you can't really remember and all day you're trying to get it back. You remember it and you try to figure out what's going on in this society of yourself. You have to figure out what that other voice inside you is trying to tell you. Once you have that little kernel you will always know when it's not quite right--and you will also know when you've found the heart of that song. That is one of the most incredible experiences you can imagine. It's the sudden quantum leap that your brain makes when all the disparate parts are brought together.

I wrote a song with a guitarist the other day and I had a melody and a bit of lyric. The whole song, the lyrics and everything popped out in like ten minutes. Its like the easy things are much stronger than the things you work and work. Its like they just appear.

TVP: I'm convinced that it comes down to the part of your brain, or your mind that you're using.

Poe: You have no idea how much that has got to be true.

A friend of mine had been doing this strange meditation stuff. She was doing some crazy meditation retreat in Seattle and she invited me up. I'd been so sleep-deprived and run down and burning the candle at both ends that I thought, "Great. I'll go do a little yoga and mud baths, and I'll get totally relaxed." I go up to Seattle and it's like a Navy Seal camp or something. It was all about training yourself to use different parts of your brain. They did exercises like walking you into a room and then 30 seconds later blindfolding you and asking you to "Describe everything in this room. What's on the north wall?" You think you can't do it and they make you stay there. If you stay long enough, and your brain stops interfering, suddenly everything stops and you see the whole thing. That's a totally different part of your brain.

TVP: I'd even argue that different parts of the brain experience completely different realities.

Poe: I'd fully agree with that too. You need to read *The Elegant Universe*. It's another *Brief History of Time and Space* type book. I spent about seven months with that book. Certain parts I had to keep going over. It's for the layman who's interested in the physics of parallel universe-- not Science Fiction but the things that they're starting to have incredible proofs for, and it really makes so much sense to me. There are these very different places you can go to in your brain, and they function in a totally different relationship to time and space, which changes your sense of who you are.

There are parts of your brain that catalogue information, and parts of your brain that create.

I will often take an idea and feed it to the back of my brain. Every night I'll tell my brain, "This is the problem, get back to me." Like when you forget a word and you're saying, "What is the word?"

TVP: Fifteen minutes later, bing, there it is.

Poe: Another part of your brain has been working on it. We think we're so smart, the way we take in perception and process information. Think about the part of your brain that's running your heart, your lungs...

TVP: Performing the calculus of catching a ball...

Poe: Your growth rate, your cell structure, everything. That part of your brain, well, the top part of your brain that controls personality has in the area of 1,000 to 10,000 neural connections per second. The back part of your brain, which also houses your subconscious mind, has something like 10,000,000 connections.

TVP: When we get in touch with that part of our brain we say, "Where is this coming from?" We're so divorced from our psychological heritage that we don't even recognize it.

Poe: That's exactly it, because there's a lot of history back there. That part of your brain, which is technically called the Reptilian Brain, is connected to the forebrain when it comes to vision. I'll stress that I'm a layman, not a scientist, but there's a theory that it's the reptilian brain that takes over to project dream images. It uses the same apparatus that your eyes do. The forebrain doesn't really know the difference.

TVP: And you would have two tracks in the brain processing the same image, the "old" brain and the forebrain.

Poe: Exactly. When you think about songs, the songwriting process, it is like shutting one pair of eyes and opening another. Artist or not, everyone has had that experience. You have it when you dream. Everyone has had a nightmare that's so frightening that it has taken days to shake it off.

TVP: That's more real than walking down the street.

Poe: That's the same part of the brain that you use when you're writing. I don't believe in the elitism of the artist. Every living person is a creator. It could be as simple as someone who's gotten in a fight with her boyfriend and is trying to find the right words to make herself understood. It's the same process; it's the will to communicate and the will to evolve.

It's the will to bring something into the world that was not there before, and what is out there needs improvement. Look at what VH1 is telling people. You need this stuff and you need this much money. This is the kind of plastic surgery all the celebrities get. I'm looking at this sometimes and saying, "This cannot be real." Kids are looking at this and thinking that in order to be a valuable human being, to win, they need that stuff.

TVP: I'm going to say that the kids for whom it matters most, reject it out of hand.

Poe: Completely, but the truth is that if that is the only thing you have access to, and fortunately that's changing because of the internet, that's a tragedy. I know that people are capable of being turned on to more interesting things.

When my brother published his novel we went on tour of Borders Bookstores together. I sang while my DJ spun beats, and my brother would do these readings. Looking at those audiences was insane. Rows of bookshelves under fluorescent lights, and fifteen-year-old kids who have gotten through a difficult 700 page book, a book that they're teaching in grad school. They have piercings and they're totally Punk Rock, alongside a 60-year-old English Professor.

Don't tell me that kids are not capable, that they have to be spoon-fed and catered to as some kind of mass common denominator. This is fascism. Don't tell me that a kid with half the education of a professor is not capable of reading James Joyce if they want to. The only reason these kids wanted to read my brother's book is because they heard about it on the radio and on MTV, and not at school. These kids were saying that it was the first book they'd read that wasn't for school. If they heard about more good challenging books once in a while, instead of just plastic surgery and $500 pillow cases, who knows what they might end up creating themselves!

TVP: Think about what that did for them.

Poe: That is what the media should be doing. I'm all over Eminem, 50 Cent, and even Nellie. Nellie has a beautiful sound and his grooves are cool and all that. But there's so much more. Why are we limited to these narrow categories? It's just this or it's just that. There's room for everything from a stupid Pop song to Radiohead to Thomas Pynchon to James Joyce. To me it's all good. What's bad is when you're convinced that the only thing is what you see on mainstream media. And mainstream media is corrupt.

I don't know how many people understand this, but radio is bought. Your votes mean nothing. I'm pretty sure that what happened with my song "Hey Pretty" on the radio could not happen today. I think it's important for every person who cares about music to know that. Oh, and that Clear Channel owns almost everything.

TVP: They don't dare play anything remotely unusual.

Poe: They're also in Bush's right hand pocket. These guys area all Texas guys and they don't want anybody at the Grammy's to say a word about the war. There's a reason that they get away with it. And there's a reason why you'll never hear challenging political ideas on the radio. It's not a conspiracy theory; it's a simple fact.

TVP: The only real conspiracy is greed, and that's universal.

Poe: Totally. So, the only way to keep culture alive is to maintain the belief in individual people. Individuals can do incredible things without the resources of these corporations. The reason the entertainment industry is so messed up financially right now is because of the technology that put a lot of power into the hands the individual and took it from the hands of a very few powerful execs. That's always good.

TVP: Certain life experiences lead people to the arts; can you tell me about yours?

Poe: For me that's true in two ways. My connection to writing came from growing up in so many different places. My life in that way lacked continuity. It's not a bad thing that we moved so often. But it created in me early on a desire to remember where I came from; a desire to glue my identity together. We lived in Africa, Switzerland, Spain, France, England, New York, India, Utah... It was wonderful, but at the same time I was never part of any community outside my own family. I was an outsider observing, participating even, but then moving on. The result of this for me was the formation of an intense internal dialogue; I talked to myself a lot. You can't really talk to the kid in public school in Manhattan about the friend you had when you were four in Africa. I had to find places within myself to keep these very different cultural and emotional perspectives.

The other thing was that landed me in the arts was the divorce of my parents--which as I mentioned was my only solid community. When my family broke up I was sixteen and it was incredible turmoil. At that point I really could not go on living without writing songs and making music. It gave me the hope that I would figure something out. A lot of those early songs were like inventing the voice of the parent that I didn't have. The songs themselves would tell me what to do next. I was using the song to ask myself what I needed. It was like the answer was coming from outside myself. When I finished the song I would know what to do, even if the song sucked. It was like the voice of my mother telling me it was okay or telling me what I had to do.

There's no question. For everyone, it is those experiences that are confusing that make us go, "How do I make sense of this? How do I make somebody understand this and understand who I am?" Human beings have so much in common, simply in being alive and going through all the things that we do. And yet sometimes it is so complicated to invent a language that can express any truth about what it feels like to be alive at any given point. It is so hard to communicate in a way that two people can really understand, even if both speak English.

To bring it back to music, the first time I saw a girl in the front row- she was a thin girl roughly 16 years old- who knew all the words to the song "That Day." I got all choked up. Not because she might think that I'm great, but because I realized that I wasn't crazy. Someone else felt the same way and understood what it was that I was trying to clarify for myself when I wrote that song. To see someone else singing it back to me made me realize that I'm not alone. It's the same experience I had on the other side, when I'd be in the audience and see and one of my favorite artist's sing something that helped me understand something better.

Whenever I talked to people after shows that did know these songs, their experiences were not far from my own. This makes me feel a great sense of kinship with the world. We're all looking for the same things and there are certain struggles that we have in common. That's one of the great beauties of music to me--it's a very direct way to communicate with people. I was so happy to get to tour with *Haunted*. I so needed to go out and play the songs on that album. Sharing music with other people is often how I figure out what it really means. And sometimes that meaning evolves which is awesome.

TVP: Now the last question, because I'm running out of tape.

Poe: I have to go in a minute too, but this is so much fun.

TVP: Let's say you wake up in the middle of the night and the perfect song pops into your head. What would it sound like?

Poe: I have no idea. When it comes, I'll play it for you. I'll definitely wake up and run to the studio. That is a call that I absolutely answer every time.

Enter the Haggis: Kicks in a Kilt

July 2007
By T. Virgil Parker

The first time I went to an Enter the Haggis performance, a dark suspicion emerged. A new, essential
vitamin has been discovered and nobody told me. The band
had plenty of it. The audience, who was dancing wildly on
every available surface, had it too. Slowly, I began to absorb
it from the atmosphere, and can't remember much more.

To be sure, there is nothing new about Celtic Rock.
In certain circles- renaissance reinactors and Wiccans for
example- the appetite for it is voracious. Nobody but the
Haggis appears to be dragging it into the full light of day
for the enjoyment of the general population. This band sus-
tains energy levels that usually accompany underwear being
thrown onstage, playing notes that would have accompa-
nied a boar hunt. Unlike most Celtic Rock, the nuances
of the traditional music are maintained while they hook
up the jumper cables; maintained and occasionally turned
inside out.

The plot thickens with their new disk, *Soapbox Heroes*.

The reels and ballads are still there, but in an unprecedented act of bravado the band has thrown in a layer of Caribbean and Calypso on top. This is a sound that is both complex and danceable, two things that usually don't happen at the same time. There is even a hint of mainstream airplay lingering over some of the tracks. I can't help but be curious about how the lusty Celts who follow them around the planet are going to react to this new sound.

TVP: Your sound feels unpremeditated and spontaneous, but the places that you go require a lot of coordination.

Trever Lewington: A lot of our tunes come out of jamming live or jamming in rehearsal. We like to change things up, keep it new. We tour all year, so we need to keep it fresh for ourselves and for the audience as well. Mark, our bass player and James our drummer both majored in Jazz. The spirit of improvisation is strong in what we do.

TVP: In the studio, do you lay a lot of tracks, or do you just bang it out?

TL: In *Casualties of Retail* we had a lot more time to record. It was our first larger budget record. I won't say large, but for an independent band fairly large. We spent about two months recording it. We did a bed track that was strictly drums, and then we worked on top of that. We're more perfectionistic in the studio and we do take our time to get where we want. On the new record we were always looking over the producer's shoulder, trying to tweak out little imperfections.

TVP: That's one good thing about a small record label. With a big label, it would have been the producer looking over your shoulder.

TL: The producer we used, Neil Dorfsmann, is absolutely a producer's producer. He was totally hands-on, with a lot of good ideas to add. He's worked with Sir Paul McCartney, Sting, Dire Straits.

TVP: Your work is increasing in complexity but it still carries that sense of mirth. Is that hard to maintain?

TL: It is definitely dance music. At a lot of our shows and festivals people want to have a good time. We do veer off of that path and do things that are a little more progressive and a little darker. A lot of Celtic bands are mixing Punk in. We find it's a challenge to find upbeat grooves that aren't just simple Punk. That's where the elements of Caribbean music and Funk are coming into the mix. We don't feel comfortable repeating ourselves.

TVP: You recently toured Scotland. What is it like going to the place where this music was invented and handing them back a truly internationalized version of it?

TL: We met up with a large group of our American fans and as a result we didn't get a real sense of how we were received by the Scottish people. Our first record, a few years ago now, did well in Scotland. Last year we did some shows in Ireland and the response was great. We were touring with two busloads of our fans. We'd be playing a gig in Galway and the locals had never heard of us before, but there'd be 40 people singing along.

TVP: There's so often a political imperative to Celtic music. You seem to have been able to avoid that.

TL: *Soap Box Heroes* has a couple of songs that are politically minded. For the most part we avoid the Irish Rock themes anyway. We started out playing covers of traditional Irish tunes, which often have political undertones about the English. We try to avoid the blatantly political anti-

English stuff. The only thing on there that might be considered political is Gasoline. It has a bit of an environmental message.

TVP: Do you ever feel pressure to be politicized?

TL: It's fun music, upbeat and danceable. That's not what we're about. What we're about is bringing as many styles of music together as possible. The music is positive; we hope it brings people together.

TVP: You have fans that cross every imaginable demographic. It looks like a random sample of the population.

TL: We have three generations of fans in one family! I can't tell you why that is, except that traditionally Celtic music was enjoyed by all members of the community. In Ireland and Scotland pubs are more of a community thing, whereas in Canada and the US people go out to bars to get drunk and pick people up.

TVP: Yeah. In Europe, they bring the kids, and the dog.

TL: And, that's where the music was traditionally played, as well as is in the household. Another reason for the wide range of people is that we're bringing so many different styles into the mix. People want something unusual and different. That's what we give them.

TVP: Any other projects Haggis has been working on?

TL: Things have really picked up over the last few years. We did a PBS Special that really helped our standing. We signed on to a label called UFO last summer, and they're bringing out our new album now. We're touring so intensely right now, I've got one night at home the next month and a half.

TVP: And the last, most essential question, have you ever tasted Haggis?

TL: Yes, I have.

Going Green With the Lizardman

January 2008
By Jessica Hopsicker

What kind of creature walks like a man, communicates, thinks, and is capable of reasoning, but bears the appearance of anything but human? A forked tongue curls between both rows of teeth; those of the top row come to an unnatural point. Above each eye is a series of five bump-like horns forming a ridge upon his brow. His ears are long and the entire face and most of his body is the same ghastly green and comprised of scales. The bipedal Lovecraftian Frankenstein described is none other than Erik Sprague: The Lizardman.

What goes into a transformation from PHD candidate at the University at Albany and a Philosophy student at Hartwick, to a sideshow performer/comic reptilian humanoid? Approximately 700 hours worth of tattooing that covers his person from head to toe, including his lips, and even eyelids. The horns are the work of sub-dermal Teflon implants and the tongue bifurcation is courtesy of an argon laser.

What may have started as a youthful obsession is now

an occupation for the inked, pierced, and plugged lizard man. Through this work, he became one of the luminaries of the modification movement: a burgeoning group that ranges from tattoos to scrotal suspension. Clearly, a man of this stature would not make his living tucked away in the office of an ad agency. Nor will he ever have the choice to do so by today's standards. He wears his freak badge proudly, as it is tattooed across his chest. Performing side-show acts nationally and internationally, his repertoire contains cringe-worthy yet fascinating acts such as suspension, and even mental floss with live little green snakes.

As outlandish as his repertoire and reptilian outward appearance is it became clear over the course of the interview that having the courage to take his identity further than any other "self-respecting stand-up citizen," makes him more authentically human than most.

Jessica Hopsicker: How is everything?

Lizard Man: Everything is good so far.

JH: Given your desire to differentiate or individualize yourself, what observations have you had about mainstream culture?

LM: Wow. That is a hell of a lead off.

JH: Well, but I did ask how you were doing.

LM: Ha-ha, yeah, that's true, you did go with a "how you doing." Wow, you make me think. I would say that "individualize myself" is a bit of a misnomer. It's not so much that I seek to individualize myself as I seek to embrace my individuality. Individualizing yourself is redundant at best, possibly impossible. Just a non-notion in a way, because we're all individuals. That's just the nature of our being. It's one of those hard rules of existence. Nobody is not an individual. We are all different. So to individualize yourself, I guess the most charitable interpretation I could give that would be what I prefer to say, which is to embrace your individuality. To focus on the things that make you unique as opposed to downplaying them and playing up the things that make you more like other people. Rather than focusing on the things we have in common, I think it's better to focus on the things that are different, things that separate us out. Not separate us from each other, but separate us in terms of our own identity. As far as how that relates to having views on mainstream culture, I think the biggest one is that mainstream culture, particularly in the West in this particular period of history, tends to exemplify the opposite. It tends to encourage us to not embrace our individuality, to join in as sort of a cultural process. And I think we're better off and would be in a better state culturally if people took an educated self-interest view; if they looked at themselves as individuals rather than identify with groups. Like, you know, Republican, or straight or gay, or whatever group. If they just thought for themselves rather than saying, "Oh, well how can I join in?" Rather than look at what makes me, me.

JH: Would you recommend a bifurcated tongue?

LM: Absolutely - if the person has an interest in tongue bifurcation I can say that my experience and that of all those I have ever known has been overwhelmingly positive. Still, like anything else in life it isn't for necessarily everyone.

JH: Do you see the world differently because of such a transformation?

LM: This is what I do for my own benefit because I want to and what I do as an entertainer and what I do as an entertainer and an artist has gradually brought my outer appearance more in line with the way people thought of me. When I was younger and first starting off, I was a freak because of my ideas and my views on the world. No big surprise there. Now, I'm viewed as a freak for the way that I look and the things that I do on stage. What's gone on before was, "oh, he's such a normal looking boy. How weird that he has these odd geopolitical notions and strange ideas about personal freedom," and things like that. Now it's, "look at him, he's a freak, he's tattooed completely green and he's shoving a sword down his throat." I pull it out and then say something outlandish about nationalism and international politics and they go, "hey, he's a freak on the outside, and he's got freaky ideas." But I always had the freaky ideas. They came first.

JH: What do your parents think about your appearance? Does The Lizardman go over well in family gatherings?

LM: My parents are very supportive and happy with what I have done. Certainly it wasn't exactly what they might have expected but like any good parent they are happy that I am happy.

JH: What do you do for the human spotlight act?

LM: I work a small powerful light bulb on a wire into my nose and down the back of my throat into my mouth while holding a crystal ball in my teeth. This focuses the light into a tight beam that I sweep over crowd. I rarely perform it but it's an interesting novelty.

JH: Has anything life threatening ever happened during a performance? Infections, misplaced sword, severe blood loss?

LM: The whole show is life threatening. I have had plenty

of cuts, bruised ribs, burns and the like but the fact that I am alive means nothing too serious thus far - bad sideshow accidents tend to be fatal.

JH: Is gargantuan alcohol consumption part of the sideshow performance? I was watching one of your YouTube videos and you're just pounding beer after beer.

LM: I do drink. Alcohol is my drug of choice, which, given time and place and culture, is not surprising. It's an easy one to end up with. It isn't really necessary to the show, there's no necessary connection, and it's just something I like to do. I could have just as easily put up a video of me eating pizza. The pizza isn't necessary to anything, it just happens to be my favorite food. That particular video, if I'm thinking of the one you just referenced, is where I took a show and edited out all the times during the show where I took a drink and made one long video montage of them. It was kind of a curious thing. I had gone up to Minnesota for this weekend to do a show for a tattoo shop. It was a really good time but those guys love to drink. I mean I enjoy drinking. I have developed a reputation for drinking and long parties and stuff like that. These guys really drank, even in my estimation. So I thought it would be funny, especially with the number of drinks they brought me while I was performing, to figure out what percentage of my hour and twenty minute show that night ended up being drinking. By stringing them all together, I had the total video montage, and it turned out that somewhere around five percent of my performance amounted to raising a glass and taking a drink.

JH: It's like concerts in a way.

LM: Yeah, it is just weird, like you say; it's an interesting thing from the performer's view. It's always customary if you get a drink on stage, and I usually do, to toast the crowd, and then I start to think about how much time do I spend doing different things on stage.

What amount are jokes? What is the content of the show? Then to say, there are a lot of little actions, how do they figure in? From a stage psychology point of view, there are things like the way that George Burns used to smoke his cigar. People are really into the craft of performance, especially comedy and stand up. His cigar smoking was not just casual. Even though he might not have been thinking about it at the forefront of his mind, he was more thinking about the story and the joke he was telling, there was a method to his actions. The pauses, as opposed to just dropping a pause when you're speaking like you might as a stage actor with a soliloquy or something- which would seem really weird for comedian to do- but if he's stopping to take a drag on the cigar, he's giving you time to process the information he just gave you. He's finding something to do that's a motivated action that makes sense while the last laugh is trailing off or something like that. So there's a definite method, there's a craft. Some comedians use the drink that's in their hands, some people smoke cigarettes, other people have weird little quirks or stage pacing, stuff like that. There is a way to study it, look at it, and make it a legitimate part of the show. Or other times it's just hey, I was thirsty.

JH: Is there anything that you wouldn't do on stage? The list of things in your act is inclusive.

LM: Things I wouldn't do on stage? Take the list of things I wouldn't do in general and I wouldn't do them on stage, for starters. As for specifics, if its things that I would do but wouldn't do on stage, it comes down to anything I thought was boring or not entertaining. I don't know that there's a hard fast rule that I would say, "I would absolutely never do this on stage," unless it's something that I would absolutely never do in any circumstance. I don't think I would ever sit on stage and clip my toenails, but who knows, maybe some weird avant-garde performance opportunity will pop up and I'll think to myself, "Wow! This is would be a great opportunity to clip my toenails as a symbol of something!" I don't think that's going to happen though.

JH: Probably not.

LM: I could go back and do some student gallery work like the one I did while I was in art school. That's the only sort of place that clipping your toenails ever gets a response. If you're maybe a freshman or sophomore art student.

JH: What did you do for art school?

LM: I attended Hartwick College, which is not far off from Syracuse, where I will be for AM-JAM. It is in Oneonta, and I studied art and philosophy there. Then I went on to study Philosophy in a doctoral program at the University of Albany. One day I woke up and realized how much debt, I was going into taking out loans for graduate school and said, "This is insane, and it's just for a little piece of paper, so I'm going to leave and go tour and make money instead of take out loans."

JH: Exactly the thing I'm trying to do, really.

LM: Right. It's weird because there was this whole time in my life where I thought I was going to be a teacher, probably a professor, and I still sort of like that idea. I grew up with both of my parents working as teachers. I guess now, as I get older it's starting to even out the amount of time I spent as a student, professional academic, versus anything else in my life. So, it's starting to catch up to a fifty-fifty balance.

But I think it still holds the lion's share. So it's not that I don't have a great deal of respect for education and want people to be educated, but it's very easy for me to come up with reasons for people not to stay in school or not to go to school whatsoever. It's one of those things where I have the weird idea, which in this case I think is just a pragmatic idea, where people go, "you went to school, you're well educated. Tell them why they should go to school." I go, "Well, first of all, they have to make a financial consideration. What are they going to school for? Can they make more money by going and getting real world experience right now? People are not going to ask me to encourage their kids to go to school unless their kid is going to be like a nuclear physicist or something where there is no other option.

JH: Then you could come up with the money to pay for the degrees.

LM: Right. And it's one of those things where I'm like, "look, in the best of worlds, given the way our culture raises children, most people at eighteen, nineteen years old, when you go and start college, are in the no position to begin the serious learning that happens there. They don't have the focus. That's what college freshmen are, by and large, and I fit perfectly into this category, fairly obnoxious. Nothing really good comes out of your freshman year, other than the parties and the people and everything else. If you're eighteen, nineteen, you're strong, you're healthy. Go work construction. Go make an ass load of money. Get a little time in the real world, gain some maturity, come back, then your freshman year would actually be a valuable part of the four years rather than the one year long hangover that it takes for you to snap out of it and then start paying attention in class, hopefully, by your sophomore year. Some people never stop paying attention. If I look at the courses, I took my freshman year and the things I did, academically that was pretty much a wash. What that was about was getting a feel for my campus, and the campus politics, meeting other people, stuff like that, and laying a foundation. But I could have done all that in a month. That would have been one semester instead of a year, maybe a week even. Now in my life, I can walk into that situation and take much better advantage of it, because I'm a lot older and I have a lot better ideas on how to approach things like that. If I had taken two years off, I could have earned enough money to put away in the bank, have a bit nicer way of living, and eat less crappy food.

JH: And you probably would have ended up a completely different person.

LM: Yeah, potentially, or it might have accelerated. Because the idea of transforming my body, the very earliest seed of it, started my senior year of high school, which I split kind of in half going to high school and commuting to take courses at the nearby state college. If I had time to go out in the world and make sense of things and approach it so I got into a framework, like the art department and the philosophy department, the people that I was working with, I might have developed it a lot better and a lot quicker. So starting later could have meant finishing earlier, in respect of if you make better time. If you take that lag of, "okay I'm just the deranged park animal with some freedom, finally," things happen a lot quicker.

JH: What are you planning on doing next to your body?

LM: Currently, I am focused on finishing the tattooing.

JH: Is there anything else that we can look forward to?

LM: AM-JAM has always been interesting. I think it's been

my first show of the year for a number of years. Usually not a lot happens early in January, just coming off Christmas and all that. This means I usually have a lot of time at home, which is where many strange ideas occur to me. They get to ruminate and I talk myself into something being a good idea whether it is or not, so it is always kind of interesting. This year it will actually be my second show of the year because I'm flying to Istanbul to do a TV show earlier in that week. When I land, coming back from Turkey, I will be getting a rental car and driving to New York right off the plane, pretty much. But for the show specifically, it's going to be nine years for me, doing stuff at AM-JAM. In the beginning, I was just kind of showing up, hanging out, and just doing odd stuff. Laying on a bed of nails and really just laying there because nothing else is happening on the stage, or other times I was a living catwalk for a leather fashion show one year. I just lay on the bed of nails and all the models stood up on top of me to show off the outfit, stepped down, and moved around. Then as I developed more and more of a stage show, things developed. Some years it would just be, do a couple of stunts, other years it was to put together a performance set. Last year we did an interesting thing where I did the family friendly sideshow stuff in the afternoons and then really dirty adult comedy. I started doing more and more straight stand up with no stunts. This year I've got a similar idea going on. There's a version of my show I've been scripting and working on ever since coming out of Halloween where I spent the entire month of October in Vegas. So there's going to be some of those Vegas elements I want to bring up. And there's going to be some magic tricks and some other jokes that I'm going to put into the mix. So really, as usual, AM-JAM is going to be the test run for the 2008 additions, revisions, and subtractions from the show. So it's a chance to see from what

I've been doing, what the show was from last year, what this year's version is kind of going to be. So, the AM-JAM people are like the test audience and such. So I know I'll have a good time and I know they'll have a good time but by the same token I'll be able to tweak and look and say, "alright, how am I going to take this throughout the year and see where it ends up?"

JH: It would be the perfect time to do that, too.

LM: Mmhhmm.

JH: Yeah, have fun in Istanbul.

LM: I'm looking forward to it! It's really one of the places that I haven't gotten to go. I want to. But there are many places that I haven't gotten to go that I'm not actually trying to, but then they fall in your lap. I got the phone call and they were like, "would you consider coming to Istanbul, Turkey?" And I was like, "yeah, I was never planning on going there, but the opportunity arises, I'll go check it out!" It should be a nice throwback. I mean I've got my possible philosophy tie. So I can look around and be like, "ooh, Constantinople, Istanbul," old buildings and stuff like that fascinate me, so I'm looking forward to it.

JH: Your media coverage is quite a long list.

LM: Yeah. The list online is very poor documenting or at least very poor transcribing onto the websites and things like that for this past year or so. So there's actually even more than what's there. I've been having and continue to have a pretty good run. It's been about ten years now that I've been primarily focused on doing sideshow and working as an entertainer and more and more things keep coming along.

JH: Is there anything else that we haven't covered?

LM: I'm sure there are things that we haven't covered, but so long as we cover things that you want to cover, I think we'll be all right.

Maybe this next issue will be what it takes to get the Hartwick alumni to be proud of the freak alumnus. They focus on, what's his name, the guy that does Dilbert. He tends to be the entertainment reference that they make.

JH: Not you?

LM: I don't seem to get a lot of love from the alumni association at Hartwick. They still ask me for donations every year, but other than that I think there's a couple of professors that maybe make an aside mention of me in a class now and then, but other than that, I don't get a lot from them.

JH: Why do you think that is?

LM: I don't know. I think it might be partially lack of awareness. Given, sort of demographic-wise, it's a lot more likely that most of the students there, falling into the sixteen to thirty-five range which tends to be the core of my fans and people who are aware of me and what I do. The students there probably know who I am, but they don't necessarily know I'm an alumnus from the college they're attending. But I'm betting that a lot of the professors don't really follow their students' lives unless they hang around, so they probably don't even realize that the student they had became the Lizard Man, other than the one or two that I know do. You know, the people who work administration, they're going to be completely out of touch. Probably some of them have kids that are coming home from elementary school with the Ripley's book that I'm on the cover of, and their looking at it going, "Oh! What a weirdo!" I was their classmate. I would almost guarantee that there are a number of people I graduated with that would have no idea that they went school and graduated with the Lizard Man. Such is life.

Jimmy Herring: A Good Catch.

March 2008
By T. Virgil Parker

We've all got a certain amount of experience with watching things fade into inertia, like American Culture, or even dramatically blow up, like student loan debt. Rarely do we get to see something come together just right.

Widespread Panic is one of those rare bands that have managed to become a byword in some, eminently disturbed, circles, and relatively unknown to the general population. How they manage to stay under the mainstream radar for 23 years, and consistently be one of the top touring bands in the US is a mystery to me. But it has given them some advantages.

They can do whatever they want to their songs; and they do. Also they don't need to entertain the groundlings, the way mainstream entertainers do.

Now we can really see something coming together. Since the most reasonable, unassuming guitarist in the world just came out of the studio as a full member of the band, Free

Somehow is hitting the streets. This is a disk fraught with significance, subtlety, and a sledgehammer, as is most of this band's work. What is really new here is a kind of subliminity, notes that seem to lead to unseen places, and songs of unusual relevance for the amount of play they contain.

About the new member, Jimmy Herring. In my experience, guitar players who are capable of hitting every note on the fret board are usually incapable of not hitting every note on the fret board. Jimmy is one of those credentialed players who can tear the instrument out of the vestibule of hell and drag it to the gates of heaven. This is no doubt why he ended getting invitations from the Dead, the Allman Brothers, and so on. But he has the soul of a poet, and his poems are his notes. He's like the Yoda of the Stratocaster, serenely parceling out nuggets of wisdom, suddenly bouncing off every wall in the room, chopping it up. With Widespread Panic, he's doing all that and more.

T. Virgil Parker: Have you ever wondered if your agent or a friend has a classified ad somewhere that says, "Willing to learn thirty years of music in one day?"

Jimmy Herring: That's an exaggeration. I couldn't do thirty years of music in one day. I had two weeks and I still couldn't do it. It's completely crazy though, isn't it? It's a scary situation, but I enjoy the challenge of it.

TVP: Not just any band, either. What can be more idiosyncratic than The Dead, for example?

JH: That was pretty heavy, man, because of the magnitude of that gig and everything. And it's the same thing with Widespread Panic, it's like, these bands have stood the test of time, and you know The Dead of course going all the way back to the early or mid-sixties, I don't even know what to say. It was huge, there was a lot of pressure, but all the people in the band really made it easy because they kept telling you "we want you to be yourself, just be yourself. Don't worry about being like anyone else.

TVP: What do you think you picked up from working with that crew? You're probably gathering some really unbelievable bits of knowledge from being imbued with these vibes.

JH: Definitely. You find out that everybody is just people, and a lot of these people you have up on a pedestal because of your developmental years. I mean I'm getting old, I'm forty-six, but when I was a kid, I remember The Grateful Dead and seeing those guys in the magazines and hearing the records and stuff. Then you work with them and you find out man, these guys are so cool, they're just like everybody else. They just want to play music, and that's the bottom line.

TVP: If there was ever a band that was more eccentric than The Dead, it would have to be Widespread Panic.

JH: Yeah, and Widespread is like, I go way back with them. Those guys are my friends. I've known them since 1989 and when I was in Colonel Bruce's band, The Aquarium Rescue Unit, Widespread Panic gave us a leg up. They pulled us out of the shadow of this crappy little club we played in one night a week and they took us on tour with them. They were already pretty big in the south at the time, and they really believed in us. They were like, "you guys need to come out and play with us, more people need to hear you." So we got to be friends that way. They would always invite us to sit in them and we started doing these gigs where we would open for them and before we even came off stage, they would start playing. We'd do a segway. They would start playing while we were still up there, and then we would start walking off one at a time and then Panic would do their set.

TVP: That is too cool.

JH: That was cool, man. That was really cool.

TVP: So first they discovered you and now you discovered them.

JH: Well honestly, if it weren't for them, ARU may have never left Atlanta because Bruce Hampton wasn't looking to tour. He provided us with an outlet, a bunch of frustrated Atlanta musicians. That one night a week we played with him, no one was telling you, "You can't wear that, go get a tux." No one was telling you, "You can't play that, that's too weird." We were doing it purely out of love, and that was our favorite gig. It was the only gig during the week that any of us had that we felt like we could be ourselves. And Panic just stumbled into the club one night and they took us on the road with them, like you said, and then years later when they needed my help I was like, "I would do anything to help you guys!" They called me when Mikey was sick and I just was brought to my knees. We weren't best friends or anything, but were friends, and we definitely had a mutual respect for each other. And we could talk. We talked a lot, we just didn't see each all the time as we got older. After ARU broke up, I didn't see Mike much anymore, but he knew and I knew that we had a mutual respect for each other. When I found he was sick, I was like, "oh no."

TVP: That must have been rough.

JH: It was rough. And here's the worst part too. Well, not the worst part, the worst part obviously was that Mikey was sick, but one of the bad things about it also was that they needed me to come out and play while Mikey was still alive. And we could play together, and he could kind of pass the torch to me. That was the idea, and we could discuss philosophies about this music. I was really moved by them wanting me to come do that, but I couldn't because I was with Phil Lesh and Friends at the time. We had just completed a twenty-one day stretch of rehearsals in preparation for a forty city tour that was coming up two weeks later. When Panic called me about doing this it was during the two weeks off between the rehearsals and the tour, so I couldn't do it. I didn't know what to do. I was trying to figure out how I could do both, but there was just no way I could do both, and I couldn't just go to Phil after twenty days of rehearsal and say, "yeah, Phil, sorry, my friends need me and I'm not going to be able to make the tour." That would have totally screwed him. He was very compassionate about the whole situation. He was really cool about it. Panic, when they found out about my situation, was like, "Jimmy, don't worry about it. We know you can't do it. We know that if you could do it you'd be here, just don't worry about it." I saw them at Bonnaroo and that was the last time I saw Mike play that year. Then they got George, who I like a lot. I like George; I've known George a long time. I mean, I don't know him, but we've been acquainted for a really long time.

TVP: You're already becoming intrinsically part of their sound, and the new album has a different character than the earlier albums. There's almost Pink Floyd-like moments in there where- and this is unlike you as well- the notes are treated like precious jewels. There're other moments where it just rips. The way it comes together is like was meant to happen.

JH: Yeah, we were kind of talking about that, because we didn't really know if it was going to work or not. When people hear you play in one group, and I've been guilty of this too when I hear other people, I can remember hearing certain people play in a group that they're known to be in and then you think you know what they sound like, and you go, "yeah, okay, that's what they sound like." And then you hear them play with someone else and they sound completely different, and you're like, "wow! I didn't know that guy could play like that! That's so different from what I thought he was!" So the point being, with me playing them, I didn't know if it was going to work or not as far as they were concerned. I didn't know if they were going to be happy with it. I love songs and a lot of people know that because they've heard me play with ARU where songs are not really the focal point of our gig, or Project Z where there are no songs and the whole point of the gig is that you're just improvising on the seat of your pants through the entire gig. But I've always loved songs, and Panic is a song band. It's funny because when I was talking to Dave, he was like, "man, we just need to get the jams going again." And I was like, "well shit, Dave, that's the easy part." The jams are the easy part, that's just the part that comes natural to me. The hard part for me was learning twenty years worth of songs. That's the hard part. We have an instant chemistry playing with each other as far as that goes, so it's just a matter of, "okay, can I learn all these tunes? Can I learn all of Mikey's signature parts? And can I try to get the same nuance he got on Surprise Valley or whatever. I don't want to copy Mike, but I don't think it would be fair to anyone to come into a band that he was in for twenty years or more and not play some of his signature licks, and try to get some type of inflection that he got on them. That's the sound of that group, so to me, that's where it starts. Starting right there with Mike Houser and listening to him and trying to at least start from the place that he was coming from.

TVP: The fans are like a cult, too, so you're walking a very thin line there.

JH: Yeah. If you copy him, then you're just copying someone. But if you don't tip your hat and don't even pay attention to what came before you, then you're ignoring what the band really is. So it is a fine line. So I agree with you.

TVP: Now you're writing with the band. What is it like to write through the focus of such a unique temperament?

TVP: It's really cool because those guys, every one of them writes, every one of them. Before we even went in the studio, I heard some of their ideas. I played on a demo of Todd's, because Todd called me up and he was doing a demo over at a local studio in Athens and he asked Dave and I to come over and play bass and guitar on it because he wanted to present it to the rest of the band, but he wanted to make it sound a little more complete than just doing what wanted to do with it. Todd plays guitar too, so Todd laid down this beautiful rhythm track on three songs, and then I came over, and Dave came over, and we put bass and guitar on those tracks. And they were good, they were really good songs. He was singing them, he sounds great. He wrote the lyrics and the music and we just added our parts to it. So we got to hear some of his stuff before we even recorded any of it for the record. And then Jo Jo's always writing, JB's always writing, JB's always got something going on. Dave has got a real thing going with Jerry Joeseph where they write songs together. I had about four songs before I started playing with Panic, but a couple of them seemed like they would be in the right kingdom for this band. So the way they do it is, they throw it in a big melting pot. But by the time everybody is done with it, it's not the same song anymore. I might have had what I thought was a song, and I bring it in to them, by the time they're done with it, it's got added section to it, maybe the time signature changed from 5:4 to 6:4, maybe there's a bridge in it that wasn't originally there, everybody brings in something big and different that wasn't in the original picture. And it's the same when they bring in tunes; they want your input on it. JB will bring in a tune and go, "hey man, here's this tune, can you put in a line right here, or can you skirt around my vocal?" Like on that song, Already Fried, I love that song. That song is like the only one on the album that doesn't have a whole lot of production it, you know? It's like the bare-bones, stripped down song on the album. It doesn't have any horns or any strings on it, which I love, I love the horns and strings, but I kind of like that one song. The absence of it makes that one song stand out to me. JB has the vocals and he goes, "can you play alongside?" So I came up with those lines to play alongside him and stuff like that. It's really fun writing with him. It's great.

TVP: I have found websites where there'll be a clip of you playing for like thirty seconds and then several pages of jazz musicians arguing about what mode you're playing in.

JH: Are you kidding me?

TVP: I am not kidding. YouTube yourself.

JH: That is hilarious!

TVP: Do you think Berklee School of Music and GIT, sort of prepped you in a way that isn't really traditional for just plain old rock?

JH: No, not really, but I would have to say that those schools are great. School is what you make of it, I've always said that, you can go to school anywhere, but Berklee and GIT are fine schools. I only went for a summer session but I ended up going for a year to GIT, and one of the great things about it is that you meet so many other people who are into music like you are. I learned so much about chord formulas and theory and other stuff that I can still draw from. But as far as the modality thing that you were just referring to, I think that's probably more the influence of Bruce Hampton than anything. Bruce doesn't tell you what to play, but he puts you in a situation where he gives you the opportunity to fail. You get in a position where they don't want to hear what you know; they want to hear something you've never played. That was the whole thing about ARU. You can sit there and play things that you played last night and you can play it flawlessly and nobody cares. They're like, "I've heard you play that, it's bullshit. Let's hear what you don't know. Let go of all that crap and just play." And that's what Bruce affords you the place to do. He gives you a place to do that. So tell those people who were arguing about what mode I was playing in, tell them it was the Hamptonian mode.

TVP: ARU was one of those bands that became legendary after it broke up.

JH: Yeah, that's funny. We couldn't make a living playing it, but later! That's what it's supposed to be I guess. I think that's great. I don't have any problem with that. We all knew that it was about the music and it was never going to a money thing.

TVP: What is this tour going to look like?

JH: It starts in early April. I'm not even sure how long it's goes. We'll be rehearsing several days near the end of March and relearning a lot of the music that's on the new album and we'll be playing it live. I'm going to be busy because a lot of that stuff came together while it was in the studio, so I might have to sit with that music for a while and remember how to play it.

TVP: And you're recording now?

JH: Yeah, I'm recording now, but it's a different project. Just some jazzier stuff that I was writing and I finally, for the first time in my life, decided to do my own record. It's tough, there's a lot of stuff going on, but I'm excited about it. There's not going to be any sort of news release, there's no record company or big global distribution or anything. There's no album release party and there's not gigs supporting it or anything like that.

TVP: It is just spooky how well you fit into Widespread Panic, I must say.

JH: Thank you very much man, I appreciate it. They're just old friends, you know? Old friends and it feels good, just like an old pair of jeans.

Joan Osborne: How Sweet It Is.

November 2002
By T. V. Parker

A ny fan of the bluesy end of Rock can have nothing
but awe for the talents of Joan Osborne. Her first
recording effort yielded no less than eight Grammy nomi-
nations - a testament to the power of her songwriting. Her
passionate vocal performances exhibit a range of expression
and texture for which it is hard to find comparison.

Her first two albums, *Relish*, and *Righteous Love* combine
the sensuous ear candy of her voice with themes both mystical and mundane, but always surging into the archetypal
and profound. The depth of content, and emotional intensity of her work has left her with a sizeable fan base hun-
gering for similar headphone ammo. So it wasn't without
a certain amount of courage that she dove into a different
project for her third CD.

How Sweet It Is is Joan's re-imagining of Soul classics
from the 60's and 70's. Anyone expecting to find her cus-
tomarily powerful performances will find intensity of an
altogether different sort.

Words like "sleek" and "smooth" do not do justice to the tone of these tracks. Pared down and toned down, there is plenty of room for the subtle, intricate vocal performance Joan delivers, making *How Sweet It Is* a uniquely pleasant listen.

I spoke with Joan about her that CD and her career in general.

Tim Parker: There is very high regard and much anticipation for your original music. What led you to embark upon a compilation of Soul greats for your latest project?

Joan Osborne: I definitely am writing music and will be putting something out hopefully next year. But there was something about doing this Soul covers record that I thought was really relevant to what's happening in the world right now. It takes a while to digest the events of the last year enough to write songs about it, unless you're someone like Bruce Springsteen. I didn't feel like I could sit down and write a whole album's worth of material about the past year and everything that's happened with the events of 9-11. Yet I really wanted to do something that was topical and had some relevance. I wanted my music to be part of -in whatever small way- people's efforts to come to terms with it, or to deal with it. I thought this would be a really great way to do it in a timely fashion.

Many of these songs that were written thirty years ago are very relevant to what's happening right now. Some of them have political content. Some of them just have that amazing soulfulness and joyfulness of great Soul music, expressing to each other how much we mean to each other. I hear people all around me talking about that and searching for ways to do that, looking for ways to make sure the people who are important to them know they're important. So this was the kind of music I was drawn to do.

TVP: A social imperative is often a component to your music. Do you think that's something that just hasn't been done enough in the last, say 25 years?

JO: I don't know that it hasn't been done much. I think that the time period that I drew a lot of these songs from, the late 60's and early 70's, was a time when music that had social consciousness was on the radio and were Top 40 hit songs. A song like "War" by Edmund Star, just a basic, flat-out anti-war song. It was a number one pop song. That kind of song hasn't received attention in recent years. If I wanted to guess why, I'd say it's less a matter of what the audience wants to hear, and more a matter of what the increasingly corporate music business has felt would be more profitable for them. Political music is being made; it's just harder for audiences to find it.

TVP: You have said that you listened to a lot of Hip Hop while you were getting ready to do the Soul project, and I was trying to figure out how they hooked in together. Is it the political aspect of Hip Hop that drew you to explore that medium?

JO: It was more of a technical consideration for me. I was interested in the minimal production and the minimal sound of a lot of the modern R & B and Hip Hop records and artists like Mary J. Blodge. A lot of her sound is just a beat and a very simple track, and her voice. It works very well because when you have a singer of her gifts you really don't need much more than that. I was interested in that as a way to take these songs and put them in a more modern context so that they'd be different from their original versions.

TVP: This CD covers material that was already very powerful in its own right. Was it hard for you to keep things your own way when you were interpreting this work?

JO: The hardest part was just to get around the fear of taking on this material, which was done originally in an incredibly powerful way. I was nervous that people would assume that I was trying to out do some of these great soul artists, and that really wasn't the case at all. It is pretty much impossible to out do Aretha Franklin singing an Aretha Franklin song, or Otis Redding or any of these people. These are my heroes. I'm not trying to go them one better. I believe that the material deserves to be seen in a little bit of a different light so that audiences could hear them in a different way and appreciate the song all over again. That was part of the challenge- to take these songs and find a way to do them in a way that was respectful of the songs themselves without imitating the earlier versions. Myself and the producer John Leventhal, worked very hard to bring something new to the productions. The minimalist Hip Hop approach was one of the ways we got to that point. I did a lot of work in my home studio before we went to the studio in New York to figure out where the song and my voice intersected in a way that was somehow compelling, interesting, authentic. The process was to strip it down and start out with my voice and a beat, or my voice and a guitar and find a place where the song and my voice were interacting in a special way.

TVP: Some of those tracks ended up with strong backing. That was part of the re-constructing process after you brought it down to its bare elements?

JO: Once we figured out what the bones were, we could go in and add things that were needed, but all the while making sure that we didn't put too much in there. That's a part of the process when you're making a record. You get all these ideas and you add all these different tracks and guitars and this and that and everything else on top of it. You have to be very vigilant that you don't put things in there

333

just for the sake of putting them in there. So that was part of the process: coming up with these ideas, adding them, and editing what we had done to make sure that it was only the necessary bits that remain.

TVP: Do you think that your status as being an independent recorder helped you do what you wanted to do right now?

JO: It helped me to make this record quickly and to get something out in this world relatively quickly. Some of the situations that I was in before with major labels were difficult in that I would make music and turning into the label and they would send me back to the drawing board over and over again. That became very frustrating, so I was happy to just make the record and say "OK, the record is done," and have it come out just a few months later.

TVP: I think it was the authenticity of your album "Relish" that made it such a smash hit.

JO: That's what I strive for. It is very easy to imitate your heroes when you're first learning. Then you need to get to a place where you're doing something original and uniquely your own- that has that authenticity to it. That's what I really strive to do. I'm glad that you're hearing that in the music. Thank you for saying that.

TVP: It strikes me that your record label decided that they wanted less authenticity.

JO: It's certainly not that cut and dry. No one came to the studio and said "I want you to do X, Y and Z, and we want you to do a song just like "One of Us." It was a case of me wanting to do something interesting for myself: add some of the influences that I had been learning about, in particular Qawwali music, to what I was doing, and work with people that I was excited about working with. I think that they just wanted a bunch of pop hit songs. I don't know what they were looking for, but it happened that I didn't give them what they wanted. That was a very frustrating time. I don't think that you have to be with an independent label to be able to follow your vision musically or that Indy labels make the best music or that major labels make the best music. I think it doesn't really matter. It's whatever situation works best for the individual. I'm happy that I'm in a situation where I have more autonomy right now.

[Qawwali is the traditional form of Islamic song found in India and Pakistan. A Qawwal is one who sings Qawwali, or the dictums of the prophets and praises of God. Though probably much older, Qawwali musical techniques have been described for over 1000 years as a means of bringing about enlightenment. Nusrat Fatah Aki Khan was considered the foremost practitioner of the form.]

TVP: I have to ask you what it was like to work with Nusrat Fatah Aki Khan

JO: He was wonderful. He was really generous. He comes from a tradition that can be very circumscribed, and closed to outsiders, in particular women. He was one of the people in Qawwali music who was very much open to working with other collaborators and very much open to bringing the music to new audiences through those collaborations and through opening up the channels to work with other artists. He was very generous in that way.

He had planned to take me on as a student and we had done a few lessons together when he had to go back to Pakistan and ended up passing away during that time. I feel that I was very lucky to spend the time with him that I did. Part of me wishes that I had met him years earlier, that

I could have become one of his students and learned a lot more from him.

TVP: He selected you to take part in his exercises.

JO: I made it no secret that I was a fan of his and that I wanted to learn about Qawwali music and I think his manager heard me saying this in an interview and picked up on that and told Nusrat about it. So when I finally did meet him for the first time, we were doing a televised special for VH1 and I finally met him back stage. He invited me into the dressing room and said "So you are the one who wanted to sing Qawwali " and he gave me a little sort of test. He said, "Why don't you sing this for me," and he played a melody on the harmonium, so I did. He played me another one and I repeated it. This went on for a few minutes and finally he stopped playing and looked around at the other men in his group and said "Oh yes, we can teach you!" I was so excited at that moment to have passed the audition or whatever it was.

TVP: The other significant performer beside yourself who worked with Nusrat was Jeff Buckley. [*Grace*, Sony Records, 1994]

JO: He was really special.

TVP: Your and Jeff's music share a profoundly expressive, emotive quality. I would guess that's what drew Nusrat to you.

JO: Personally I think that's the kind of thing that music is here for on Earth, to allow people to step outside that sort of day-to-day consciousness or reality or dealing with business, or whatever, and get to a state where you're more aware of yourself as a spiritual being and you're more aware of expressing your emotions and your spirituality. I feel that that's music's mission in the world, at least one of the things that it can do. So I've always been drawn to that kind of music.

Whenever I saw Jeff I could always see that this was obviously part of his approach as well. He obviously felt that kind of freedom and release when he was making his music. Then you would meet him and he was always this shy, quiet kind of person. I think music enabled him to get to places that he wasn't able to get to in his day-to-day life, which is what I think it does for everyone who loves music.

TVP: This is a good time to ask you a question that I've been dying to ask you. How did it feel to be covered by Dr. Evil and Mini Me in *The Spy Who Shagged Me?*

JO: I'm sure they sent me some kind of a thing to sign to let them use "One of Us" but I had completely forgotten. A year later when the movie came out a guy I was dating at the time said "Let's go see a movie." We went and sat in the theatre and we got there late so we had to sit right in the front row. So of course the screen was looming hugely above our heads. And the minute Dr. Evil started singing that song I was so embarrassed I just wanted the floor to open and swallow me up. [Laughter] It was definitely a bizarre moment.

TVP: Can you tell me a little about your time at N.Y.U. when you first started performing?

JO: I'd actually stopped taking classes and was working a couple different jobs to save some money to go back to school and finish my degree. I was putting myself through school, and NYU was expensive, and living in New York is expensive and film is very expensive, so it was always a real struggle for me financially to keep it together. So I was in a period where I had stopped taking classes for a semester. I was working a bunch of jobs and trying to save money for that. That's when I discovered this whole scene that was going on in New York City at the time, people doing Roots music and Blues music. It was purely by accident. I didn't think I was going to do music for a living or anything. I was still very focused on studying film.

But a friend of mine in my apartment complex said "Hey lets go down to this club on the corner and get a beer." So I went and this place was a Blues bar. It was very late and the band had torn down but there was this piano player there who was playing for himself or the few people that were still there. My friend dared me to go up and sing a song. I have no idea why, he had never heard me sing. He was just trying to embarrass me or something, and I said "Ok, I will." I went over and sang "God Bless the Child," a Billie Holiday song and when it was done the piano player said "Hey, that was pretty good. You should come back to our Open Mic Night that we have every Tuesday night." I started doing that. This place was right around the corner from where I lived.

There was something about the act of singing that really turned my head around. I think there was something about the immediacy of it that was in contrast to the very lengthy process of making a film. Film is much more of an intellectual pursuit, and music, for me, is more of an instinctive thing. There was something about it that captured my imagination, and I kept coming back. I found out about other places that had Open Mic nights and I went to those places. I started meeting musicians and putting together my own band out of people I met. And after a while I actually started playing gigs in some of these little clubs. It slowly grew and grew to the point where I was doing five or six nights a week. I was able to quit my day job. At that point it was "Do I go back to school and forget about this, or continue on with this thing that seems to have a life of its own?" I chose to follow it.

TVP: It's almost like the universe gave you a little nudge in the direction of music.

JO: Yeah, I've thought about it many times, the hand of fate or whatever. I was on a completely different path and it was totally by accident that I ended up doing music.

TVP: When you played with Bob Dylan, did he have anything to say about "The Man in the Long Black Coat" from your album *Relish*?

JO: He didn't say anything to me about covering his song at all, but his manager was very complimentary and had told me several times "You know, Bob really likes the way you did that song." But Bob never said anything, so I don't know if it's true or not.

TVP: It's an astonishing song, the way you performed it.

JO: I love doing that song, and I loved the moment of doing it, when we were on the Relish tour. There were a lot of young girls in the audience, and for me the song was very much about this dangerous person who comes into a girl's life and sweeps her away and I could tell there was something that really struck a chord to these girls who were like 14, 15 and 16. They always reacted very strongly to that song, and for me that was a wonderful thing. These are girls who will never go see a Bob Dylan concert, yet they're able to appreciate this song in a way that's in a completely different context and with a different reading than the one the original writer gave to it. That's just one of the wonderful things about music. Someone can write a song and perform it, and have it mean something very wonderful and very specific to them. Yet, another artist can come along, take the song, do something different with it, and magnify the impact of the song.

TVP: What kind of advice would you like to impart to young musicians trying to break into the industry?

JO: My first piece of advice would be to do it because you love to do it and because you enjoy doing it even at the smallest level, playing for free or for only a handful of people. If you can love doing that then that's the best reason to do it, for the love of music. It is such hard work and you have to dedicate yourself to it completely. You end up spending many, many months away from home, away from your family.

It's not the most stable occupation in the world, so if you're doing it for the money, you're definitely in the wrong business. Do it for the love of it. You can write songs if you're a songwriter and spend as much time as you can writing the best songs you can, because that's where you live or die, by your material.

TVP: In conclusion, do you have anything you want to say in general?

JO: I really wanted to make a record that was very relevant and very topical with what people are dealing with right now, and that's why I chose the songs that I chose, the ones that are political and the ones that are talking about brotherhood, peace. These are the things that I hear people around me talking about all the time, the things I think about, the things you see when you turn on your TV. I really wanted to make a record that could be part of this moment.

Ryan Montbleau:
The Montbleau Mystique

May 2007
By T. Virgil Parker

When a band manages to keep a low profile it is usually for a good reason; such as: They suck.

Meanwhile, The Ryan Montbleau Band is quietly popping out here and there, making people see God, packing up and sneaking down the dusty trail. It is just possible that they don't want to be *too* famous. Another reason this band is not at the tip of every tongue in the world is very different.

The fans want to keep The Ryan Montbleau Band to themselves, in short to be theirs, and nobody else's.

I can't deny feeling this way myself. There is an intensely personal relationship between this music and the people who listen to it; this music is about me!

I have thought that the government might be covering up Ryan's uncommon skill for security reasons: Ryan's voice is so compelling that if he sang about tennis shoes you'd wonder why you were in line with a box under your arm. Imagine what that would do to the economy. Fortunately, his lyrics transcend petty consumerism. In fact, the unearthly combination of the personal and the archetypal in this body of work is what drives the bonding experience.

TVP: There's an authenticity in you work that runs deep, but it must have taken a good deal of crafting to get it there.

RM: I didn't really plan on doing this. I slowly started. I played guitar when I was little, and I played a bunch in college and finally started singing. I was writing the whole time and it just naturally came together. Since then it has all been a slow build, I just throw it out there and see what happens. I hope that translates into authenticity. We've been playing so much as a band-two hundred gigs a year-that allows you to get deeper and deeper into the music. You start to hear things that you never heard before. We've still got a long way to go.

TVP: That's an unbelievable onslaught of touring. Can you write in the middle of that, or do you need a break from touring to write?

RM: I need a break but I don't get one. I'm looking out a van window right now. I wish we had more time home, but it is all part of the process. We bring it out for the people as much as we can. That's fine. I'm starting to get a little tired, but we roll with it. I have to write on the road.

TVP: It is also the perfect testing ground for ideas, I'm guessing.

RM: Yeah.

TVP: Do you get a feel for the response while you're rolling out the new material?

RM: You can tell, especially over the years, what the people like. The road actually is a pretty good place to try out new material. I still want to write more story songs and songs about the rest of the world. A lot of my stuff comes from introspection.

TVP: You majored in English?

RM: Yeah.

TVP: There's a narrative strand through all of your music. Do you start with a music idea, or a story idea?

RM: More often than not a musical idea. It usually starts on the guitar. I can already hear a melody over it. I start to sketch out words. Sometimes I'll get a musical idea that already comes with the words. I'll have to start jotting it down. I rarely try to fit something that's already written to music. I try to write something fresh for music that's already there. I'm just starting to dig into my old journals and look for pieces I like, and try to fit those into my music. I did that more on the record we're recording now.

TVP: You spontaneously discovered that you have a voice, but everyone seems convinced your voice was trained extensively. The level of complexity of the vocal treatment is unusual who hasn't spent years behind the baton.

RM: I sort of have been singing in my head, since I was little. I never let it out and was never sure that I could. It was always kicking around in there. In middle school I sang in front of a friend once and he told me I was no good. For years I didn't sing after that. I guess now that he was a little concerned that I could sing better than he could. By the time I was in college I started singing to myself in the car. Of course it wasn't like it is now. I try to work on my voice and figure out what my limitations are. I feel like I need lessons now. I'm happy that I can sing at all.

TVP: The things that you say are your influences don't resemble your music at all.

RM: Like who?

TVP: You listen to a lot of heavy music, metal. Your work is in a category all its own.

RM: There're so many influences in there, especially with the band as a whole. We never set out to emulate anything. We embrace each tune as it comes.

TVP: I notice that the sun is used as an image in a lot of your songs. It is like a leitmotif throughout your album.

RM: I didn't do that intentionally across all the tracks. It just kept popping in there on its own. I like to evoke as many emotions as I can in the music. To me the sun is such a strong symbol. More than a symbol, it gives you a certain feeling. I think I've used it too much. I didn't realize it until after the fact. Now I won't even do it. I get tempted to say sunshine, and I say something else. On this last album I wanted to say sunshine and I changed it to sunlight. A lot of my favorite music makes me think of sunlight. I find myself wanting to emulate that.

TVP: When you look at a piece of poetry and see solar imagery in a systematic way you start digging at thematic elements. I found myself digging into your lyrics that way. You must have taken your study of literature seriously.

RM: I definitely take the lyrics seriously. I play guitar and I sing, and the third part is the words. They're all equal. I could play and sing amazingly, but if the words were meaningless, the whole thing would be meaningless.

TVP: There's a lot of that out there.

RM: There's too much of that out there. I don't think there's a lot of strong voices out there, saying something. I'm really just trying to look into myself and be as honest as I can. Hopefully that is perceived as true.

I was a chemical engineer, then business school, then I was majoring in English for my last two years, reading all the time. I'm still not as well read as I'd like to be. I studied poetry, which changed everything for me. That stuff is indispensable to what I do.

TVP: Usually with this much devotion from fans a band becomes huger than huge. Are you making an effort to prevent things from getting too big?

RM: I'm not intentionally keeping it small. I do want more and more people to listen. We have made an effort to keep it grass roots, one room at a time, independent, all on our own. I'm not against somebody coming in and helping us, but I've yet to see that the way I want it. I'd like help doing it the way we're doing it now. We've done a slow build for years, and that's how we've done it.

TVP: We are in a time when people crave content; it has been largely unanswered need.

RM: Not to many years ago I used to think that all my songs belong on the radio. I see now that a lot of my stuff doesn't fit into that format, a lot of it isn't that easily grabable.

TVP: I'm not sure that you want it to be. You have the right kind of momentum. I've heard promoters rave about you. That doesn't happen.

RM: I feel very lucky. We just try to be genuine with the music and with the people. The entire band, I'm just proud of the way we come into a town and treat people with respect. And it comes back to you.

TVP: You're doing some festivals in our neck of the woods this summer. How's that environment for playing?

RM: Festivals are my favorite; they're just so much fun. Hanging out at them is so much fun too. They can be some of the best experiences ever. This summer is the festival season I've been waiting for, for around five years. We're in Gathering of the Vibes, moe.down, Sterling Stage.

Playing for those crowds is the coolest thing in the world, but makes me think we should be doing crazy improvisational stuff, though our strength is really in songs. That scene is really where my heart is. My head is more in the folk thing and the singer-songwriter thing. The real core of that scene is people who are open to new things.

TVP: The real connoisseurs of music are at the festivals these days.

RM: If you can get those people going, you're doing something right. What's the alternative, the radio?

Billy Howerdell: Chiaroscuro

January 2004
By T. Virgil Parker

We forget that Modern Rock is an art form only because it makes so few demands. A Perfect Circle's most recent offering is an authentic workout. You can try to figure out where Thirteenth Step is going, only to be diverted by the pervading sense of edging toward the unknowable. This is music that forces you to become a passenger on an excursion through radiant landscapes strewn with the wreckage of contemporary existence.

It is more than a little ironic that the band looks suspiciously like the front row at the MTV Awards. Tool front man Maynard James Keenan is covering the vocals, and the lineup includes veterans of Smashing Pumpkins and Marilyn Manson. The fountain of inspiration in this band, however, flows from someone you might have found backstage wrapping up a cord for one of these luminaries: Billy Howerdell. Prior to his emergence into the limelight Billy was a guitar technician Nine Inch Nails, Tool, and Smashing Pumpkins.

There is an astonishingly imaginative range of expression coming from his guitar. He has the astounding gift of being crunchy in a way that can only be described as evocative. This is a sound that lends itself to interpretation.

Timothy Parker: A Perfect Circle started with its own mythology. You're in a back room in Tool's Studio laying some tracks and Maynard comes up to you and asks if he can sing on them. You say "Na" but he gradually wins you over and the next thing you know you're an international rock star. Is that how it actually happened?

Billy Howerdell: Not exactly. Maynard and I had met years earlier. We wound up bumping into each other again in Los Angeles and ended up roommates.

I kind of went and did a temporary guitar tech gig for Tool. They were all friends of mine. I wasn't really interested in teck-ing anymore; I just did it to help them out. Part of the deal was that I got to set up my studio in the back room and I was just working up some tracks. He actually heard them a little later and said that he wanted to sing on them. I didn't put much weight to his words because he was just about to launch a Tool album and tour. I just kept doing my own thing; I didn't really think much of it. I took it more seriously when he started putting vocal ideas down on songs, and two years later it started to come into reality.

TVP: It's very interesting that his voice found your work- they come together so naturally. Was a lot of the work on the first album put together prior to his emergence into the project?

B.H.: Around 70% of the blueprints were done before he came onboard.

TVP: Do you find yourself writing a little differently now that you have an idea of the makeup of the project?

BH: I don't write differently, I just decide what to show these guys. I filter what I present to them, or just know that some things will work for this band, and not others. There are some other tracks that I know aren't appropriate for this band that I'm going to do something else with.

TVP: Is there a sense now when you're writing, that you're writing for a full stadium, as supposed to writing for yourself?

BH: No. In a way the music writes itself. You can't really think about it that much.

TVP: Art Rock is usually a term for a band with fifteen fans. Your work is probably the first popular music since the seventies that has earned that title. What goes into the success of music that has more content, more depth than people are usually willing to accept in Rock and Roll?

BH: I don't know, I'm not good at the Biz part- what sells and what doesn't. Things surprise me all the time. I hear a demo and I think "This is going to be the biggest thing in the world," or "This is never going to work" and it's never right. For me personally, I'm putting my honest heart into it and I know everyone else in the band is as well and people are picking up on it. Hopefully that's what people are drawn to.

There are a lot of other factors that got us off the ground. Maynard had a built-in audience with Tool, for example. Getting on the Nine Inch Nails arena tour right out of the box was good. David Finch is producing our video. Nancy Berry at Virgin Records taking us under her wing certainly was one of the biggest things. Doing music we're really proud of helped us put it all together. The timing was right.

TVP: There seems to be a sincere effort to make your music sound accessible, even though the work itself is relatively arcane.

BH: It isn't intended just to be accessible. The music that I've been inspired by is a factor. I think that musicians are the product of what they've been inspired by. If you took all the bands I've ever liked and put them in a room, that's what comes out of me. And I guess that those bands are just accessible.

TVP: What do you consider your influences?

BH: The Cure, early on, when I was a kid, it was Blue Oyster Cult, Elvis Costello. During the first record it was Fiona Apple, OK Computer by Radiohead was big. This time out I think Interpol had a lot of influence on me and White Stripes' 'White Blood Cells", Cat Power. Mazy Star as far as overall atmosphere.

TVP: The only thing I can think of that is remotely comparable in smoothness to A Perfect Circle is something like *Gish*- very early Smashing Pumpkins. They shared the trance-like quality, but minus the crunch.

BH: I can't tell you where it comes from, it just comes out.

TVP: Does anything you write strike you as coming completely from nowhere?

BH: Yeah, and I get scared. I'm like "Am I accidentally ripping off some song unconsciously?"

TVP: With so many aspects of your life having changed, does your inspiration change?

BH: No. But with so little time, it is hard to find time for the pure enjoyment of music. I don't give myself a lot of time to simply listen to music. If I get spare time it's usually to watch a movie or listen to a book on tape.

TVP: Did you ever suspect that the music you make would find such a huge mainstream audience?

BH: I'd hoped, but I never thought that it would get to this level. I'm a realist when it comes to the music industry just because I grew up working behind the scenes. I know how hard it is. It's even harder now than it was in the early nineties when I started.

I feel blessed and lucky to have the success that we've found.

Its great and I think it's a really difficult time to be successful if you judge it by records sold or attendance at concerts.

TVP: I think a lot of people have been getting signed for the wrong reasons. There are so few bands available for a young person to become passionate about that it leads to lukewarm sales and so on.

BH: I agree. I'd be very surprised if many of the bands around today will be around for more than five years.

TVP: Is it challenging to work with an avatar like Maynard?

BH: It's what I know. From working with a lot of talented and successful performers, more specifically, front men when I was a tech. I would always get hired for dealing with the "star". They've all got something special and they've all got a lot of baggage. You can look at it two ways. You can be with someone who is easier to get along with and with less talent, or someone who is slightly schizophrenic and has something interesting to say. Not to say that these people are totally insane, but people ask me if they're like regular guys and I have to say no. You can't be. These people are where they are because of what they were before; there was something that drove them to be out there in front. I'm not going to sugar-coat it or condemn it. But it has to be noted that these people are different.

TVP: There's a mindset where it is more important to create, express, than anything else.

BH: Yes.

TVP: A Perfect Circle's music sounds very much like it was built around ideas, themes. It doesn't feel like you got together to bang out songs and then tacked the ideas on.

BH: In a lot of ways this music feels ghostwritten to me. I guess its how people explain going into hypnosis. You're not unconscious; you're just not totally there. I feel that way when I'm writing music. I only know that from getting interrupted in the studio. I'll be sitting in front of the screen and playing, and my girlfriend would walk into the room and stand there staring at me. She would swear that I would see her and I don't. As soon as you snap out of it, it takes a while to get back into it. It's like sex from the female perspective; you have to be in the mood for it to get the right result. That's the way I see getting in the mood to write music.

TVP: Your music specifically has a trance inducing quality.

BH: I'm not sure about that.

TVP: I don't mean that people are running off to join the Moonies, but you go to a Godsmack concert and everyone is trying to jump out of their skin. But this is something you only see at an APC concert: people are receptive. They're seeing their favorite band, and rather than throwing their bras up onstage, they're engaging the music on a different level, more trance-like.

BH: That's been a big issue for the band on this tour, seated venues versus non-seated shows. Last night was a seated venue. And it was the best seated show we had on the tour so far. Every other seated show the crowd has been quiet. Our best shows are open floor. The kids are not moshing but certainly having a good time, you feel the energy, and you see people smiling. Other times we look out at the audience and we wonder, 'Are people looking at their watches waiting to get out of here?' A friend who was out there will say, no, people are just taking it in.

You believe that like you believe your mom when she says she likes your music. The show is as good as the crowd. When we don't feel that we don't give as much. It's a chemistry thing. We feel silly getting physically into it if the crowd doesn't

TVP: I'm not going to say that your music is more a cerebral experience- because it's so heavy, but there is a strong cerebral component that makes people want to let it in rather than jump around. People are processing it.

BH: I have some friends who feel compelled to compare Tool's music with APC, and say things like they need a paring knife to listen to Tool. It is really a more musician-oriented music. I love it and I would have to list it as one of my influences.

TVP: The only similarity aside from the vocals is the complexity.

BH: Have Beck sing with APC and tell me if it sounds like Tool.

TVP: Exactly.

BH: I've got a call on a wrap for this.

TVP: What are your plans in the near future?

BH: We're finishing this tour and then we're hitting Europe, Australia, and Japan. Then in March our big US tour, ten weeks.

TVP: Any advice for someone just trying to break into the business?

BH: I don't know if I would even try. It's an interesting time and I really don't know what direction I would go. With or without a record company? As the digital age becomes more of a reality in the music world, the live experience is the last pure form of expression and the last authentic way to break out. Bands will value the live experience more.

TVP: The only thing you can't dump onto a disk-

BH: is being there.

No Prima Donnas: Method Man Exclusive Interview

November 2006

By Jessica Hopsicker

The party is for the most part over, but not in the literal sense, though, far from it. It's the point that Method Man conveys in his latest album, *4:21...The Day After*. The disk released in August and expresses the aftermath and the moment of "clear headedness" that follows. The deal is that the party's over and it's time to get back to business. The name and the contents within couldn't be truer. After a steady bout of media pitfalls and a fair share of nay-sayers, Meth was ready to go at it again.

Clifford Smith began in Staten Island's Park Hill Projects, a child with two other siblings and separated parents. There he gained his infamy for being a comic book aficionado. Later after a bout of drug dealing and shit jobs, his rhyming abilities served a far greater purpose when he joined the renown Wu-Tang Clan; where he was aligned with the likes of ODB, RZA, GZA,

U- God, Ghostface Killah, and plenty of others. While still a large part of Wu-Tang, he branched into a solo career

355

where he was and still is releasing many albums including: Solo, compilation, soundtracks, and collaborations. Acting soon followed.

The FOX sitcom entitled *Method & Red* in which he stared with his label mate Redman aired June of 2004. The fish-out-of-water comedy that bore the tagline "Puttin' the urban in suburban, " was cancelled only after a few months. Meth and Redman publicly bashed the network's control, and how it lorded over the show's style, and the sheer unwillingness to compromise. What drove the screw in further to the ill-fated series was the travesty of having a laugh track, and deeply unprofessional editing skills. It was as if the viewers had to be told when the sitcom was being funny. The prestigious pair also played in a 2001 Stoner Film *How High*, as Silas and Jamal who basically smoke some mystical herb and find themselves in Harvard. A few years later, Mr. Meth's acting career went from canned laughter and slapstick stereotyping to hardcore The HBO series *The Wire*. The hard-hitting drama delves into the lives of junkies, dealers, politicians, and police, which make up the nefarious Baltimore drug scene. It is very different from the processed and produced fake humor.

With the latest album and ongoing tour, Meth is a testament of determination. Perseverance is the game, and everyone else be damned. He has a successful music and acting career under his belt as well many aliases to carry his name, and a discography that will not quit. Sadly, not even the high and mighty Method Man, actor, musician, and media mogul could escape the clutches of the first class bug that recently gripped the nation.

Jessica Hopsicker: Good afternoon Meth, how're you doing?

Method Man: I'm sick

JH: The theme of your new album is basically about keeping it real and being yourself, has there been any time or situation that you haven't felt that way?

MM: No, there ain't never been no time like that.

JH: Through out your career, you appear to be an artist of many names, who was your favorite persona and what does it say about you?

MM: My favorite persona?

JH: Yes.

MM: I don't think I understand the question ... persona, what do you mean?

JH: Umm- your pseudonyms.

MM: Oh no I name-dropped all those like last album, the album before that, I name-dropped all those pseudonyms. That was just a little kid's game. It was fun while it was on, but you know, I grew past that.

JH: It also appears you have issues with the media, who or what do you have the biggest beef with?

MM: Well, you see that whole part about it, I don't have issues with the media, they have issues with me. And it's not a who issue its how many, you know what I'm saying. These mothafuckers is all, basically, it's not even a beef anymore. It's like I said what I said and they did what they did, and you see the results of it. You can't win against them so, I ain't got no beef with the media.

JH: While branching into acting, how different is it than music?

MM: What music?

JH: Yeah

MM: I mean as far as me being about music is not really different. I'm still doing the same thing I've been doing, you know. Business wise, though, they're not putting much effort as they used to inside these records.

JH: What's life been like since Wu Tang?

MM: What do you mean since Wu Tang? I'm still Wu Tang; we still a group.

JH: So tell me about your heroes.

MM: Heroes?

JH: Yes.

MM: I'm from the hood we don't have any.

JH: Are you pleased with the way your new album is going?

MM: Am I pleased?

JH; Yeah.

MM: Hell no, I'd be an idiot to say that. No I'm not.

JH: On to TV, it seems you've gone along way from the canned laughter on Method & Red, to The Wire, how's that going?

MM: The Wire's cool, I always wanted to do dramatic, comedy is a little pain in the ass sometimes.

JH: And laugh track, that's a bit much.

MM: Yeah, the laugh track, yeah.

JH: The Wire seems like a really intense set. What's it like shooting the scenes?

MM: Its pretty laid back everybody's real cool. Nobody's complaining, no prima donnas, none of the bullshit. I love it.

JH: Is there anything we haven't covered, new projects? Your upcoming show in Syracuse, NY?

MM: Well, I just hope that everybody comes out to have a good time, no prima donnas and shit. If they're coming to see a conventional show they in the wrong spot I don't do conventional.

JH: Well I hope you feel better.

MM: Yeah I hope so too, I got a show tonight.

Chuck Klosterman: Articulating the Unintelligible

June 2006
By T. Virgil Parker

t is uniquely fitting that the man who is being called the voice of Generation X uses cultural debris the way a flasher uses a trench coat. Eloquence suddenly emerges from his deceptively chatty prose, imparting momentous meaning from sources that can usually be called humble. Chuck Klosterman's voice is compelling to the extent that he writes convincingly about the significance of cereal commercials. It isn't a case of making something out of nothing, the conclusions he arrives at are frighteningly substantial, though somehow funny at the same time.

What fascinates me about Chuck is that every time he speaks it's like he's tossing out new material. The Klosterman process is operating constantly: A casual mixture of hedonic mirth and profundity that veers to the edge of neurosis and pulls back triumphantly. This is how he manages, I assume, to write for Spin, Esquire, and ESPN while churning out a steady stream of book titles. I suspect that it would be hard for him to turn it off.

Killing Yourself to Live is theoretically about Chuck's cross-country pilgrimage to the death-places of Rock stars, but that's kind of like saying that tennis is about balls. The real journey is a relentless tour of one of America's more original minds. The even more recent Chuck's *IV* is a profound gathering of his work that has expanded significantly.

T. Virgil Parker: You have a unique ability to bring significance out of minutiae. What draws you to the original ideas?

Chuck Klosterman: I'm always interested in doing two kinds of cultural criticism: Taking really big ideas and trying to make them very specific and personal, or taking very small ideas and trying to look at them in a much larger context. I use my own life as a literary device. I'm working under the premise that under the right circumstances, to the right person, anything can have social meaning to somebody. I just take the things that I'm naturally interested in, and use those as a starting point. I'm much more effective writing about things that I'm actually interested in, than trying to figure out what other people might be interested in.

TVP: Pop culture has begun to gain parity with higher art forms. I think you're doing a lot more to evoke its significance than other people are willing to do.

CK: I think that almost everybody wants to think critically about the things in their life that are important to them. I think there are a lot of people who want to understand why things are important to them; what is the meaning outside of them? Some media does that very well: The New Yorker, Atlantic Monthly, National Public Radio. The problem is that a lot of the people reading about these things have no real relationship to the actual cultural artifact. They may not have listened to those records or seen those films. I want to apply that same sort of critical approach to popular culture; the universal things that people have a relationship with. When I write about *Saved by the Bell* I'm not trying to say that it was a really important television show, I was thinking that it was a show that a lot of people of a certain age will have a relationship with. Maybe they enjoy watching it and they understand things about the characters, but it almost seems ridiculous to take this inherently bad show seriously. I'm going to be the person who does that.

I think that people sometimes view this stuff backwards. They think that something begins the process of being important by being great. That isn't really how the world works. Something becomes important because of the way the audience reacts, not because of what it is inherently.

TVP: One of the things that you achieve is to imply that low culture is formative in ways that people wouldn't want to admit.

CK: Yes and no. To say formative is to say that it shapes the way people look at life. That might be true, might not be true. A statement I agree with more is that life and this show have some commonalties. I try to look at this poorly written but somehow entertaining program and find the elements that would make someone understand their own life better. That is the purpose of art.

TVP: Most of the people writing for the magazines you're working with are writing with an implied audience of people like themselves. You seem to be writing for a broader audience, but without dumbing it down.

CK: That is my hope. I've been fortunate. Besides book writing I've been able to write for <u>Spin</u>, for <u>Esquire</u>, and the <u>New York Times Magazine</u>, and <u>ESPN</u>. I don't know how much crossover there is. I'd like to think that I'm writing cultural criticism for an audience of people who don't normally read it.

TVP: Exactly. Do you think that it helps to have grown up in the mid-west?

CK: Probably. It is odd to say that because it's like I'm implying that because I'm from North Dakota I know what real people are like. That's not how it is. The reason there might be a relationship is that culture gets there last. It starts on the east coast and on the west coast and gets to the middle of the country last. So all the culture I experienced growing up was the most populist stuff. It was the stuff that was universal to being alive in America during the 1980's and early 90's. It's hard to live in North Dakota and be an elitist. You get used to the idea that there's value in things that a lot of cultural critics would not see as valuable.

The single unifying characteristic in everything I write about is that I'm always more interested in the audience than the actual artifice. I'm always more interested in how people respond to Rock music opposed to the music itself. I'm more interested in how books or film affect peoples' world view as opposed to the actual elements of that piece of art. You still have to break down the art itself, but what I'm interested in is the consequence.

TVP: You come to Rock and Roll from a Rock and Roll perspective, as opposed to an academic perspective. That makes your critical and interpretive work a little more authentic.

CK: I hope it is. You can talk about music and authenticity. Talking about authenticity in criticism is more complex. There's a certain element to any performing art that is inherently inauthentic. Bob Dylan knows he's onstage.

He's acting the character of Bob Dylan onstage. When you're a writer it's a little different. If you accuse someone of being an inauthentic Rock Critic it's almost like they're pretending to like or dislike bands. What's weird, is that there's tons of people who do that. I never thought to myself as a kid that I was going to be a Rock Critic. I didn't really think of that as a job, it never even occurred to me. We had Rolling Stone in the library and the only thing I remember about it is that they hated all the bands I liked. It's so interesting to be in New York now because I meet people whose career goal is to become a Rock Critic. They were listening to The Velvet Underground in the sixth grade. They were in the mindset that this is what they were going to do. Until I got to college I had a completely normative experience of Rock music. I was really into it, but my interest was entirely based on my own personal interests and the culture I was in. I wasn't into the canonized, dogmatic qualities of what was good or bad about Rock music. You say authentic. My response would have had to be authentic. I had nothing else to base my experience on.

TVP: That word does have to be suspect in any context, but what I mean is that it helps to perceive music as an experience rather than interpreting it as a cultural artifact.

CK: The key is being able to do both. Take a band like Radiohead. There's a visceral experience to seeing them live. There are also elements of Radiohead that are fun to think about- that have nothing to do with being there in concert, or even listening to the album. There are ideas not just in the lyrics but in the construction of the song and the way the band has positioned itself. I think that people who write about music want to go in one of two directions. They either want to look at these songs as math and prove that Pet Sounds is the best record from that year based on that criteria, or go in the exact opposite way; if you think about music at all, you're missing the point. It just has to blow your mind away. I try to be exactly in the middle. You try to think about things intellectually and write about them emotionally.

TVP: You're the only Rock Critic I know of who is willing to admit that you like bands that aren't cool.

CK: I suspect my book *Fargo, Rock City* helped perpetuate this in a back-handed way, but actually, writing about bands that aren't cool now is half of the criticism I read. It used to be really hard to write about music and get it published for any audience larger than a 'zine. There were only a few publications. The people who wrote about Rock music thought they were in this rarified class, so they came up with these shared opinions. Now there are lots of places and ways to get published, it's just hard to get paid for it. There are so many people writing now, the only way to stand out is to have insanely contrarian perspectives. I see this more and more. People base their aesthetic on whatever appears might become something. Or, if something is getting big, their position is going to be the opposite, so you'll see something like, "Wilco is Terrible". I have no problem about somebody having that opinion, but it's weird when someone has that opinion on purpose.

TVP: That's what I mean I guess. There's a sincerity level when you talk about a band that isn't part of the cannon.

CK: I'm lucky for two reasons. One: Because I never identified myself as a Rock Critic I never had the pressure to be accepted by the peers of Rock Criticism. The vast majority of Rock Critics are only writing for other rock critics. I'm not in that position because I didn't know any of them until I moved to New York.

The other thing is that I've been able to write books. I'm really a generalist at this point. I can write about sports or religion or politics. I do happen to write about music a lot. I can write about Creed or Yo La Tengo and since I'm not a Rock Critic I don't have to worry about someone looking at my perspective and saying that I'm just accepting what everyone else believes or is just trying to disagree with people. I don't have to worry about them anymore. I will be able to publish books regardless.

TVP: I do have one Rock Criticism question I'm dying to ask you. Granted, the last Red Hot Chili Peppers album is great, but no one had anything ambivalent to say about it anywhere.

CK: Those guys are so annoying. I was just thinking that today in fact. I had just woken up and one of those VH1 top videos of the week shows was on. *Dani California* is actually a pretty good song. I liked that song more than the vast majority of their catalogue, but they're one band where watching the video makes me dislike the song because those guys are just idiots. They remind me of when you're in college and some guys start a band and they go out of their way to make sure at all times that everyone knows they're in a band. And, because they're in this band they're in this artistic venture- they're allowed to embrace the most obviously eccentric public posturing and act like they're on drugs all the time even when they're not. They're like a college band that's now super successful.

TVP: This reminds me of your idea of what I would call personality templates: People who say they're creative are not creative.

CK: If you tell someone to act spontaneously they're going to act the way they assume spontaneity is represented- which is the opposite. For the most part, people are bad at understanding their own dominant quality. In fact they assume the complete opposite. When I think about the things that accelerate culture -the proliferation of media- has had a positive effect on people, but there's a negative effect too. There's less self-awareness among people. Their recognition of their own insecurities and their own failures leads them to identify themselves the opposite of the way people perceive them. My biggest fear in life is that there's something about me that absolutely everyone knows except me. I've seen other people like this. Their dominant quality is clear to everyone and they're absolutely oblivious to it. You never know the things you don't know.

There's things that we know we know, and there's things that we know we don't know. We don't know what's going to happen when we die, the big existential questions. Then there's all these questions we don't even know to ask. A lot of people are unaware of the things that construct who they are.

TVP: I think that a lot of your most important work revolves around that. Most people who think about culture believe that there's some social engineer out there trying to mass produce contemporary consciousness. It's more likely that a good deal of contemporary mass consciousness is a byproduct of selling soda.

CK: The hardest thing about cultural criticism is dealing with the element of chance. I was working on this column about *Snakes on a Plane*. Esquire wanted it. They went back and shot scenes based on what people wanted on the internet. They changed the name of the movie and changed it back based on what they thought people wanted.

I think this is a bad direction for filmmaking to go for two reasons. One: If you look at the entire blogisphere as a focus group the movies are going to become less personal and more idiotic. The other problem- and I wonder if the movie studios even realize- is not only will it make the movies worse, but even if they do their research perfectly it will only work half the time. It's the same as having one guy pick. If you asked 100,000,000 people everything they wanted from a film, and made that movie, it might be popular and it might not. There's still that element that people don't know what they want until they get it. Whenever you're writing about culture you always face that mystery, like why is Led Zeppelin huge?

I can give a whole bunch of reasons why Led Zeppelin is great. I can use musical reasons, reasons about their iconography, timing, the world-view of youth in the 70's- all those things, but there's still the question of why it was them. Why not Blue Cheer? Was it because the music was inherently better? I would argue that it is, but I don't really know. There are tons of examples where the opposite is true.

TVP: My wife read the passage in *Killing Yourself to Live* about Led Zeppelin and she said that you hit the nail on the head except for one thing: Why are there generations of female fans obsessing over Zep?

CW: Some people have brought that up, that it was a somewhat sexist point. I wasn't saying that only guys like Led Zeppelin, I'm just saying it's a really formative part of being a guy. Every guy will, for whatever reason, find the music of Led Zeppelin to be, at least briefly, the only good music in the world. Whether it's for eight days, or eight weeks, or their whole lives. I'd guess women would like Led Zeppelin for less gender-specific reasons. Maybe they just think it's good.

Especially for guys who were totally into Zeppelin for like six weeks in tenth grade, in all likelihood it wasn't their most successful romantic era. I don't know if any guys have ever gotten laid because they like Led Zeppelin.

TVP: You're working on a new book project?

CK: The soft cover of *Killing Yourself* comes out in June, so I'll be touring for that. Then in September an anthology is coming out called *Chuck Klosterman IV,* like *Led Zeppelin IV*. It's a collection of things previously published plus some new material. There's a 40 page novella at the end. There's a story, half true, half fiction, and I added some new questions. Most of this book, 85 percent, is previously published. I'm working on a novel right now.

TVP: I've been saving this one up. What if a sumo wrestler joined Kiss?

CK: What instrument?

TVP: Doesn't matter, but I would have to say drums.

CK: Would I be enthused about that? No. But if any band was going to attempt to add a sumo wrestler to the lineup, and somehow not destroy their fan base, or the iconic meaning of the group, Kiss is the only one who could do it. Somehow Gene Simmons and Paul Stanley could convince me and all the other idiots who love Kiss, that bringing in the sumo wrestler would encompass the history of Kiss being super popular in Japan. They'd represent the idea that Kiss was always larger than life, and who's larger than a sumo wrestler, that their music was always written with that sort of Godzilla mentality.

TVP: I thought I was the only person in the world who thought that Ace Frehley's solo album was not only listenable, but fun.

CK: In the world of Kiss people, that's a given. We all

369

think Ace Frehley has the best delivery. Basically he made a normal Kiss album out of songs that he couldn't get on Kiss records because Paul and Gene wouldn't let him. It's comparable to the first George Harrison solo record, which is all stuff he saved up when the Beatles wouldn't let him put it on a record, a comparison can be drawn there, except Ace Frehley is not George Harrison. Both geniuses; but in very different ways.

TVP: Do you think there's an inverse ratio between the fame of the people you interview, and the value of the things they have to say?

CK: One thing about this job is that people want to know what Brittany Spears is like, what's Bono like? For the most part, celebrities are less interesting than normal people. They have a vested interest in not being interesting. When you talk to Brittany Spears, she's working. I don't know what she's like at all. She's doing something to promote the idea of Brittany Spears. It's hard to get these people to say what people want to know about them, or something out-side the character of what they've already constructed. In my experience, the best interviews are old Rock guys.

TVP: Yes.

CK: Like Robert Plant or Ozzy Osbourne, Donald Fagan or Bono, because they've done this a whole bunch of times. They don't care anymore. The best people to interview are super famous, super established, and know that journal-ists don't really affect their career that much, or bands who have just begun and are still in the process of creating who they think they want to be.

The worst people are really successful bands who are on their second album. They're doing media all the time, and they're sick of it. This is when the record company decides that they have to become Pearl Jam and do thousands of interviews a day. Being interesting can only hurt them. Also, it's hard to get a pro athlete to say something interesting because it's impossible to convince them that they have a motive to do so.

Bono was very interesting to talk to, and he loves being interviewed, but he's different from most musicians. I suppose it is a case-by-case situation.

TVP: I'd interview someone like Poe -who disappeared off the face of the earth- and they'd be consistently brilliant.

CK: When somebody falls off the map like that they tend to learn a lot of life lessons, and they have a lot to say about the way the music industry works.

When I interviewed Brittany Spears for <u>Esquire</u> something dawned on me in the middle of it: It was probably her first real interview. She'd been talking to media for like ten years. However it was always either Teen People asking her questions like "why are you so awesome' or she was surrounded by her handlers who dictated what she said. I'm asking her these questions that seem almost too obvious, and she was completely oblivious to them. She had never even considered that there might be this dichotomy between being a virgin and being a sexual object at the same time. She didn't think about things like that. I suppose, if she did, she'd go insane. If she really thought about her iconography and the bizarre impact she has on the world- she'd go insane. To be that famous, maybe you have to be the kind of person who doesn't understand the meaning of what they do, whereas someone like Poe is not in that position.

TVP: I wonder if you can be an icon and think on any level of complexity.

CK: The degree of complexity isn't as overwhelming as

the degree to which it has to consume you. If you're Bob Dylan or Madonna or any of these super famous people, I assume that there's no aspect of their lives that they don't see through the prism of their fame. No matter how much they say that they're just a normal person. If they perceive that going to a convenient to buy a box of cookies or a Pepsi will be perceived as interesting to people they've never met, that would alter the way they perceive the act themselves.

TVP: I suspect that the relationship between a person and their favorite celebrities bypasses the parts of the brain that have evolved in the past 40,000,000 years.

CK: It depends on what point you consider celebrity starting. What's so weird now- and media like Us Weekly have really accelerated this- is that there are so many celebrities that are famous to people who really don't care about them at all. There's a difference between the way Joe DiMaggio was famous, and the way Nick Leshay is famous. There are all these people who know that Nick Leshay is a famous guy and would actively identify themselves as not being a fan of him, or actually disliking him. They're the same people who read the magazines that make him a celebrity. He's on a television show, but there's shows that are more popular than that, and there's people who are more popular than that. He exists in this world where he's famous for being famous. The people who drive that industry, the people who care about who he's dating and things like that, very often don't like him. He's in this weird position of being beloved by people who hate him.

The Tossers: Free Booze and Tossing Off

March 2008
By Jessica Hopsicker

Rarely has there been such a collection of stalwart musicians. For over fifteen years, The Tossers have pioneered the great burgeoning genre known as Celtic punk. With rowdy pub sing-a-longs, coupled with powerful polemics, and age-old traditional folk tunes, their music goes down twice as smoothly when lubricated with whiskey or a hearty stout. The Chicago-based ruffians have successfully established an entirely different sound than their successors: the Dropkick Murphys and even Flogging Molly.

With a band that was originally indefinable, they were able to tour with the likes of Clutch, The Reverend Horton Heat, and The Mighty Mighty Bosstones, successfully spanning the gap between Hardcore, Rockabilly and Ska. Still, after all this time, they have managed to stay true to the Tossers' gritty hooliganesque signature sound.

In live performances, they seem to defy the meaning of the phrase "opening act," for it is rather easy to forget there ever was a headliner. The newest album under their belt, *Gloatin' and Showboatin:' Live on St. Patrick's Day*, is a compilation CD/DVD that is a fitting example of this fact, combining previously unreleased tracks with fan favorites. Charting the course of numerous albums, Gloatin' and Showboatin' brings the band to a fine foaming head.

After interviewing the likes of Flogging Molly and the Dropkick Murphys, it only seemed natural that The Tossers should aid in fueling my recent infatuation with all things Celtic, including the drinking. The bassist, backing vocals, and squeezebox man Dan Shaw was happy to oblige. Given the allotted time, however, and the mass amount of ground to cover, I felt a little bit cheated with the interview... or maybe we were both just too sober.

Jessica Hopsicker: So, Gloatin' and Showboatin' is coming out now?

Dan Shaw: Yes indeed.

JH: Do you think that will get a nice rise out of the fans?

DS: I hope so. It's really good, so I'm sure everyone will enjoy it.

JH: I've enjoyed it. So how has Chicago shaped your sound as opposed to, say, bands from Boston or Los Angeles?

DS: I've never really thought about that because we're from Chicago, so it is what it is. But I would say that anywhere where there is a very large blue-collar environment that definitely impacts your sound. You end up with more, a harder edge to things.

JH: As a musician, how much responsibility do you feel towards the traditional roots of Celtic music?

DS: I don't necessarily think that there's a responsibility as much as it is that you have this great surplus of songs that obviously are good songs because they've been around for hundreds of years, and in a way, we're repackaging them. Updating them a little bit, to make it more palatable to people. A lot of times, let's say you're sitting at your grand-parents' house. It's a great song, but you don't even pay much attention to it because it's coming at you in a very hokey way. When you repackage that a little bit and give it the energy and everything, I think it's more palatable to the youth especially. Because they might have heard a song a couple of times before and never paid much attention to it and when you put a little bit more soul behind it, and energy, then people perk up and listen.

JH: With fifteen years under your belt, you've seen the genre explode, and you were there from the start. Was it gratifying to see the genre grow so much?

DS: Yeah!

JH: Do you feel like any of your thunder has been stolen?

DS: Not at all, not at all. For years and years and years, no one knew what to do with us. No one knew what type of band we were, no one had any idea. So when it came to playing rock shows, the though was, "well, they wear suits, so they must be a Ska band." So, we ended up playing with a lot of Ska bands for a long time, because no one really knew what to do with us. Now there's definitely a broader appreciation. So, people know when you say, "We're a Celtic punk band," people know what that means now. Which is great. I like it a lot. And I like the fact that this type of music can be played with any bands. It goes with everything.

JH: You've also toured with rockabilly gods and hardcore favorites. Has that rubbed off on you in any style?

DS: No. As much as we can, we try to play with bands

that we really like and respect. I wouldn't necessarily say anything rubbed off on us in a genre style. So many of us independently listen to different types of music from each other. Like I listen to a lot of R&B and old soul. That's what I like. And I like old rock and roll; I like a lot of rockabilly. Our drummer likes a lot of Indie rock. Our old time highland player is a total Prog Rock guy. So, we have all these different elements contributing to everything that we do. And, it's always been that way.

JH: How does the band come together to write music?

DS: We all knew each other. We were friends and all of us had our own bands that we were doing. We all had our main projects and then we did this as fun. Just to get together, play some tunes, get some free booze, have a good time.

JH: That's always a plus.

DS: It is a plus. On one hand, we didn't really take it very seriously. We never started out ever to have the band be a full time anything for us.

It was just for us to have fun. For us to start thinking business-wise took a long time. But it brought us all closer together as people and as friends and we enjoyed ourselves a lot more than a lot of other bands do, if that makes any sense. So, it's great. Now this is our full-time thing, and we do other stuff on the side.

JH: Like what?

DS: Oh, everybody does something. Everybody's always doing something. Sometimes the same genre, sometimes it's different. But all of us are musicians and all of us like to play, so we're always trying to do something new, fun, and fresh for ourselves. It's great.

JH: Do you feel any responsibility towards the geo-political realities?

DS: I think that goes with, "does art impersonate life or does it influence life?" I think it does a little bit of both. I think all artists job is to communicate ideas and I'm speaking for myself, but you want to leave the world a better place than when you started. Or at least you want to try. So to see things in the world as they are and also be able to imagine them being better and to influence that any way that you can, I think is important and a responsibility for all artists. You can tackle subject matter in so many ways. You can force it down people's throats and be like, "this is wrong, this is wrong, and this is wrong." But that's very preachy and I think that you end up not gaining or reaching the widest audience that way. Then there's also the bring it up, roll it over in your head, and come to your own conclusion. And the funnier way, try to make people recognize things in the world, the injustices in the world in a fun manner. And I think that is something that we are fairly able to do. Like "The Ballad of N.A.T.O." on Long Dim Road is basically an A Capella, but we do play that live with the whole band. I think that's great because it builds all that energy behind it so that the audience is more interactive, and the lyrics seep in. Then people walk away and think about things later.

JH: It plays in your head over again.

DS: I think that's great.

JH: A friends turned me on to that song.

DS: It's a really great song with a whole lot of lyrics.

JH: My friend turned me onto that song. Saying something like, "He's just singing there, with a mandolin and he's angry. It's a great song, really fucked up. I love it"

All right, everyone has a great bar story. What's yours?

DS: A great bar story? I've been in a lot of bars. Well, I think one of the more fun times that I ever had was when we were out with Flogging Molly and The Mighty Mighty Bosstones, and after one of the shows some of the dudes from Flogging Molly and some of us all went out to a bar together. And all of us being multi-instrumentalists, we just sat around in a circle and drank free booze all night and played traditional songs all night long. So if I felt like playing guitar on one song and banjo on another or mandolin on something different, I could. And everybody was able to do that. So having all those people there with all of their references of musical ideas just built for a very fun, energetic, and diverse amount of songs. That was a lot of fun, so I'll put that down as one of my favorite bar moments. Another favorite bar moment was when we were in Nashville and we were taken to a bar that had a mechanical bull. So we all rode the mechanical bull and got drunk, for free. And that was fun. That was a good time. That was more fun than the show we actually played. It was a blast. We played the show and ran out as quickly as we could and went to this bar. Denim and Diamonds, it was in Nashville. We just had a great old time. It was fantastic.

JH: Any upcoming events or anything?

DS: Well, we have the Metro show coming up. I think that's the fourteenth.

JH: Where is that one at?

DS: The Metro, in Chicago. That is Friday, the fourteenth of March. I'm looking very forward to that show. Then we're also playing in Washington DC and Milwaukee. It'll be a good time.

JH: Sounds like you're keeping busy.

DS: And hopefully recording a new record soon.

JH: That'll be good.

DS: I agree.

JH: So are you working on any new songs for that yet?

DS: Oh yeah. It never stops. It's a constant, so the next record is usually pretty well planned out and thought of while we're in the studio recording its predecessor.

JH: Are you going to take this one anywhere different, music-wise?

DS: I don't know. I think there will probably be a very good cross section between some heavier hitters, more punk rock back to the stuff that we used to do. Plus all of the stuff that we do now, with the bigger orchestrated numbers. I think it will be a cross-section all across the board. It'll have its light ballads, it will have its drinking songs, and it will have its energetic punk rock tunes as well.

JH: Is the rest of the band is in Europe right now?

DS: Yes they are. Just got a couple of more days and then they will be home. It sounds like they're having a fantastic time. So, I'm super happy about that.

JH: Excellent, I think we've covered just about everything.

DS: Fantastic, if that's it, I'm gonna go and play piano.

Elvira: Mistress of Darkness

September, 2007
By T. Virgil Parker

It's late at night. You're lying on the couch. You feel a lump under you and you hope it's the TV remote because you have a suspicion that an infomercial is headed your way. But no, the dulcet intonations of horror movie music reverberate around the room. The iconic goddess of the fright flick comes into focus and you know the evening has just begun.

Many people think of a hot bod, horror, and beer commercials when they think of Elvira, Mistress of Darkness. However, the talent behind that image is one of imposing magnitude. Writer, director, actress, songstress, dancer, and all-around comedic mastermind, Elvira's creator- some might say alter ego- Cassandra Peterson is a woman of unique ability.

She took off for Los Vegas at the age of 17, and became its youngest professional dancer. Elvis Presley quickly took her under his wing and told her to start a band. She packed off to Italy with her band and landed a role in Frederico

Felini's *La Roma,* a film, and a director, worthy of deification according to the majority of culture vultures. Paying her dues slowly back in the states, she landed the MC role on a Los Angeles late night horror show, where the irresistible character was created.

Since that time she has done everything from directing to becoming a comic book character- a unique resume to be sure.

TVP: Everyone wants to be someone else for a while. How does it feel to have consistent access to an alter ego with a frightening amount of creative license?

Cassandra Peterson: Feels great! I can do all the things that I wouldn't do in my normal life. I have this outrageous personality that I can withdraw from when I want to. I can hurl the most incredible insults and be so incredibly truthful to them and they think it's cute; they love it.

TVP: Do you find yourself being nicer in compensatory fashion when you're being Cassandra?

CP: People who know I'm Elvira- I want them to know that I'm not always that forthright. I do withdraw a little bit, as if to say "See? I really am a nice person."

TVP: Is it safe to say that your die-hard fans are numbered among the more unusual people?

CP: That's definitely safe to say. I've sort of figured out my fan base- there's a lot of different components- old ladies to little kids, to the Metal crowd, and the Goth crowd of course, prisoners, bikers, soldiers. It's just weird. The one thing I've noticed about my really big fans is that they're the misfit's of the world. I always considered myself the same type of person. I seem to hold some kind of connection with those people who don't seem to fit in. Those people usually turn into the really coolest kinds of people when they grow up; more creative, more in control of their lives, not following the same old crap that everybody does. But they feel like I did, completely out of it, total social geeks when they're growing up.

TVP: All creative people seem to share that need to create an alternative to the circumstance in which they found themselves.

CP: That's right, and I did that with a vengeance! I went for that literally, you know?

TVP: Given the unique nature of your fan base, I'm going to guess that a lot of interesting interactions crop up.

CP: Where do I start? A thing that used to be bizarre but is now so common that I hardly even blink is fans getting my image tattooed on their various body parts. When that started I was like, "Wow that's so cool!" Now every time I appear someone comes up and says, "Hey, check this out," and they have my whole entire image on their thigh or their shoulder or their butt, which is very common. Or I'll be signing my autograph on their arm and I'll say, "Go have it tattooed." A couple hours later they come with this bloody scab. I always think I should've told them to knock over a 7/11 and bring me the cash.

I had a girl come up to me and say, "Elvira, I love you! I've been practicing this for years now just for you!" I told her I couldn't wait to see what she was going to do. She took out a 2 by 4, a hammer and some nails, and nailed her tongue to the wood. I had to say, "Gee, that's great!"

I've had people put screwdrivers up their nose into their skulls for me. Just a bunch of wacky fans out there.

TVP: You have a resume that says "Destined for greatness".

You were discovered by Elvis, appeared in a Fellini film- only the greatest film director of all time, worked in a troupe that spawned a slew of comedic geniuses-including yourself. Does it seem a bit surreal to you that it was Elvira that threw you into the limelight?

CP: It's kind of funny because I always say to people "I'm going to write my autobiography." They always say "You're too young to write your autobiography." But, it would probably stop at the point where I became Elvira. That's when my life got boring. I had a much more exciting life before that. Say from 14 to 30- that's when it was really happening. This is my job now, not that it's a boring job.

People ask me what my mother thinks of me wearing the Elvira dress. In fact, she's relieved that I'm wearing any clothes at all. And I have a steady income.

I've had a pretty diversified and varied past, I can tell you that.

TVP: You had a parallel musical career that it seems you could have taken very far.

CP: That's how I started out, dancing and singing. I was really depressed when I took up acting and gave up my singing career; all those years working on that, and then quitting. The funny thing is that it is coming around. As Elvira I use singing for a lot of things. I did this IMAX movie that was basically a music video of one of my songs, "Livin' in a Haunted House." I have several CD's of Halloween music out. I still use those talents.

I wanted to stay in the music world. At the point when I got the Elvira part it was the 80's and there was the whole New Wave thing. I was so into music and musicians. Crissie Hinds was my idol, and Joan Jett. I probably would have gone in that direction.

TVP: I can easily envision you at Ozzfest with a Metal band behind you.

CP: That's scaring me. I still get to hang out with a lot of bands and musicians because I always do the intros. All the old 80's metal bands, everybody from them to U2 I've introduced for shows. Alice Cooper, Rob Zombie, Kiss, Motley Crew, all those guys. Right now I'm friends with that group Roony that did the Lollapalooza tour. I've always been crazy about bands and music. I guess that translates into the way I put the Elvira character together in some ways.

TVP: You spend a lot of time in character.

CP: I do

TVP: Not just on sets but in a lot of live appearances. Do you ever find yourself thinking in Elvira mode?

CP: Oh yes! I like that. She has the more healthy personality. It's definitely the more confident, strong, woman. I'm not afraid to say what I'm thinking. It's a character that I wish I could incorporate more into my real life. And actually, as I get older, I am and I think it's a really good, healthy thing.

I get so many letters from teenage girls who love the character of Elvira, and I know why they love it. She's an incredibly sexy-yet powerful, empowered woman. Just because she is empowered doesn't mean she has to look like Hillary Clinton or Opra Winfrey.

TVP: There's an unfortunate thing in our culture where there's a dichotomy between female empowerment and beauty.

CP: There really, really is. I just really realized that. Either you're incredibly smart, together, empowered and you look like Eleanor Roosevelt, or you're a big breasted sexy bimbo. People can't seem to incorporate the two. Elvira is the perfect incorporation. She's not a brain surgeon, but she's powerful. She knows what she wants and she goes after it.

That's the appeal in Elvira for younger girls. There's not much out there that brings beauty and empowerment together. I get so much mail from preteen, teenage and twenty-something girls.

TVP: Young girls are incented not to appear intelligent.

CP: Yes, they're rewarded for it. And there's little else in the media. Take Laura Croft for an example. She's basically just a two-dimensional robot character. She can kick some ass, and she looks sexy, but where's the rest of it, you know? Where's the vulnerability, where's the femaleness of all that. It's not really there. She's like a guy in drag.

TVP: A lot of that has to do with specifically American culture. Intelligence in general is not considered a survival skill here.

CP: So true. It's not really rewarded like it is in other countries. Here, looks rule.

TVP: And youth.

CP: I was trying to forget that. Really, I was stressing out about not being really young anymore but I decided not to bother. I plan on bringing the Elvira character into animation. Or, I don't care if Angelina Jolie plays Elvira in a movie. To me, the character can make that transition.

TVP it's not just a character, it's an archetype.

CP: Exactly! You are so smart, I love you! I tell people that all the time. It doesn't need me behind her to keep playing her. How many actors have played Batman in the movies, or 007? Agent 007 doesn't disappear when Sean Connery gets too old to play him, or Santa Claus, someone with whom I align myself closely.

TVP: Do you think in about a century kids will be waiting for Elvira to come down the chimney on Halloween?

CP: If I can get that going, yeah!

TVP: Not a bad gig. Can you tell me a little about your movie, Haunted Hills?

CP: It's out there in the video stores now. It's very much a parody of the old Gothic Horror films that I grew up with. In the 60's Hammer and Roger Korman and A.I.P. were all making these incredibly slow movies, but scary as hell. They would put people to sleep now, because images move so fast and special effects are so advanced. Back then they were the scariest movies around.

What we set out to do was to make a parody of that genre of film. A lot of people in their teens and twenties have seen those movies because they've become camp classics. We set out to do to that genre what Austin Powers did to the spy movies of the 60's.

TVP: The horror of that era had a lot of unintentional self-satire built in. You showed an unusual amount of dexterity in bringing that to its furthest logical conclusion with *Haunted Hills*. That film was released in October of '02, and it's already becoming something of a cult classic.

CP: I'd like to think so. Anybody who's into horror movies is going to enjoy this movie. It doesn't make fun of the traditional horror films, as much as just pulls the fun out of it. People watching it can tell that I'm celebrating it.

TVP: My wife is always quoting a passage from that film,

"Oh Mr. Pirate, please don't pillage my booty!" That's a terrific line!

CP: I thought it was funny. Most of he time, in the theater when it plays, I don't think anyone hears that line. I'm laughing to myself, and I look around, and silence!

TVP: You shot it for under a million bucks, I believe. It doesn't look like it, at all.

CP: Looks pretty damn good, doesn't it? I have to give myself and my producer Mark Pierson a little pat on the back, because I think the quality is amazing. If you noticed, we had a real original score with an orchestra, which is unheard of these days in any low budget film.

TVP: Or many high budget films for that matter.

CP: It's all electronic, you know? We went to Russia and had the Russian Symphony Orchestra record the soundtrack. The producer, Mark Pierson, was really adamant about that because these old films had that kind of score. If you tried to fake it, you're going to lose a lot of the quality.

TVP: I hadn't noticed it, but that's where the uncanny ring of authenticity comes from.

CP: We' even used tungsten lighting, because that's all they had in Rumania, and that's what they used in the sixties. It gives off a special light. That lighting gives this quality that you can't get with the lights they use now, a different quality, and different colors. We used that ultra- saturated color so the red is really red and the colors really pop out not in a realistic way, but in a way that really captures the look of the 60's low budget films.

TVP: It was an advantage that anything you really couldn't afford would just add to the cheese factor.

CP: That was a great thing. We tried to find a black cat, and apparently they don't have black cats in Rumania or something. I'm a real animal rights person so I wasn't going to have another cat dyed black. The producer said, "We have to have a black cat! Every Roger Korman movie had a black cat!" I told them to go out to a toy store and buy the best looking stuffed black cat they could find. They came back with a brown stuffed kangaroo, which is as close as they could get. We spray-painted it black and we still used it. We used a piece of the tail sticking out from behind the curtain, and cut to stock footage of a cat running away.

That's what shooting was like almost every day in Rumania. In the end all those things worked out. Like, the thing with that actor who plays my love interest, that big hunky guy. We wanted Fabio, the Italian model who does all the Romance novel covers. He wanted more money than anybody in the film. We dropped negotiations with him and started looking for the Rumanian version of Fabio. We auditioned hundreds of guys. There was only one guy who had the muscles and long hair.

We took him despite the fact that he knew no English.

TVP: I saw that in the Special Features of the DVD. You did an intentionally awful lip-syncing job for the film.

CP: What else? We had the bad B Movie dubbing job edited in. It turned into one of the highlights of the film.

TVP: With that kind of creativity you don't even need a budget.

CP: Next time we'll go somewhere even worse than Rumania! It's a wonderful place with wonderful people. I guess you get a little spoiled when you want this or that and they can't be found.

TVP: Other than the accommodations and the food, what was the scariest thing that happened?

CP: The accommodations and the food were pretty damn scary. We wanted four black stallions to thunder across the road. What we ended up with, was two ancient nags from the dog food factory. Every day was scary. I was the only writer there; I had to show up on the set two hours before everyone else to do my makeup. Somebody would show up and say they couldn't do this or get that and I'd have to rewrite the scene right then.

It was the hardest thing I ever did.

T.V.P: You think you're going to do it again?

CP: I might be directing straight to video or TV some books I wrote a few years ago. One of them is called Camp Vamp. Somebody else is going to finance that one. I learned my lesson- never do that again! We financed ourselves to the tune of $1,500,000 and that is really scary, when you know you might be losing your own money. You work really hard when you know that's happening.

TVP: You're probably that much more deferential to producers.

CP: Yes! No producer uses their own money. Nobody would be that stupid.

TVP: Are you appearing in Hollywood Squares this year?

CP: I usually do. I got to sit between Tammy Fae Baker and Rue Paul, perhaps the two people on earth who wear more makeup than me.

TVP: Is there anything our readers should be looking out for besides *Haunted Hills*?

CP: I've been working up the whole reinvention process of Elvira. I hired a whole new team of people, marketing people, PR, and licensing people that I'm really excited about. So we're really kind of reinventing the character and concentrating more on the icon of Elvira because she's become a very iconic kind of symbol, and less on me being Elvira and running around playing Elvira.

TVP: That's where the reality show comes in?

CP: Yeah, well that plays into the whole new reinvention of Elvira and that show, which I'm doing this October, is about looking for a few good Elviras to sort of be Elvira. But not to take my place, that's where people have been getting confused. I've read several little articles that say, "Oh, Elvira is retiring and somebody else is taking over her place!" That's not what it's about at all. It's having more Elviras, just like Santa Claus does. You know, those little helpers who go out and are Santa Claus in the malls and all around at Christmastime. Well, there can be other Elviras that go to shopping malls. So the reality show is to find other Elviras to go out and do my evil bidding, you know?

TVP: So here's the big question about the reality show that everyone mentions as soon as I tell them that you're doing this. Are you going to let drag queens go for it?

CP: Absolutely! Some of the best Elviras are men. I have some amazing drag queens. We're inviting every ethnicity, gender; I even had somebody apply who I'm not even sure at all what their gender is. It is so frightening. They are somewhere definitely in the middle. And I'm not talking about your typical tranny (who I welcome), this is something beyond that. Some combination, a human-animal hybrid of some type, I don't know. I've never seen anything like this picture in my life. So we have a little bit of everything, you know? Who's to say there shouldn't be a male Elvira and an African American Elvira and Asian Elvira and Latino Elvira and a Little Person Elvira, and you know, what the heck? Something for everybody.

TVP: I heard recently that Elvira is the longest standing comic book character in print.

CP: Yeah! We just found that out. I broke the record of Bob Hope and Jerry Lewis. That was the last time that a comic book was done on a living human being and that was a while ago. The Elvira comic book this month will be the 167th issue, which will be my last issue with Claypool Comics, who did a fantastic job. It's the last issue and it set a record for the longest living human being as a comic book.

TVP: The next frontier would be Elvira cereal.

CP: Yeah. Elvira cereal, you mean the kind you eat?

TVP: Yes.

CP: I was thinking, "Do you mean serial like the old movies?" But, yeah, Elvira cereal. They're boob-a-licious!

TVP: Just think about all the free toys inside.

CP: Oh God, wow! I don't think we should think about the free toys inside. Could be interesting!

TVP: Could you talk to me briefly about Elvira's Box of Horror?

CP: Yeah, the Elvira Box of Horror was with Time Life, that's pretty much come and gone. But I have a new DVD series that came out last Halloween from Shout Factory. It went over so well. We did seven of them, I believe. And they're making thirty more for this Halloween because they sold like hot cakes. So we're doing it again, only with more movies. And that is actually my television series, my original TV series, Movie Macabre, which was local here in LA market, and also syndicated across the country. These DVDs are of the original show. And hopefully we'll put some extra added bonus stuff on it this time. The first time was kind of a test. They just did six or seven, threw them out there to see how they'd do, and they really did great. So now we're going to beef them up a little bit.

TVP: And now you're starting to work on some other Indie projects?

CP: No. Are they like Tomoko's Kitchen or something like that?

TVP: Yes.

CP: No, those are just a couple of little acting gigs I did for a friend. I just did these really brief acting things as myself. One of them might have been Elvira. I was paying back favors; that's what I was doing. To be in somebody's independent film when they ask you, it was like "aw, okay." I have very small parts. So those were favors. Something out there.

TVP: When you think about iconography in acting, PeeWee Herman immediately springs to mind. Have you every thought of a vehicle for Elvira and PeeWee?

CP: We joke about it sometimes. I see PeeWee fairly frequently these days, we go out together. Actually, we love going to parties and stuff together because we love to scare and shock people when we tell them who we are. So it's sort of a double whammy when it's him and me together, we get a kick out of that. But we haven't really ever talked about a project, I don't think that would work. I think PeeWee and Elvira would be fighting too much. The only time it worked was in Big Adventure when I got to beat him up and threaten to kill him. Then it worked great. But I have a feeling that PeeWee would drive Elvira insane and she would have to kill him. I always say that I was in PeeWee's Big Adventure getting to play the role that every woman in America dreamed of; killing PeeWee, always beating him up. He rubs people that way and Elvira wouldn't put up with his crap for two minutes.

TVP: There's a strong crossover in California between the entertainment industry and politics. When are you going to throw your hat into the ring?

CP: I'm throwing my bra into the ring! I thought Elvira really should run for president. I've always said that they've got two boobs in office now, why not mine? I think Elvira would be very good. Anyone would make a better president than what you've got now, anyone.

TVP: You're continuing to champion PETA?

CP: Yeah. I've been involved with them for a long time, though I'm not as involved with them now. I love and adore them and what they do. But right at the moment I'm so involved in this Elvira thing that I don't have a lot of time to devote to charities, but I hope the end result is that I will have a lot more time and money to make a bigger impact when Elvira is more visible.

TVP: I have to tell you, I had been talking to the CEO of Sea Monkeys. He had seen my last interview of you on the website.

CP: Sea Monkeys?

TVP: Yes, Sea Monkeys.

CP: The little things that you put in the little jar and they come alive?

TVP: Yes, he's a scream. But in any case, he said, "I wonder if Elvira would be a good sponsor for Sea Monkeys?" I thought that was the most mind-blowing idea.

CP: Wow. It is. I've done wacky products in my life but I think that would be about up there with the wackiest. Wow, a sponsor for Sea Monkeys. I don't know, does that involve animal abuse?

TVP: That's what I was wondering. You should really set the Sea Monkeys free, shouldn't you?

CP: Yes, I'm going to be the first person to save the Sea Monkeys. My new Save the Sea Monkey campaign.

TVP: So that will be your foundation.

CP: That's right. When I make all these gazillions of dollars I'm setting up the Save the Sea Monkeys foundation. That's going to be my priority. Thank you for that, your residual check will be in the mail.

TVP: If you had anything to say to someone who was trying to launch an acting career now, what would it be?

CP: I regret not having gone to college, I could have taken acting in college and gotten a strong background; I now think that's important. Also, stick to it. If it's really what you want, just do not give up. You will eventually get what you want.

I always think about my girlfriends and myself when we were in our twenties. We were all actresses. The reason I finally made it was that I was the only one who kept going. They dropped out one by one and got married to a lawyer or went into real estate. They all had their expensive cars while I drove a beat up Volkswagen and lived in a hovel. It's like, "How long can you live with suffering?" But eventually you will get it if you do not give up.

BALLS OF STEEL:
Future World Emperor
Dr. Phineas Waldolf Steel

April 2008
By Jessica Hopsicker

Life is short, and far too much of it is spent being miserable. This is a tragic fact, but the truth has been hard-wired into the human psyche for generations upon generations: that we can never truly be happy. We dwell on our own mortality, strive for stability, and want what our neighbors have. In order to fill the void, many turn to alcohol, medication (prescription and otherwise), or to gods. Some of us may just as soon wallow in misery rather than do something about it. In the tired old age of today, unhappiness has become an excuse, a crutch, and a staple of everyday life. Our formal education, forced us to cast off our "childish" dreams of grandeur and thrust us headlong into the real world, where we must sacrifice ideals and embrace the social norms of becoming an adult. If you don't conform, you're ultimately labeled with some sort of mental illness.

Dr. Steel constitutes a threat of this dehumanizing process, much like a wrench shoved into the spokes of a passing bicycle. Not only is he turning this modern day travesty completely upside down, but he has taken upon himself the ultimate dream of grandeur: taking over the world.

The mad scientist musician, media persona, and big buckled- bootstrap marketer, propagates, envisions, and strives for a Utopian Playland based on entertainment, self-actualization, and of course, robots. The basis of such a revolution exists in toys. In the New Dr. Steel™ World Dictionary, the definition is simply put: toy n., an object that makes you happy

Although he prides himself on his insanity, it isn't some sort of tin foil-hat- wearing-new agey polyrazzmatazz. The man has a point, not to mention a goal to make the world a better place. With the help of his Toy Scouts, nursemaid henchmen, and an ever-burgeoning Army of Toy Soldiers, some are already touting him as such. Lets face it, establishing a new world order really takes a pair.

Q: What was it that planted the notion of global domination in that fine brain of yours?

A: My plans for global domination are but a reflection of what I see happening all around us. There was indeed a moment in my life when I began to see the manipulative tactics of The System. Since then I have only learned more and more about the agendas and techniques of the individuals who seek to control us. Their power exists only because we believe that they have power. What they are doing is engineering reality through propaganda. My interests lay in educating the masses in the ways of these magicians, for when the technique of their "slight of hand" is revealed; they cease to have special powers. Each of us has the potential to be a great creator, but it is fear that keeps us confined and domesticated under a blanket of misinformation. I have found that the best way to educate the masses is not through aggressive preaching but through entertaining. One must not indoctrinate by force but educate by example.

JH: I must state that you have an impeccable sense of style how important is your image while obtaining your ultimate goal?

DS: Thank you for the kind words. I'm glad to hear that you enjoy my particular sense of aesthetics. Though many of us were taught not to judge a book by its cover, our natural instincts tend to do just that. Our visual perception is designed to inform us of safety or danger in a very quick way through visual stimuli. To this end, as the advertising world certainly knows, image is very important. Unfortunately, many of today's modern productions take this a bit too far by placing image before content. The result is a wide array of recycled garbage presented to us through shiny packaging. For me, it is important not only to provide quality content but also to maintain a unique sense of overall style throughout everything that I do. I myself am a canvas and I present myself accordingly. We inevitably judge books by their covers, so I aim to present the most interesting cover that I can. I trust that others who find my style interesting will also enjoy the many other aspects of my world since they come from the same mind.

JH: After all, my good Doctor, isn't marketing and mass media, for that matter, a multi-trillion dollar industry these days? Does this mean you've chosen to become the beast, infiltrate, and tear it down from the inside to reach your goal?

DS: Absolutely. One must utilize The System to the best of their ability...and then destroy it with giant robots.

JH: How are your robots faring these days, Doctor?

DS: Ah, well there are many a technical issue with the current model. Likewise, my time has been monopolized by a variety of other more pressing issues at the moment. My passion for building the robots is great, though my resources are forever dwindling. I look forward to the day when I might be able to put together a team of robotic engineers to execute my specific designs. In the meantime, I shall continue to tinker as my schedule allows and wear protective clothing.

JH: I hope that more music is among those pressing issues. I must say your audio experimentation is hauntingly familiar to an old version of "The Teddy Bear's Picnic" that still gives me nightmares to this day.

DS: Ah, grand. I'm delighted to know that my audio experimentation conjures up such childhood memories. I have drawn much inspiration from the entertainment I recall from my youth. I find inspiration in creating contrast and I greatly enjoy playing sounds against one another. To take a project in a direction that one might not expect is my underlying modus operandi. I encourage such inspiration on a daily basis and I do indeed have many musical creations lurching about my hard drive at the moment. I look forward to unleashing them on the masses in the not too distant future.

JH: Well, it must have been quite an interesting youth to derive such a result, Doctor.

DS: I suppose it was, though I spent a great deal of time alone as a child. I found it awkward to interact with other children and spent most of my time exploring my creative interests in the privacy of my own mind. I attended a strict, private school and it may have been in this environment that I felt the desire for such isolated creativity. In an environment where one is expected to conform, often a desire to escape is great. My escape was through my imagination.

JH: Outside one's own imagination, life can be exceedingly drab, mindless, and rather annoying at times. Which brings me to my next question, about your Utopian Playland: is it progressing well?

DS: It is developing and growing larger each and every day. Though I have some very specific plans for the physical incarnation of the world of tomorrow, a Utopian Playland begins from within. It is a state of mind and a way of looking at one's reality. To envision a Utopian Playland is to recognize and actively pursue your sincere passions and talent with the confidence in knowing that you are capable of great things. To this end, as The Army of Toy Soldiers grows and more people embrace this creative empowerment, the collective consciousness of the world is shifting. This is the single most important stage of building a Utopian Playland and it is very exciting to witness.

JH: Eloquently stated, Doctor. Now, what can the gentle reader of this publication do to become a member of Toy Soldier Army?

DS: Ah, it is easy. Simply visit my website, www.doctor-steel.com and click the "enlist today" button. Do feel free to peruse the rest of this digital labyrinth as well. There are a great many tidbits of brainwashing fun to be enjoyed throughout.

JH: What is your defensive strategy for the Orphan Works Act?

DS: I have become vocal about The Orphan Works act, which is rare for me as I care not to spend much energy or attention on legislations and political minutia. They are but symptoms of the real disease, which is how The System controls us. The Orphan Works Act, however, is a cut closer to the artery of our very being. The real issue is that The System fears us a great deal. We hold immense potential, and the key to this potential lies within our imagination. As children we are quickly conditioned to look at the world in an accepted way and to cease our "day dreaming." Thus begins our enslavement and domestication as a species of blinder-wearing zombies. The few of us who do put forth great effort to follow our dreams are rarely encouraged. Now, with this Orphan Works Act, the elite are paving the way to discourage our acts of creative passion by owning them. This isn't about stealing an image of someone's grandmother for an apple sauce jar; this is about striking increasing fear into the masses with the intention of removing any form of creative thought. This, combined with many, many other tactics to numb our minds, has been in the works for a very long time. The thought police are actively tightening the screws during a time of growing awareness. It is time to open our eyes.

JH: Now in conclusion: creamy or crunchy?

DS: I would have to choose crunchy with a creamy center... and with a hint of purple.

Music, Mythos, and Throwing a Song at Fascism: The Bob Weir Interview

April 2005
By T. Virgil Parker

I can easily envision the members of The Dead coming from another dimension. I can see them materialize on stage; just long enough to create the music that inspired millions of fans to remove themselves from the rituals of daily life and create a world to call their own. Then I imagine the band dissolving back into the mythos, where energy and ideas are communicated by producing sonic landscapes.

This feeling of other-worldliness intensifies when I talk to any of the more ardent Dead Heads. He may find bootlegs of a show more important than food or soap. His house may serve the sole purpose of containing his recordings and his recording equipment. No other band- and very few religions- have been able to inculcate such fanatical acolytes.

This phenomenon becomes less mystical, but more ponderous when it becomes clear that the members of the band had no intention of creating so fanatical a response. It is possible that this is part of the reason that Bob Weir throws so much energy into RatDog. Unburdened with a colossal cultural spectacle, the music and the mirth become the message. Any other member of one of the most famous bands on Earth might be accused of mere dallying in a side project. Nobody calls RatDog a side project. When Bob tunes up for a show with his *other* band, he's playing for keeps.

The Crier snagged Bob on break while he was rehearsing for tour.

TVP: So you just stepped out of a hefty rehearsal?

Bob Weir: We're in rehearsal right now and I'm taking a little break.

TVP: Do you feel exhilarated or a little blown out from a hefty workout with the band?

BW: It gets your blood up a bit.

TVP: You're working on a set that you're going to dismantle in any number of ways while you're on tour. How do you rehearse that?

BW: The deal is we rehearse tunes, and we play what you could call little exercises to see what emerges. The basic set is different every night. In the thousand or so shows we've done I don't think you'll find the same set list. Even if we did play the same set twice they wouldn't sound remotely alike.

TVP: Rat Dog's tenth anniversary is coming up. How different is touring with Rat Dog from touring with the Dead?

BW: I don't think it's all that different on stage. We state a theme and take it for a little walk. That's what we do, same as The Dead. Some of the material is different, and the guys are different. The chemistry of the players is necessarily quite different. Aside from that, not that much is different.

TVP: There's a significant cross-fertilization of sound in RatDog. How did you dig up that talent for that band? Everyone seems of a piece, while contributing in very different ways.

BW: We ended up with the players we've got by using the left foot/right foot approach and stumbling our way into them. It just happened.

TVP: There's a natural dynamic and a natural personality to the sound. Nothing seems forced.

BW: I didn't decide the people I wanted and go out and get them, I found my way into working with them one by one. Over the first five years of the band we tried various people out and what we learned early on was that having people who weren't local was difficult, we needed to get together at the drop of a hat. Somebody would get an idea and we'd all get together.

TVP: The shows sell out on the east coast. That's not happening a lot these days. To what do you attribute that kind of success?

BW: We have a good time. We jump, and the kids jump too.

TVP: The synergy between the band and the audience?

BW: Same as it ever was.

TVP: People always describe going to one of your shows as almost a warp of space and time- a sense of otherness. You don't hear concerts talked about that way, usually.

BW: We live in another realm. That's where we do our living. Day-to-day stuff, we're normal humans, but when we work, we go somewhere else. Mickey Hart used to say that we're in the transportation business- we transport ourselves and anybody else that's there with us. The audience is part of this endeavor- we're all going somewhere. That's the whole point of the evening.

TVP: You've lived in that realm for a pretty large chunk of your life. What has it taught you?

BW: It has taught me a bit about who I am, and what it is like to be me, and what it could be like for other humans to be them. The place that we go- when we're doing a show- is more real for me than anyplace else.

TVP: Do you ever feel like you're contending with your own legacy?

BW: Always. Any artist is going to have that, good or bad. You're tied to your legacy but at the same time you have to constantly out do yourself. It is jihad in a classical sense.

TVP: It has to be gratifying too to have such an imposing magnitude of work behind you, and you're continuing to create, to add to it.

BW: When we're doing older material, the challenge as well as the payoff, is to recreate it.

TVP: That can't be easy considering the transformations even the most recognized, most standard material has undergone under the tutelage of the Dead.

BW: The more you love a song, the easier it is to do. The more that you love a song, the more it will show you about itself.

TVP: Looking back over your life do you feel a certain responsibility for spawning at least two generations of improvisational musicians and an entire culture that goes along with it?

BW: I don't think we spawned it. The Jazz tradition far pre-dates us, and really we just brought that modus operandi into what you would call popular music, though I think this whole Jam Band ilk exists apart from the popular. When we started off we were playing popular music. By virtue of the fact that we were listening to a lot of Jazz and a lot of Classical for that matter, we just started drifting into a practice where we used more improvisation. We stretched stuff because that's where our ears told us to go. We found ourselves taking the music on a little walk in the woods. We started applying it to different kinds of scales and different kinds of lyrical renditions.

TVP: Do you ever look back with pure amazement at the music you helped to create?

BW: I don't often listen to stuff from the past, but someone will play me something they think will be of particular note to me, and I admit to being kind of tickled by what I hear.

TVP: There are thousands of people, perhaps millions, in basements around the world listening to concerts that were recorded twenty, thirty or more years ago. I believe that that's an unprecedented phenomenon.

BW: If it gives them direction and it spurs them, if it opens up their creative flow, I couldn't be too much more pleased.

TVP: There is also a culture of social consciousness and activism that comes along with the tradition. Do you feel that that's being kept up?

BW: I feel like we did our part last summer and fall, but it might not have been enough. We're still in deep shit with the drift of our country and its leadership is going. There may or may not be anything we can do about that.

TVP: It may be too late?

BW: As far as I can see the other end of the deal is that uneducated people tend to breed more than educated people. The people who are actually creating the wealth in this country will be increasingly less represented in our government. People want to be spoon-fed what to think, want to be told things that will make them feel good. By virtue of their numbers, those kinds of people are going to run the show. The people who know how to tell them what they want to hear will be leading them. The future looks pretty rosy for people like that, not for people like us.

TVP: You have to concede that your efforts are part of the solution.

BW: There could be a solution if more of us get dedicated to being active. It may be that democracy is a dead deal, but we'll see.

TVP: Democracy has always been contingent on the comprehension level of the populace.

BW: Yup, if people don't want to know, and they've demonstrated that they don't want to know. Furthermore, you can't tell them. People are very comfortable being willfully ignorant.

TVP: I've always tried to understand how an entire world view can be conveyed through music.

BW: I've got no answer for you on that. I don't know where we caught it, but it sort of caught fire with us and the people who listen to us, and they lend their energies to us.

TVP: It strikes me that its all been done in a spirit of mirth.

BW: And in the spirit of quest.

TVP: At this stage of your life you find yourself at the reigns of an economic powerhouse, but still having very crucial social concerns. Is there a balancing act there?

BW: I just try to live my life properly, according to what life has taught me, and hope the other peoples' lives teach them similar things.

TVP: You have a really demanding schedule; you're known for exciting, flawless performances. Do you see yourself performing for the rest of your life?

BW: Close to twenty years ago I went to the Venetian Room in the Paramount Hotel here in San Francisco to see Count Basie. It was wonderful. They sang like angels. They had an eighteen-year-old drummer, but everybody else in that band had been there close to fifty years. They had a cohesiveness that you can't get any other way. It was an incredible night. After the show, since that was the end of his run in San Francisco, he packed up his suitcase and flew home to Florida, put his feet up and checked out. When I read that in the paper my jaw dropped, I caught Count Basie's last show. I felt like I sort of got passed a torch there. Whether or not that's true, I came to the realization that I have nothing better to do, so I can't imagine not playing. What great musician ever retired?

TVP: What's exciting that you're listening to now?

BW: Basically what I listen to is Jazz and Classical music, and what we call World music, but actually might be East Indian Classical, or African Classical, which is basically drum stuff. When I listen to music I like to go as far as I can get from where I live, otherwise it's not a vacation for me. Branford came through town the other night with a really swell quartet. They did "A Love Supreme" and they really nailed it. It was sublime.

TVP: You've been performing longer than many of your listeners have been alive-

BW: Most of them-

TVP: Your comprehension of music would have been continuing to grow over that entire period. Not always true with listeners. Do you ever find it challenging to maintain a kind of relevance to your fans?

BW: I have a great deal of difficulty with the fact that a lot of Dead Heads won't listen to anything else. To me that's fundamentalism and I'm philosophically opposed to that. The fact is that they're missing the point. If they can't hear our influences, they should attempt to, and then go there. Jerry, Phil, myself, all of us were eclectic in the extreme in our tastes. We would go to the farthest reaches to get music because once you develop a facility with your instrument people are going to hear what you're listening to in the music. People will hear what I'm listening to in the music that I play. I want to take them somewhere.

TVP: You've never stopped, for a moment, creating music.

BW: It is my great love.

TVP: What do you do to keep it fresh, to not box yourself in?

BW: Generally speaking, if I start to feel boxed in, it's my own damn fault. Nevertheless, when that happens, the music always takes care of that for me. I'll hear something out of the corner of my ear that grabs my attention and it'll spark me up again. I make every attempt to be eclectic. I think I was born that way, but I make every attempt to live up to that.

TVP: Where do you feel the music going right now?

BW: I don't listen to enough popular music to really have any notion of where it's headed. I know my own music- at least a dozen major projects- to learn this kind of feel, this kind of scale, this or that harmonic development. That keeps me busy, that and just chasing whims until they open up to kick in some new revelation.

TVP: And you're probably still going places you never imagined prior to having gone there.

BW: Yup. I try do that on a daily basis. Sometimes, on a weekly or a monthly basis, something big arrives for me.

TVP: You exist in a world that is constantly expanding, changing.

BW: If isn't expanding, it is dying.

TVP: Music itself is in a way concretized for listeners. Is there a way you manage to convey that expansion to listeners? If you compare the world-view of your fans to that of a typical CPA for example, it does seem to be a great deal more encompassing-

BW: -Or even certain musicians. I saw a television special, I've always been curious about this particular performer. She was doing her act and it was a great big, fully orchestrated act, but all the songs were predetermined and all the passages within the songs were predetermined. I watched with some amount of fascination to see how people could actually live through that kind of experience. I couldn't, I'd go completely fucking nuts playing a note-for-note show every night.

TVP: You've seen Rock and Roll become part of the establishment. You may have been invited to a few ribbon-cutting ceremonies.

BW: Yeah, all that stuff. I don't know how much real Rock and Roll is available these days. I have a fairly classical notion of what that is. If you want to listen to real Rock and Roll, listen to Chuck Berry, Little Richard. That was Rock and Roll. A lot of what gets played these days doesn't have the lilt. It's more marching music than anything else.

TVP: Is it still possible to subvert the more negative aspects of authority through music?

BW: That's what I'm up to.

TVP: You've seen a lot of the developments that evolved from the sixties get systematically erased.

BW: Yup.

TVP: But you've also seen literally third generation members of a counter culture that exists in opposition to that.

BW: There's going to be a struggle for a bit. All we have budding in this country right now is fascism in the pure sense. Study up on what the Romans, who invented fascism, did and compare that to what happened in Washington recently when the rule of law was replaced by the rule of people [Ed. Note: In the Terri Schiavo case]. People were running the show rather than laws. When a State Supreme Court can be overturned by a bunch of people who have an 'in' to the President, and the President tries to do that to please a constituency of his; that is definitively fascism.

TVP: There have been relatively narrow pockets of history when fascism wasn't the rule.

BW: Well, Absolute Monarchy is not fascism. There have been numerous dictatorships that weren't fascistic. If you have a fairly illiterate population, fascism or a dictatorship will be the logical result, not Rule of Law.

TVP: I suspect that over-literalism is the source of all fascism, and that anything that can't be easily defined or processed, anything with a certain amount of irony simply causes fascistic ideology to wilt. In a literal sense, creating something that people truly enjoy is a political act.

BW: And they will try to shut us down, I'm pretty sure. It was done in Germany. For what it's worth, abject literalism goes hand-in-hand fundamentalism. Once again you have a people with no or limited imagination, and therefore are almost necessarily drawn to literalism because they can't accept ambiguity. They can't deal with it.

TVP: Who other than yourself is carrying the torch of what you and The Dead initialized.

BW: There are lots of bands, lots of artists and writers, so many that I can't weigh in because I'd be neglecting this or that person. There are plenty of us around.

TVP: Anything you want to bring up?

BW: Not really, time to get back to rehearsal.

the love kills theory: Sneaky Medicine

September 2007
By Jessica Hopsicker

the love kills theory is like a candy-coated pill, the surface is comprised of an electro-pop psychedelic rock that goes down with inexplicable smoothness. Nevertheless, something in the music sticks, like boiled spaghetti tossed at a wall. The medicine lies within the lyrics. As it dissolves into your mind, you can't help but wonder what it is exactly the band is spooning out. Hidden in the words is a heady dose of contemporary philosophy from such notable writers and thinkers as Aldus Huxley, Guy Debord, and H. L. Mencken. That by itself is a hard pill to swallow without the flashy instrumental wrapping, for the band documents the demise of art in modern culture. The result is rather hypnotic, for even after the music is over, the words rattle around in your brain, perhaps even making you think.

the love kills theory front man, Cevin Soling is no stranger to such a lofty subject matter, since he was after all, obtaining his M.A. in Philosophy at Harvard. As it turned out, he wasn't just another man with a band. Not only does he head up his own record label, Xemu Records, he's also the president of Spectacle Films and World Watch Productions. He is the writer/producer/director of numerous Indie films... and to top that off, he's a South Sea God. The research material was abundant, for I was up to my eyeballs in contemporary philosophers, cargo cults, "children's books," and the Church of the SubGenius. The more I dug up, more was there to be uncovered. I couldn't help but suspect that this guy might be a bit full of himself... until I actually spoke with him.

JH: I've been doing some research and you're like this modern day super Renaissance man. Writer, producer, director, musician, you're president of various companies, and you're a South Sea god. Cevin Soling S: Yeah, among other things, that kind of sums it up.

JH: That's quite a résumé.

CS: I'm also in school right now and I've got paper due right when I get back. So that's the other thing I'm kind of dreading because I have a book to read and paper to write on it and I'm going to have to do that on the plane.

JH: So how's the master's degree in philosophy treating you?

CS: Okay except I'm looking to transfer to apply for the Ph.D. program. So after this semester I'm going to submit my application, so I'm trying to keep my 4.0 going.

JH: With the band heating up, is that demanding a lot of your time, too?

CS: Kind of, but I don't really think about it that way because I enjoy it so much that it never feels like work. I'm planning on getting some kind of pretty decent tour together in the late winter, early spring. That will coincide with our various breaks. So I'm waiting to see, booking is supposed to put us together with some various high-profile bands. They promised at least one date, if not more, opening for The Zombies, because I like The Zombies a lot. Not that we really have the same audience or anything like that, but what a thrill to open for The Zombies. I guess The Sex Pistols are doing some kind of tour. It would be fun to play that, but I don't think that will happen. It would be cool.

JH: Yes it would.

CS: Actually, I don't know if I should say this yet because it's in the early stages and I don't want to blow it for them, but some friends of mine have really good potential for opening for Led Zeppelin and they're pretty thrilled about that. They both have the same booking agent and they've booked for Robert Plant before so it's just a really natural fit if it works out for them.

JH: And your sound has a ton of retro elements, but souped up. What attracts you to a sound?

CS: Basically, when I set about working on the album, I wanted to do something that was kind of distinct, because I felt that there was no point in throwing anything out there that's already been out there. I spent a lot of time trying to come up with distinctive elements that were also contributing and moving the art form forward in some way. I think I sort of gravitated toward the ear candy of the different sound effect noises. And also use them in a way that compliments the content of the song. As far as the other elements of the song, I like things that are melodic and catchy and pop-based in that way, but also still kind of a harder edge. And there are also various instrumentations

415

that I like. I love the monophonic keyboard sound, and I like strings, and I think it's really just an amalgam of noises that I happen to like. I also try to weave into a storytelling tapestry with the sound effects and also to create something that complements that content.

JH: The message is something else entirely, too.

CS: After the music was written I spent at least two years or more working on the lyrics and developing some sort of consistent philosophy. Devo has done something to that effect when they started out, as far as developing philosophy is concerned. But combined with my other pursuits, I really wanted something that was self-consistent and truly heartfelt that I believed in and in that way, it would be a concept album in the sense that all the songs would tie in to the philosophy. The album The Hurting by Tears for Fears did something to that end, although the philosophy in that was Arthur Janov's that they were reflecting, and intermingling my own with elements of a lot of other people that came before us. An amalgam of different works. I wanted to show how these elements apply in different aspects of life.

JH: I read something a while back about trying to put art back into pop culture.

CS: That's sort of the situation. The movement in itself was sort the art of everyday life. I think it's sort of trying to give meaning to existence and not just being a cog in the machine and living without questioning. I don't know if there is more questioning going on or less, it seems like in the 60's there was this whole raise in consciousness and that sort of led into the 70's where there were all sorts of anxiety about that. Even though his films are humorous, Woody Allen I think utilized a sort of questioning of why we're here in a humorous existential sort of anxiety. And than after that those questions sort of went away and there seems to be a lot less of any of that going; it just got harder and harder to get by. There wasn't time for the luxury of any type of that thought. We're sort of reintroducing that and trying to make it accessible.

JH: That's quite a task.

CS: The hardest thing is trying not to make it either preachy or too heavy and to try to be serious but still have a sense of humor about things. I'm sort of walking that line. I think that was the hardest and that was what made things so challenging lyrically was trying to walk that balance.

JH: I was listening to it earlier today and for some reason it was sort of reminiscent of "Bob" Dobbs.

CS: Yeah, I can see that. I was actually hoping to sort of, as far as on the video element of it, I've been trying to work on the video for each song and so far two of the songs have videos, so I've still got a ways to go.

JH: That's what I was watching.

CS: But certainly, in the video, I was going for that sort of "Bob" Dobbs thing. I guess a little less humor than "Bob" Dobbs, but still certainly that element. But that was one of the influences there. That was definitely on the forefront of my mind when I was working on that.

JH: And which one was that one you were working on?

CS: For The Love Kills Theory, for that particular song. Nice that you picked up on that.

JH: Thanks.

CS: In a way Lee Harvey Oswald is used in that "Bob"

Dobbs sort of way. It's like anti-"Bob" Dobbs, but it's actually more like iconography.

JH: Your film work also has an Indy feel, but a lot of heavy hitters are giving it some attention.

CS: Yeah, things only changed recently. I've kind of been avoiding even doing interviews and doing the whole marketing push. Just because in the past it really slowed me down in terms of creative output. It takes a lot of work and a lot of time to actually promote things. Then also, I worked in so much of a vacuum. I have virtually no industry connections in film or music and everything I've done has been very insulated. It's been good and bad, I think mostly when you get involved in a larger community you get people who tell you all the things you can't do and the reasons why certain things can't be done. There's a lot of other negativity in other layers and it makes the process of creating that much harder. Yeah, I mean it's nice and useful to get attention because it enables you to do other things, mostly in terms of access to capital, but there's always a price to be paid when that's involved.

JH: Yeah, without actually whoring yourself out to the other marketing aspect of your work.

CS: I've managed to successfully avoid that for this long. I think at this point I can have a little more security in terms of reaching out now. Now I'm sort of engaged in the marketing push and getting some exposure. I can do things on a little bigger scale.

JH: Did The War on the War on Drugs make you any enemies in high places?

CS: It's funny I was expecting it to. It's funny as far as critical review; it fell very hardcore along party lines. In some cases I thought was kind of amusing, there were people who simply attacked it because they failed to understand the whole concept of irony. There's just no way to respond to that. If you just take something as literal that was never meant to be literal then of course you can quote it and when you see things in print, they only read literally, especially if you take only small sections. It's kind of frustrating to see that although, what are you going to do? No one had a middle-of-the-road opinion on it. I was actually concerned, there were a number of people who worked on the project who used pseudonyms, but there was a case where one journalist named Daniel Forbes who I'd spoken to in the process of doing the research. He had exposed the government's policy of paying TV programs. The financing wasn't straightforward. They got credits in return for the public service announcement dollars if they had TV programs that had anti-drug themes. Shows like Beverly Hills 90210, things like that, would have episodes that were anti-drug propaganda. The same thing would happen in articles and print and different places and they would all get government money under the table. He ended up getting seriously harassed by the feds for writing this article. The article was followed and all sorts of pressure was placed on him. I was sort of gearing up for the worst, and to the best of my knowledge there hasn't been any impact on that end. Which is fine, I have no desire to have my life complicated that way.

JH: So you weren't the least bit disappointed?

CS: No, quite the opposite. The last thing I want was that kind of hassle. If anything it was more of a relief and more reassuring that one can make statements like that and some of us can be left alone even if we are making statements against policy.

JH: The concept of irony seemed completely lost on some of these people?

CS: To some of the critics, I mean the right-wing papers like The Post and The Daily News in New York. If they want to criticize that the movie wasn't funny or was poorly made or something like that then what can I say, you know? That's a criticism. But when you're criticizing it for the wrong reasons and holding that up because you didn't understand that things weren't meant to be taken literally. You just wonder how these people got jobs in writing.

JH: Tell me about your adventure as a South Sea God.

CS: Oh gosh. I've actually made several trips to off-the-beaten-path places. The first one was actually in Borneo where, before I was even in film, this was immediately after I got out of college; I went to Borneo just for the sake of doing something different. I ended up staying with a tribe of headhunters there. That sort of got me hooked on wanting to go to these remote places. I then had done a film in Uganda, which I'm still editing. There's this tribe called the Ik that this anthropologist Colin Turnbull had written about. It's a required reading in Intro to Anthro in most colleges. The book is called The Mountain People and he writes about the three years that he spent with this tribe that in the mountains of northeastern Uganda near the border of Kenya and Sudan. What made his trip kind of remarkable was how he came to thoroughly detest these people and openly recommended that the tribe be dispersed among Africa and be broken up with no remnant that they even existed because the tribe so depraved. And they were at the time he was there, each person was completely self-interested and they would starve the elderly and starve their children and each person was kind of out for themselves. The treatment was worse than simply that. But that was kind of the last that anyone had ever heard of them, so I decided to set up and expedition to try to track them down and find them and also see what they were like. That was a really intense journey. There pretty much wasn't a single day that I wasn't in fear of my life when I was there, and for good reason. We got shot at, got ambushed by gunmen, lions surrounded our tents one night, all sorts of bad things, but we did eventually find the tribe. The following year was when I went to Vanuatu where there is, they're called the Cargo Cult, which I've since talked to anthropologists about and they sort of question the whole description of what a Cargo Cult is. It's hard to even define that anymore. But the more you know, the less it is to use words unfortunately. But this movement began as result of extreme oppression due to missionaries. This group of people took waiting for the return of this spirit named John Frum. Around that time also they came to hear about America. This was right before World War II and they'd been having just beginnings of America coming into that area and eventually the Americans had set up their head operations on one of the islands of Vanuatu. Vanuatu consists of eighty-three islands, and on the island of Santo was the main operations for fighting Japan. The experience that the natives had had with Europeans was predominately either the people being used for indentured servants in work around Australia or had been these horribly oppressive situations where missionaries had come and they'd be forced to convert or have their huts burned down or people killed. So when the Americans arrived it was the first time they had seen white men and black men working together. To some degree there was segregation at that time in the regiments but soldiers were still soldiers, and the natives were treated very well. They were paid well for their work, they were given free medical care, and clothes and food, and the scope of the operations was beyond anything they had ever seen before that the Europeans ever had. So when the war ended America just kind of took off and left. This also happened at the time of the rise of this John Frum movement and it got tied in with the worshiping of America. So they've been waiting for America to come, as well as the return of John Frum, and there's supposed to be this gift of tremendous amount of good brought to the island and that's sort of Cargo Cult aspect of it. But there's a Millianism aspect where it's sort of the return of this messiah as well. So when I came to the island I got a number of corporate sponsors to donate a tremendous amount of goods for humanitarian reasons as well as product placement for the film. All the goods that I got were thoroughly consistent with the lifestyles of the people which would be cooking utensils and cooking pots and fishing tackle and gear, nothing that the people hadn't had some contact or exposure with. Not necessarily things that they had, but things that wouldn't alter their lifestyle, it would complement it.

JH: So, no TV's or anything like that?

CS: No, no TV's. You know, lighters, coolers, stoves, generators, solar panels; I mean globalization is taking effect so there is the arrival of a number of things there already. So as a result of me bringing all these things, it resulted in a sort of elevated stature. There was a lot of resistance on the part of the government; the government is in cahoots with the missionaries. There's one central government of all eighty-three islands. They have a small presence on each island. The government wants to see the movement extinguished to a certain degree, except that because there is curiosity it brings some attention to the region, but they really want to see them become Christianized. They saw my presence there as reaffirming their traditional customs and beliefs which is this historic struggle that goes back hundreds of years and persists today. They are still trying to extinguish the traditional customs and culture and have them all convert. So they were deathly afraid that my presence was going to make it that much harder to convert them. So there's a lot of pressure and resistance from the government and a lot of effort to basically impede me from seeing the people and that led to a big conflict with the people and the government. They had threatened to burn down the government presence on the island if I wasn't permitted free access. So the basic conflict over me kind of magnified my stature there. So the following year I was asked by the government to return because there was so much demand from the people for me to come back. They had a huge ceremony for me. All the chiefs of the island were there. They gave me land on the island. They adopted me into the tribe and announced that the whole island was essentially mine even though they were legally giving me one chunk of land. And the legend has sort of grown, and continues to grow.

JH: Sounds like fun.

CS: I respect the people greatly and I'm not trying to exploit them in any way, it's walking that fine line between having a presence while respecting their ways and traditions.

JH: Is there anything else you're working on?

CS: Yeah. There's the most recent film project that I just sent out to Sundance. The tentative title is The War on Kids. I'm going to change the title, but I've already sent it off that way. It's a two part documentary, I've just finished with part one, which is problems with public education in America. It's not simply just showing how bad public education is or the education system itself as being this autocratic, fascist institution. It's basically an indictment that people will voluntarily send their children to places like that. That's essentially what the film is about, although it looks predominately like it's just an indictment of the public education system as well as the amount of pharmacological abuse through the drugging of kids with Ritalin and Adderall. Then part two will deal with society, things like curfews and the rise of boarding and reform schools, and hotels and villages and all sorts of different places where kids are not allowed at all. It's just this overall societal attempt to marginalize kids and keep them out of public fear. One thing I'm working is also a series of books. They're written kind of like children's books but they're for all ages. There sort of more for a college audience.

JH: The Rumpleville Chronicles?

CS: The Rumpleville Chronicles, yeah. Book number three just got back from the press, although I guess it won't come out until January. There's a series of ten. I'm in pre-pre-production on a documentary on the phenomena of enlightenment.

JH: Really?

CS: Yeah. It's in it its very early stages right now; I'm just sort of reaching out to people who have contacts and access with a number of people. Things unfortunately take on a life of their own much faster than I ever like and I get sucked into situations before I'm really ready. I ran into someone who has pretty good access to the Dali Llama and I know I only have a narrow window of opportunity to talk to him. So I'll probably get sucked into making that before I really want to.

JH: Is there anything else I haven't covered?

CS: Probably, but that's a bunch of it.

JH: I suppose I should let you go back to your vacation.

CS: This is the last day of it anyway. I should be home today. I have to work on that paper for class.

JH: That doesn't seem as adventurous as lions or battles or anything like that.

CS: No, this is a vacation that was anything but. I remember it was just day after day in Uganda of some kind of real present threat. We'd be in a village and people would have anthrax. It was just a constant, every day thing. Each day you'd think you'd have whatever you were confronted with the previous day under control. Although being in a war zone with a large resistance army as a clear and present persistent danger was never easy. We were driving through these abandoned refugee camps because the LRA was in the area. And always having to worry about that was intense. But there was a point when a threshold was exceeded. That was when we were hiking and came across some elephants. African elephants are not like Asian elephants, African elephants are not trainable and they're not friendly. Allegedly, the Natives insist that they have a collective memory of all the poaching and if an elephant wants to kill you, it will. There's not much you can do about it. It can outrun you and there's just not much you can do. So we came upon these elephants and they started expressing their unhappiness at our being there and started trumpeting and kicking up dirt and threatening us. It was at that point that I really lost it. I was staring one of the elephants in the eyes and saying, "you'd better just fucking kill me and get this over with, or just shut up." I kind of really lost it at that point. And then after that everything was a lot easier because I had just reached my threshold. Nothing really mattered too much after that, after the elephants didn't kill us for whatever reason.

JH: Wow.

CS: Then we were ambushed later that day. There were these three gunmen. We had this vehicle we had driven just a certain distance to a missionary outpost, and then hiked the rest of the way. Then after we hiked and retrieved our vehicle there were these three gunmen blocking the road. There isn't really a road there, just a dry riverbed, so there wasn't any place to turn around. We had to jump out of our vehicle when we saw the gunmen. They'd shoot the driver, or everyone, and rob whoever's there. So we saw them about a hundred yards ahead and jumped out of the vehicle and ended up walking up to them with our cameras and started filming them. Somehow we managed to engage them. I had taken a Polaroid camera with me and we showed them a photo of them I had on the Polaroid. They saw themselves and they were just kind of amused. We got out of a lot very unfortunate situations like that; where they for whatever reason let us go. So no, my homework isn't like that.

The Beautiful Girls:
More Than Skin Deep

March 2006
By T. Virgil Parker

There is a kind of purity that comes from knowing nothing at all, and perhaps a much more profound purity that comes from knowing enough to avoid the things that swallow so many of us. It matters whether your motivations are coming from yourself, or from what you think the world wants you to be. This has a direct bearing on what you give the world, and what you take from it. We often find ourselves doing things we don't like in exchange for stuff that we don't really want.

When we listen to music, are we sharing experience? Are we helping someone buy a Lexis? The question goes to the heart of the way Aussie band The Beautiful Girls serve up their uniquely pristine music. If most bands are trying to hack away at a diamond, The Beautiful Girls are planting small seeds here and there, and letting the fruit ripen as if by itself.

Talking with Mat McHugh is very much like listening to the music of his band. You don't get the slightest clue that he has a huge following in Australia, and is beginning to make a serious splash here in the States. You wouldn't guess that he has a new disk hitting the stands. It is obvious that his devotion to Roots music is the result of his unusual talent at getting to the core of meaning, and shaving away all the petty spirit-killing distractions.

TVP: A lot of our readers are from New York. It looks like New York had a profound effect on your vision as a musical artist.

Mat McHugh: I lived in New York for almost a year, back in '99. I came there inspired by a singer/songwriter called Chris Whiteley. He used to perform in Washington Square Park and he used to play on the streets and I thought that was a pretty romantic notion. I had lived in India for a year and when I moved to New York, I played wherever I could.

TVP: It seems like you tuned in on a different New York than a lot of New Yorkers tune in on.

MM: The inspiration for me playing music didn't come from New York. If New York did anything it kind of gave me a kick in the pants. It made me realize that there were so many amazing artists out there struggling to be heard. If you're going to get heard in this world then you're going to have to get your stuff together. It was motivational for the most part but t was also inspirational because it was such and amazing city. I get inspired by the vibe I experienced on the beach, growing up. I try to be honest as to where I came from, rather than trying to manufacture some spirit or vibration or whatever.

TVP: Most people who are trying to make an impression in the music industry try to take it as far over the top as they can go. You appear to be doing the exact opposite.

MM: I like spacey music. My favorite records are all Jazz and Blues records. Miles Davis, Coltrane, there's spaces all over those records. They're not filled up with studio stuff that will sound good compressed on MTV or VH1 or whatever. It's actual music in conversational form, which is what music should be. It shouldn't be a thick chunk of information just dumped on your head. It should stay a living and breathing thing, and that involves space and subtlety. I'm interested in those things.

TVP: There's a real purity to the sound, nothing extraneous. Does that require a lot of discipline on your part?

MM: It depends on what kind of aesthetic you get stuck in your head. I think you can go at things in certain ways. The tendency in our day and age is to make things huge. If there's space, fill it up. It's kind of like cramming a million ideas into one little space. There's a million jump cuts in every video, like the attention span has been reduced to one second. It's just all slammed in together and it doesn't really sit with me too well. I like to just chill with things. It doesn't require too much effort to just strip things back. You have to have the confidence to go with it and be prepared for people the say that there isn't enough music. It's nice to stand out because of the spaces in your music as opposed to other things, I guess.

TVP: You spent some time in an ashram. Did it help you to get the internal space required to get at an open sound like that?

M.M.: I think definitely, in a lot of ways. I spent a lot time thinking about my motivations. I tried to get to the essence of things as closely as I could. What's the reason I'm playing this song, or why am I even playing music? What am I trying to communicate, of myself, in the music. It instilled in me the idea of not just doing something for the sake of doing it. I just wanted to do it for a purpose and a reason. It's in there now, that approach to making music.

Anything you do informs your output creatively. That had a huge effect on myself and on whatever music I'm involved in. I would say.

TVP: Do you feel that there's a lot less authenticity out there now?

MM: People who look for authenticity have to find other ways of looking for it. Because everything is such the industry now, it's all packaged and processed and really easy to digest. It's served to you on a plate, and if you don't go looking you'll just eat what you're served. It's like sitting down at the dinner table and having the same meal over and over again. You have to be thinking that there's nice, tempting food out there and you just have to go and look for it. There's a lot of people who react to one side of the music industry and go straight to the other. In our travels and in the bands we've played with and at the places we've played, I think that there's a lot of authentic people and musicians. I don't think they often make it to the top of the charts, but I like it that way too.

TVP: At this point in the band's history I'm guessing that the industry is talking to you, and I bet that the band is going to stay as independent as possible.

MM: Our first set of demos became an album in Australia and one of our songs immediately got heavy rotation nationally on the radio. We've had major labels dangling brass rings ever since the band started. They talk big deals and money and tell us we're the next big thing. None of us have ever been interested. We have different agendas. We're happy with being independent because there's nothing more fulfilling than being able to work, and employ your friends and have all the creative control that you require. All the things that are great about being independent are worth too much to throw away. It is a lot harder, but it's all the more satisfying in the end. We enjoy how we do things and it keeps us in a good enough mindset to keep us making music that means something.

TVP: That's unbelievably refreshing.

MM: I can't look at it any other way. I'd be selling myself short, and I don't think I'd be able to go to sleep at night, really. It depends on what value you put on what you do, as opposed to what you can get out of it.

TVP: What is the band's composition style like, is it more spontaneous, or is it more structured?

MM: The songs are all skeleton-structured, so they go from A to B, but how they do that depends on what goes down. We try to get into the space of what the song's trying to get across. That's why it's still really fun to play the songs. Every single night we inhabit the songs, so they change, they grow. It's all living and breathing music. I've been in and around bands where it's all very heavily structured, where every little pick attack on the guitar strings is all militantly observed. We're not like that. If it feels good, it feels good. That's the main criteria.

TVP: I'm thinking about the song, "Girl, Lately Things Have Been Changing" on the new disk. It's almost like a chemist or an engineer sat down to synthesize a complete fusion of Blues and Reggae. I have to wonder, did you just do that, or did you sit down and plot it out?

MM: That was the fastest one that we did. We were in the middle of recording and I was at home watching television and I came up with the riff, brought it in the next day, and within five minutes we banged out the song. The lyrics are just off the top of my head.

TVP: That's a melodica lead in there, right, a little piano that you blow into?

MM: A lot of the horn lines on the record we play live with the melodica. It's a sound we really like. There's a lot of early dub records that use that. You can get melodies and set a kind of mood with that sound.

TVP: You're touring a lot in Australia and in America. How different is the American audience these days.

MM: The only difference really, is the size. We're pretty big in Australia right now. So, the only difference is the size, since we're just beginning to catch on in the U.S. The people are surprisingly similar. It's surprising how similar it is all around the world. It's bizarre and refreshing at the same time. We go to Japan or Denmark and wonder what the people will be like and aside from a few cultural differences; most people's hearts are the same. Of course the people we see are like-minded enough to get into our music. The weird thing is how similar people are.

TVP: You can almost hear the sunlight pouring out of the CD. Do you think there's a sense of local color in the music?

MM: Where we grew up is a pretty nice area, nice as in the environment. We grew up on the beach, not too different from Southern California or Hawaii. The bands we grew up around were all pretty Punky and pretty tough. To me those bands sounded like bands from elsewhere. I wanted to honestly represent what it felt like being from where we were from. We've tried to make that an underlying thing in our band. We're not from an urban area that has drive-by shootings and such; we're from the beach. The east coast of Australia is pretty nice. We didn't want to represent ourselves in a false way.

TVP: A lot of heavy bands seem to be going out of their way to be generic, limiting themselves to, it seems, the same three notes.

MM: There are only twelve notes. I don't want to point a finger, but you can train yourself to any degree to play music. A lot of bands see a band on MTV who make a lot of money and get laid every night. They aspire to those things, and they use the music to get to those things. So they play the same kind of music. A lot of people make music as a means to an end. There's a huge difference between doing that and making music because you have to and because the world gets to you. You have to have something to say back to the world. Listen to a generic metal band and go listen to Bob Dylan. You'll see the difference. Without real inspiration there's only so many notes you can play over and over again.

TVP: Because being real is a strong motivation for you, how do you know that you've got it right?

MM: You know when you've got it wrong. I get an uneasy feeling if it isn't right I have a sound in my head and I know how it should be presented. If it isn't that way, you keep on chipping away, if necessary until it's all gone. We brought in a great percussionist and got him to play all this great stuff, and when it came time to mix it down, we were like 'let's take this out' and so on. We were left with one little tiny conga hit every four bars, and it was just right. He was wondering what happened to all his tracks. Then he really listened and it made sense. The best thing to do is leave your ego at the door. If you're worried about people thinking you're a great musician, you're missing the point. The best stuff you can do at times is the most innocent, endearing stuff that won't land you in Percussion Player Magazine.

No Stranger to Fate:
Dave King of Flogging Molly

September 2007

By Jessica Hopsicker

I received my copy of Whiskey on a Sunday from a co-worker during my weekend job as an adult video store clerk. When I wasn't working seven days a week or drinking on my downtime, I finally had time to watch the disc. It was then my stomach flipped, "I'm gonna interview these guys," I thought to myself as I sprawled out on the futon completely entrapped by the band's full length documentary. The pre-interview jitters I took as a sign, that perhaps it wasn't some sort of childish delusion, interviewing a band that I've loved for years. Sure enough, here it is.

Dave King, the Dublin born singer/songwriter/guitarist of the punk infused Celtic menagerie known as Flogging Molly, is no stranger to fate himself. There was a time he almost went down the same path as his some of his friends who joined the IRA, but King figured there was a different means to bring about social change. Partially due to his upbringing, he found it through music. But his career didn't start right off as the enduring band so many of us have come to love. In fact, the traditional music path had been something he wanted to escape. The mandolin was replaced with an electric guitar and he joined up with Motorhead guitarist Eddy Clark in the late 80's group Fastway. It proved to be the proverbial rags to riches scenario; until he started do his own thing.

He found himself in LA cleaning the clubs he used to play, plugging away on an acoustic. Then he met the young fiddle player Bridget Regan. It was then the music, as if by unforeseen circumstance, was brought back to his parents' home in the old English Barracks of Beggar's Bush with the fiddle and tin whistle. Much like the rest of the seven-piece ensemble he happened upon her by chance. They became part of Dave King's musical movement with hardly an audition. Melding the traditional Irish Folk instruments with the driving elements of punk rock wasn't an easy feat. For years, every Monday night they played flogging away at small LA pub called Molly Malone's, and there couldn't have been a more apt name for such an outfit.

I caught up with King in Ireland, where he and his band mates were working on songs for yet another album. He was an exceedingly pleasant guy to talk to even though I interrupted his morning routine of running errands. Or, I think it was morning there. Either way I couldn't think of a better way to spend my afternoon.

Jessica Hopsicker: I've been a fan for a while.

Dave King: Oh, thank you. Thanks very much.

JH: So you're in Ireland now?

DK: I am, yes. Just writing some new songs and we're going to be heading back to America on Monday, and do a little bit more roading and get ready for the Warped tour.

JH: Are you pretty much used to such a strict touring regime?

DK: At this point yeah. I mean, we've been touring for quite a while and we just got back from Europe where we had a few dates that went very well. You have a few weeks to work on some new stuff and take some time off with the family and then you're back out again, you know? We are a live touring band, you know?

JH: What do you look forward to upon coming home?

DK: Ohhh, all the things that are broken down in the house. All the things that stopped working while you were away. But really, it's just nice to be back home. I like the quietness. I find that like, away from the road, I like to lead a very quiet life. You know, go down to the local pub, hang out with local people, take it mellow, cook at home, read a lot. Just catch up on things, you know.

JH: Looking back, what was the epitome of a Flogging Molly show and has there been a time when you felt it wasn't worth it?

DK: Oh, no. Our live show is the pinnacle of what we're all about. It's the combination of the people who've followed us for years and us doing what we do best. When it all comes together it's unbelievable.

JH: I gathered from one of the quotes from the Whiskey on a Sunday DVD that if you don't leave a Flogging Molly show sweaty, covered in beer, and don't have some sort of spiritual awakening, it isn't your thing.

DK: I don't know what kind of spiritual awakening that would be, I don't know. Maybe spirits awakening, I don't know. I mean a lot of songs are about life and hardship and it's time to celebrate that at our live shows. So, you know, there's no airs or graces. It's all like real stuff, you know?

JH: All right, what do you feel would be the best song that you've written?

DK: Oh, Christ. That is a very, very difficult question because I'm in the middle of writing a whole lot of new songs and it's hard for me to even think about the songs I've written. God, I have no idea. That's a very good question actually. I wouldn't have a clue, I really wouldn't. Every song means something different to me. Every song has a special place. It reminds me of certain things and you know, and probably in a year's time when I go back and listen to the album, it will be very interesting. It'll be a nice map and a guide of where I was in my life at that particular time. But I don't have a favorite song, no I don't. What's yours?

JH: Oh, yeah, that is a good question.

DK: I have no idea, I really don't.

JH: Yeah, ever since I found out about the interview, I've been listening to Flogging Molly before I wake up, before I go to bed, research, you know.

DK: So where are you at?

JH: Holland Patent. It's a small town in Upstate New York.

DK: Oh, nice one, nice one.

JH: With all the Irish fests up the wazoo this summer, how do you describe the Celtic pride in America?

DK: Once again, it's a celebration. It's a celebration of hard times. People from Ireland had no direction, unfortunately, but to leave Ireland due to hunger and no work, no anything. I think it's a celebration of triumph that America is such a great country for people of ethnicities to thrive in. Ireland is a great example of that. It's lovely to see people have been aroused and are having a great time to fiddles and accordions and mandolins. At one point, music was all the Irish people had, and to see people from different nations and different countries and different backgrounds enjoying that, it's a wonderful thing.

JH: I'm excited. If you weren't fronting such a band, what would you be doing?

DK: Oh Christ. Probably painting houses. I mean, I used to paint houses, drive trucks, do stuff like that. What I've always wanted to do was just find myself and to discover myself and to do the best that I can with what I did with myself. That's been writing music. I want to be a father. I want to be a good father. I just want to do the best I can, you know? But what would I be doing, God knows.

JH: You think you're getting there, though? You know, doing the best you can?

DK: Yes, I think so. I'm trying to look at each scenario the best way that I can. Look at it the best way that I can. I take in all around me and put it towards my writing and hopefully I write music and lyrics that I can be proud of. That's most important to me, to write songs and lyrics that I am proud of. Then we see what happens after that, you know.

JH: How much of it would you attribute to luck, good or bad, that got you where you are?

DK: Oh absolutely, luck has so much to with it. Meeting various people, being in the right situation at the right time. Luck is something that you don't see at the time. Luck is something in hindsight that you see. This band has been together since 1997. You can look back at all the luck that we've had and we've been very fortunate and that's why a band like us takes nothing for granted. We walk out on stage and there are people there. We're going, "Christ, there's still people coming, this is great!" But a lot of it is luck. Anybody who thinks that luck isn't involved in what they do; it's a big part. You can say the luck of the Irish maybe, but I don't know.

JH: Yeah.

DK: We've actually had a summer here that it's pissed rain every day. There's not much luck in that.

JH: Oh man. We've been in a drought.

DK: It's rained here every day. But you know.

JH: Do you think it would be harder to pack up and leave home nowadays?

DK: I've been on the road for a long time and when people have started families or want to have families; it's always a natural thing that people want to spend more time at home. All we're focused on right now is the Warped tour. Finishing the Warped Tour and producing the best album that we possibly can. That's the most important thing to us right now. That's what we're here to do and that's what we're doing and we just want to do the best that we can. We've been working over in Ireland now on and off for the last month or so and we've been sitting in the garage writing songs and some the songs are a lot different from what Flogging Molly would be accustomed with. Lyrically, maybe not, but there's a lot of ground being covered in this next album. To me, it's really bringing a lot of traditional music into the twenty-first century and it has all the traditional elements. We're taking chances that I don't think anybody else has ever done.

JH: What possessed you to meld such genres together?

DK: When I heard Bridget playing fiddle it sort of sparked off something in my heart. I've always been involved in other genres of bands, whether it be rock bands or punk bands or whatever, and then I heard Bridget playing fiddle and it was like, it seemed jell-able stuff. It just seems to melt stuff together. There wasn't a huge effort to, shall we say, mangle the two together, because it was very, very easy. Traditional riffs were fitting over what I was writing and it just seemed to be a powerful statement and that's the way we went forward. It wasn't as hard as people would think it was. - I'm gonna do a u-turn right now and hopefully I won't get a ticket or a truck up my ass.

JH: So it also seems that there is an ever-renewing crop of sixteen-year-olds donning Flogging Molly shirts.

DK: Yeah, it's unbelievable. Obviously I spend most of my time in Ireland but every time I got to America or Europe I always see people wearing Flogging Molly shirts. It's over-whelming, it's breathtaking. We started as this band in a little tiny pub in Los Angeles and it's been very good to us. It's very exciting and it's fun.

JH: Did you ever think that it would turn out this way?

DK: Not at all, no way. Did we believe in ourselves? Absolutely we did. Did we believe in the music that we were playing? Absolutely we did. Nobody could tell us to do any different. But did we think it would go this way? Of course not, you know. Of course not.

JH: Yeah, but as luck would have it.

DK: There you go. You go back to that again. I mean there's a lot of that, you know?

JH: I think it was luck that got me this interview.

DK: Hopefully it's good luck.

JH: I think so.

DK: Alrighty then.

JH: Well, I think I've covered all my questions.

DK: Well you did a great job, thanks for calling.

JH: Thank you. Is there anything else we should add?

DK: We're looking forward to the Warped Tour and looking forward to being back on American soil again and playing to a wonderful bunch of people, as we always seem to do in America. We're looking forward to it. - I nearly knocked down a little black dog, where you going, move over, get off the road. You have to imagine it, I'm driving down the road, and only one car fit at a time, and it's a small country lane.

JH: That's too much...

DK: Okay, well until I talk to you again, all the best.

Haale: Finding Her Comet

April 2008
By T. Virgil Parker

Does it ever bug you that nearly every major media company in the nation assumes that you; yes you, have below average intelligence? Record companies, MTV/VH1, magazines, all seem to be earning their keep by exploiting the assumption that your idea of culture peaks out at Fox Reality Network.

And why exactly do people in other countries assume that Americans are idiots? Could it be in part that most of our global media empire is obsessing over certain august personages? (See: Lohan, Lindsay; Hilton, Paris). Go ahead and assume that the world judges us harshly on this point, even though Americans have no monopoly on the decline of Western Civilization (See: Murdoch, Rupert).

I choose this moment to vent because Haale's music is exactly the kind that easily falls victim to the industry; an industry, in fact, that she and her kind are rescuing from oblivion. She and a score of other unsigned artists and

Indie film people are kitting a shroud for the myth of the ignorant American.

What about her music could be particularly scary to the big AR people? As melodic as it is, as accessible as it is, it insists on taking you places. She did not name her new CD *No Ceiling* without reason. We resist mysterious journeys because we know that it is not us who arrives at the destination; it is who we will become.

The rugged among us plunge into demanding art. The part of the brain we didn't get from lizards needs to get stoked up now and then. Dare I say a good chunk of North America needs this treatment?

Now, on the subject of Haale herself. Getting ready to talk to this breakaway talent, I was afraid that she would impart life-altering wisdom that would send me immediately to an ashram, or a commune. But talking with her is more like collaborating, even conspiring. She, like the music she creates, represents a seamless synthesis of Eastern and Western concepts. It is evident that art is sacred to her, but it must also be beautiful, and satisfying as well.

T. V. Parker: You had other plans; music almost kidnapped you. Is that accurate?

Haale: Oh yeah, definitely. But in a way, it was always there. When I was a child it was something I wanted to do, and I kind of took a detour. Then it definitely stole me away. Thank God.

TVP: Writing has such a very different reward structure from music. Do you think you benefit from that immediacy of the way people receive music?

H: Absolutely. Especially when you're singing in another language. I could stand up and speak in Persian, and except for the rhyme and the rhythm of the language it probably wouldn't be that interesting, but music carries some emotional quality that allows you to transcend linguistic barriers.

TVP: I noticed right away that your music is highly trance-inducing.

H: I think it's something I just naturally gravitate towards. My favorite Beatles song, for instance, when I was a kid was *Tomorrow Never Knows*, which is their droney, trancy eastern song. So I always have been gravitated towards that and it's definitely part of the tradition in Persian music. But I also find it in American music bands like Velvet Underground. There is this trancy, droney element in a lot of Western music too. I've always liked it, so it's pretty natural for me to do that in my own music without much thought.

TVP: It's interesting that it's part of the main culture in Persian music, but it's part of the counterculture in American music.

H: That's true!

TVP: You have to be experiencing a lot of, say, consciousness expansion, while you're performing the music.

H: Performing, yeah. In performing there's a certain time period where I can lose certain things. You know like dialogue in the mind. I can just listen and sing. And definitely as sound travels through you, it's pretty intense. It is in itself trance-inducing. Even when I just sing and do vocal practice in the bathtub, which I often do, I can be transported.

TVP: You manage to combine a contemporary world view with something that seems eternal. What kind perspective does that come from?

H: There's certain poets that I've found to be most

compelling, like H. D., and Allen Ginsberg, and Eleni Sike-lianos, and then the Persian poets like Rumi. I've read a lot of poetry and I definitely come out of that tradition of post-beat poetry.

TVP: The lyrics do stand up as poetry as well. I don't know anyone who's using complex imagery in lyrics like you're doing right now. It's got to be a benefit of the study of creative writing that you've done as well as having fertile soil for it to grow upon.

H: Definitely. When I listen to music I always listen to the lyrics, so that's one of the most important things to me. Definitely when I write, I do write poetry. I don't want the music to limit language because it doesn't have to. And actually it's funny because this morning we were staying at someone's house in Nashville. I was looking at their CD collection and I pulled out Hejira by Joni Mitchell just to read the lyrics. And it's amazing, her language and how many words she can fit into a song and how courageous she is with language! She's definitely one of my inspirations. So I definitely write poetry when I write songs.

TVP: Did you have to learn Persian culture or was it intrinsic to your household growing up?

H: It was definitely swirling around the house, that's for sure. My parents had a lot of books in their library. There's Chekhov and James Joyce and there's Sohrab Sepehri, a Persian writer. And they would be playing Persian traditional music in the house as well as western classical music, and the Persian traditional music often has lyrics like Rumi, he's the big one. And Hafiz. So I was hearing it as I grew up, but I wasn't so interested in it. I think I started noticing it, really allowing myself to pay attention to it and dig into it and relate to it, later in life, past my teens.

TVP: Music in the house as a child is kind of like wallpaper. But what really startles me is that you are inherently an intersection of what I find most compelling of both eastern and western modes of expression. I have to wonder, how is mainstream culture processing that?

H: All I've seen so far really is audience reactions at shows. We just played in a town called Hot Springs, Arkansas. I never thought I'd be playing a show in Arkansas. It was a wonderful space. It was called the Low Key Arts Building. It was a very beautiful space with lots of art on the walls and a cool audience and they loved it! They were really yelping through the show and gave us a very warm standing ovation and bought a lot of CDs. So I think there's something happening even when we go to places where there might be more conservatism or less exposure to eastern culture. There's definitely an interest. I think that people want to hear new sonic territories. We have a huge library of rock. Drum kit, bass, and electric guitar, lyrics in English, we have so many bands we can listen to like that. We're saturated with it. So one of the things I think that people in the mainstream want, it seems to me, is something a little different. There's an emotional quality to this music that's pretty intense, and there's a relevancy socially politically now. I see pretty good responses in the audiences so far and nice reviews from the audiences so far. So that's about all I know about mainstream. We're not on top 40 radio and I don't know if we'll ever be, but that's okay with me.

TVP: You don't really want to be, I don't think. With The Beatles as an influence, it must have been mind boggling to work with Sean Lennon.

H: It was amazing! He came down to the studio. We were recording downtown on the lower east side in a studio called Woodshop Recordings. He came down and he listened to the song. I don't even think he was definitely going to play that day. Basically, the producer that we found invited him to come down and hear it. We weren't so sure if he was actually going to do anything on it. Then he listened to it, and he really liked it. I wrote down the lyrics and he looked them over. First he played bass. He listened to the song twice–it's got kind of an interesting chord progression, it's not the easiest song in the world–and he had it down in two takes. Just beautiful, very Beatles-esque harmonies on the vocals and even saying a couple words in Persian. He really did a beautiful job and it was wonderful to watch him in action. And to really feel the tradition that runs through it, you can hear it. And his album, Friendly Fire, is awesome.

TVP: Yes, it is. It's intrinsically him. People are looking for other things, but it's him. When you're creating, do you feel a big difference between artwork, like a painting, and music? Or does it feel like it comes from the same place?

H: I think I have to be in the same space to do it, mentally. I remember hearing Allen Ginsberg once say that I only write when I'm in my right mind. I understand what he means by that. I think sitting down to do a collage or to write music or to write lyrics, there is a certain mental space that I like to be in. That I need to be in, essentially. The sensor has to be somehow present but shut down simultaneously.

TVP: It's not the part of the mind that orders a pizza, that's for sure.

H: I think it is a relaxed mind. You've got to be able to bend and twist and enjoy it. So I can't do it while I'm feeling pressure.

TVP: Here's the question. You've suddenly got a first-class disk on your hands. Do you feel the pressure to kick out another one, or do you just do it?

H: I can't wait to do the next album! We've written a bunch of songs, and now we're on the road. We're doing twenty-five shows in thirty days. We're going to get back to New York in mid-April, and we have a little bit of time before we get out again, so we're going to work on the songs and try to map out what we're going to do with this next album a little bit, then probably get back after the next round of touring and start recording. So we were thinking of starting in June with the actual recording process. But basically, I want to keep writing and recording. It keeps my juices flowing, it keeps me in a good place. I know what you mean, you make a good piece of art and you wonder if you can live up to it and do something better next time. I am definitely in a space of wanting to evolve and do better work, just to keep it real. I'm definitely on the planet here and experiencing and engaging in things. I think as long as there are engagements happening, the ideas come and it's possible to keep creating.

TVP: You know what I was going to ask you about Joni Mitchell now that I'm thinking about it; she's a painter as well. She talks about the color of her sound. That just totally applies to what you're doing.

H: Yeah I think it's black, and shimmers in gold, too.

TVP: The funniest thing about the way you've built a song is that it draws people in to a certain point and then it forces them to go where the song goes. And that's almost a key of Sufi music, that it requires a certain amount of effort on the part of the listener. Did you study Sufi music deeply, or are we going back to the landscape of just growing up around the music?

H: I would say growing up around it and listening to it now. I never studied with a Persian music teacher, but listening.

TVP: The immediacy is certainly evidence of not going hardcore into the Sufi thing, and I think that's what's making people seek it out who wouldn't normally.

H: I think that's true.

TVP: So what are your plans now?

H: We're actually moving. We're in the van, we're going to Ashville. We've got a show tonight, and a show tomorrow in Chapel Hill, and bunch of shows lined up until mid-April and then we'll be back in town. So we'll hit some of those new songs, and then we'll go back out, and come back, and record. I think my plans are just to continue writing songs and recording, working on my voice. This is it, this is my water. My water and drink.

TVP: You're certainly in the right place. Is there anything you want to add?

H: I think we covered a lot of ground. I guess my favorite song on the album lately is "Zero to One."

TVP: Yeah, that's strong. I'm trying hard not to be too "fanlike," because the stuff is so good.

George Clinton: One Nation Under a Jam and Funkentelechy for All

February 2006
By Jessica Hopsicker

Funkentelechy: "The actualization of funk rather than its potential."

In other words, it means turning all that pent-up potential funk into something ass-shakingly kinetic. It's based on the belief that everyone has the funk bone somewhere inside. It's all the matter of catching the funkafied vibe and rising against the status quo, stupidity, and the rigidity of society. The credo lies in the Funkadelic phrase and album title, "Free your mind ... and your ass will follow."

George Clinton, the grandmaster, unimpeachable president, era-spanning madman made his start some 50 years ago. In the process, he created a whole funkin' universe. The seeds were sewn with the Parliaments, a quintet inspired by Frankie Lyman and the Teenagers, formed in a New Jersey barbershop. If "Funk is the DNA of Hip-Hop" P-Funk is the pure uncut stuff or Plainfield, NJ Funk. The Sci-fi driven doo-wop gospel group was the vehicle that spawned the whole mythology. In years to come, Mothership became a household term, forever known as the great mystical interplanetary chariot that transports Dr. Funkenstein and Starchild to Earth when all the world's peoples are in the need of a great global spanking.

Due to some legalities, mainly the Parliaments label going under, he formed the acid rock primal funk politically infused band Funkadelic, a concoction psychedelic soul, driving guitars and of course that P-funk goodness. Together they knocked out albums such as America Eats its Young, The Electric Spanking of War Babies, and Uncle Jam Wants You. They tackled the meaty issues such as injustice, poverty, hypocrisy consumerism and the stratification of the classes with the awesome power of overt lyrics and Hendrixian guitars. Funkadelic became the sonic backdrop to a generation. That is until legal wrangling with former managers ground the whole thing to a halt.

This is where it gets confusing. After he loses the Parliaments, he makes Funkadelic. He gains Parliaments back and drops the s. He loses Funkadelic, goes solo, releases more albums, after a 12-year battle, the interplanetary funkmaster wins Funkadelic back. Even after all that P-Funk stands to have another definition, an abbreviation for Parliament Funkadelic.

Now, finally, after years and years of creation and litigation, the whole P-funk Empire is under the one roof of the lord and master of all worlds funky. Ten years beyond his last disk "T.A.P. O. A. F.O. M. or *The Awesome Power of a Fully Operational Mothership,* George Clinton resides under yet another label, this time its his own, The C-Kunspyruhzy, LLC. The aptly named shiny new self-released double disk How Late Do U Have 2BB4UR Absent? features Parliament, Funkadelic, the symbol formerly known as Prince, Del the Funkee Homosapien, Joi and Jazze Pha, his granddaughter Sativa and the ever increasing funk mob. The disk is dripping with the stripped down funk, do wop roots, horny allegory and those booty bouncin' jams. " I can't wait to grow this Pfunk thang all over again," he laughs, "I got the old roots with the live concerts and the new branches with the various band members, as well as my own solo projects."

Amazingly enough, it's 2006 and he has yet another generation of followers. We flagged down Dr. Funkenstein himself, George Clinton, at a Los Angeles hotel via a phone and a space age voice activated tape recorder. It appears the crazy music making galactic funk man doesn't appear to be letting up any time soon.

Jessica Hopsicker: On your quest from NJ hairstylist to interplanetary funk machine, did anybody think you were just crazy?

George Clinton: Oh, I've been there a couple of times. The madhouse a few times, I think I'm crazy myself.

JH: I was going to say, 50 years of funk later, do they still think you're nuts?

GC: I don't think so, they're funkin' by now.

JH: Can you talk to me about the struggles and challenges you faced while bringing this new disc out?

GC: Well, it's all fun there; I wouldn't say there are challenges. It's been fun and I say we're just getting started.

JH: With your new label, The C Kunspruhzy, are you happy with the outcome so far?

GC: For sure, like I say I never want to get to the end of a result. Because I like doing it and as long as I'm doing it I'm fine.

JH: There is a generation of kids who don't know that you were the inspiration for the Chili Peppers, Outcast, and Dr Dre.

GC: They're finding out in due time, that's keeps new fans always coming along. They find that out there's always the new possibility of new fans comin', and were still working with a lot of new acts.

JH: How do you hunt down these people?

GC: They find me. I don't know what the requirement is. If they're crazy enough to want go for their ride, then jump on the Mothership, we'll take off together. Usually they find me; I wouldn't know what to look for.

JH: Since you're considered one of the most sampled musicians, is it hard to maintain your originality?

GC: Oh, I'll just sample myself back, sample myself over their records. Somebody sample us I'll sample myself back.

JH: What other projects are you working on?

GC: Just my granddaughter Sativa. You know we got a new album out now right? How Late Do U Have 2BB4UR Absent? And it has a lot of band members on it, a compilation of Parliament, Funkadelic and as well as the band members individually. After that I'm working on a doo-wop one doo-wop techno, techno doo-wop. There's some techno music from the fifties.

JH: You have realized "the awesome power of a fully operational Mothership". You couldn't just bring together "one nation under a groove"; you had to go galactic too?

GC: I had to do all of that; I'm getting ready to go to the dimensions now.

JH: Dimensions?

GC: The sixth and seventh dimensions, we're gonna skip the fourth and fifth, they booby-trapped already. We're going to the sixth and seventh ain't nobody been there to taint it yet.

JH: And what's that going to be like?

GC: I don't know, that's what I like about it. I don't know what's gonna be there. Fourth and fifth, we probably got some kind of notion of what they should be like. At least the fourth anyway, but I don't want to take the precaution and go to someplace I know, and just go to where nobody has contemplated yet. The sixth and seventh.

JH: Back to the old Funkadelic Politics, with the albums "The Electric Spanking of War Babies" and "Uncle Jam Wants You" Can you do anything about the current political situation?

GC: Its time for the spanking again.

JH: Indeed

GC: We need it, we need it real bad right now, that's why the Mothership, will probably taking off again in the New Year.

JH: We'll be waiting for it.

GC: Okie dokie.

T. VIRGIL PARKER lives in Rome, NY, with his consort and son, where he witnessed the destruction by fire of the Woodstock Music Festival. He has formally studied music, Shakespeare, Milton, and student loan statements. After an unpleasant excursion into banking, he currently publishes the College Crier and plays in the Renaissance and World music group Arethusa with his son.

JESSICA HOPSICKER was born in the wilds of Upstate New York. She spent most of her life in the outskirts of the Adirondack State Park in the small town of Hinckley; a town with possible ties with a notable would-be assassin. She majored in graphic design at Pratt Institute in Brooklyn, until May of 04. At the end of her junior year, she left art school to follow a career in piracy. Instead, she found journalism. Jessica is currently back home working full time at the College Crier and dreaming of leaving for a warmer climate.

CARRI ANNE YAGER lives in Rome, N.Y. with T. Virgil Parker, their fifteen-year-old son, T. Blake Parker, and a sadistic cat named Enoch. She has a B.A. in English and is working on an M.S. in Counseling Studies and is studying belly dancing. She has held positions in the fields of Education and Writing as well as face painting, in her spare time has done advanced work in trying to get T. Virgil Parker to work on the basement.

Printed in the United States
213458BV00004B/19/P

9 781592 993611